THE
ILLUSTRATED
ENCYCLOPEDIA
OF
HELICOPTERS

THE ILLUSTRATED ENCYCLOPEDIA OF HELICOPTERS

Giorgio Apostolo

Advisor on English-language edition
Elfan ap Rees

Illustrated by Amedeo Gigli

BONANZA BOOKS
New York

Produced by ERVIN s.r.l., Rome
under the supervision of Adriano Zannino
editorial assistant Serenella Genoese Zerbi

Photographs of the following helicopters on pp. 126-136
by kind permission of Helicopter International:
Agusta A129, Bell 400 TwinRanger, Bell XV-15, Bell-Boeing JVX,
Brennan Helicopter, Cierva CLTH-1, Hillman 360, Weir W.5

Translated from the Italian by Valerie Palmer and S.M. Harris

This 1984 edition published by Bonanza Books,
distributed by Crown Publishers, Inc.

Printed in Italy by Arnoldo Mondadori Editore,
Officine Grafiche, Verona

Library of Congress Cataloging in publication data

Apostolo, Giorgio.
   The illustrated encyclopedia of helicopters.

   Translation of: Atlante enciclopedico degli elicotteri
civili e militari del mondo.
   1. Helicopters-History. I. Title.
TL716.A6413   1984   629.133'352'09   84-9626
ISBN 0-517-439352
h g f e d c b

CONTENTS

INTRODUCTION

For all its apparent clumsiness and lack of clean, elegant lines, the helicopter is a highly complex and remarkable machine which has become an indispensable means of transport and has proved invaluable in both civil and military contexts, as well as for para-military tasks such as policing, air-ambulance work and traffic control. During the 60 years which have passed since the first successful flight of a helicopter, progress has been startlingly swift, and this book sets out to trace the development of rotorcraft during this period of rapid technological advance, charting the history of the helicopter from the unstable and rickety contraption designed by Breguet to the gigantic Mil which can carry 65 passengers, the elegant Agusta A.109, and the high-speed Hughes AH-64 gunship. Today the rotorcraft can be said to have fulfilled its potential – flying at over 186 mph (300 km/h), lifting and carrying extraordinarily heavy loads, and generally showing itself to be astonishingly versatile.

The opening sections of this encyclopedia give the broad outlines of the helicopter's history and of the attempts by inventors, enthusiasts and scientists to understand the principles which govern vertical flight.

The Pioneers section traces this process from Leonardo da Vinci's airscrew, to the invention of the autogyro by La Cierva many centuries later, and the development of the first successful pre-war helicopters.

An over-view of major advances made since the Second World War is given in the Civil and Military Helicopters section, which is then complemented by the detailed entries for individual aircraft arranged in alphabetical order by manufacturer. Each helicopter is illustrated in colour, often by three views, to give a clear and comprehensive impression of its construction and appearance. A number of perspective drawings of some variants complete the picture and bring these fascinating machines to life. The descriptions are accompanied by outlines of the basic technical data for each aircraft. The book also includes tables with scale views, information in chart form, and a photographic section with plates dating from the earliest examples of helicopters and autogyros to the most up-to-date contemporary models. The result is an excellent and comprehensive guide.

THE PIONEERS

1493 — Leonardo da Vinci's studies on mechanical flight included the invention of an "airscrew" where the screw surface forms a continuous spiral suitable for vertical flight.

1843 — Machine for vertical flight designed by Sir George Cayley, one of the great precursors of flight.

1870 — Simple elastic model by Pénaud.

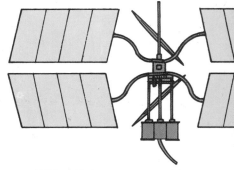

1877 — Twin-rotor steam-driven model by Dieuaide.

The first studies on helicopters were well in advance of the first airplanes. Leonardo da Vinci is credited with having first thought of a machine for vertical flight, the "airscrew," the design for which, dated 1493, was only discovered in the 19th century. It consisted of a platform surmounted by a helical screw driven by a somewhat rudimentary system, not unlike that of rubber-powered model aircraft. The great Tuscan genius wrote that if this instrument in the form of a screw were well made of linen, the pores of which had been stopped with starch, it should, upon being turned sharply, rise into the air in a spiral. However his design was never put to any practical use.

The first firm historical evidence of such a machine being built dates from 1784, when two French artisans, Launoy and Bienvenu, devised an ingenious toy consisting of two propellers made of birds' feathers fixed to the tips of a shaft, around which two strings were twisted, tensioning a spring in a crossbow arrangement. As it straightened out, the spring caused the propellers to rotate for a few seconds, sufficient to send the toy spinning a few meters.

The question of vertical flight was confined to drawings and more-or-less working models for another century, but a number of people were passionately interested in the subject. In 1842 W.H. Phillips built a scale jet-propelled helicopter in Great Britain, and a year later Sir George Cayley, the father of British aviation, invented his "Aerial Carriage" which had four "rotors" arranged coaxially in pairs. This strange vehicle was an improvement on other contemporary projects, but Sir George did not succeed in finding a suitable engine, so the machine remained on the drawing board.

Finding a satisfactory powerplant was long a fundamental problem with helicopters. At the beginning, steam engines had already been invented, but only with limited capacity and their weight:power ratio was prohibitive. Thanks, however, to the efforts of a few "aeronautical" pioneers, some designs really did fly, such as the spring-operated models by Bright (1861) and Castel (1878), and the steam-driven ones by the Frenchman Ponton d'Amécourt (1863) and the German Achenbach (1874), while Alphonse Pénaud (1870) tested a series of models of various shapes and with various propulsion systems.

One of the most ingenious solutions was that adopted by Enrico Forlanini, who flew a model helicopter in 1877 with a pair of two-bladed, coaxial, contra-rotating rotors, using a steam engine fed by a small boiler heated by a stove which also served as a stand for the model when at rest.

However the helicopter as such was still to come. It appeared more-or-less contemporarily with the airplane, when Volumand — chosen as pilot largely on account of his modest weight of 64 kg (10 stone) — was lifted clear of the ground at Douai in France on 29 September 1907, in the elaborate Gyroplane built by Louis and Jacques Breguet under the guidance of Professor Charles Richet. The aircraft achieved a height of only 60 cm (2 ft) and was totally uncontrollable, to the extent that it had to be steadied by four assistants. But it was the first time a mechanical device had raised itself vertically from the ground with a man on board, using a rotary wing system, even if it could not be described as a free flight.

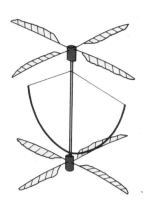

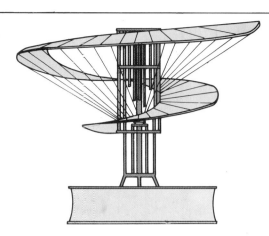

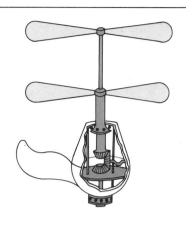

1784 — Model helicopter by Launoy and Bienvenu, presented to the French Academy of Science.

1818 — Another model of a vehicle for vertical flight invented by Lambertgye.

1861 — Little aluminum model by Bright.

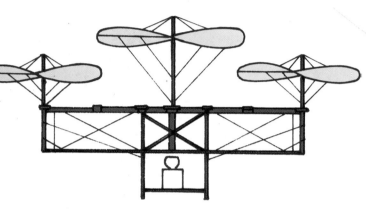

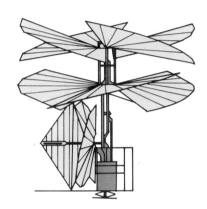

1845 — Three-propeller vehicle by Cossus.

1861 — In this model by d'Amécourt, the two big propellers are contra-rotating.

1862 — A steam-driven version of the 1861 model by d'Amécourt.

1871 — Model by two Frenchmen, Pomés and de la Pauze, which anticipated rocket propulsion.

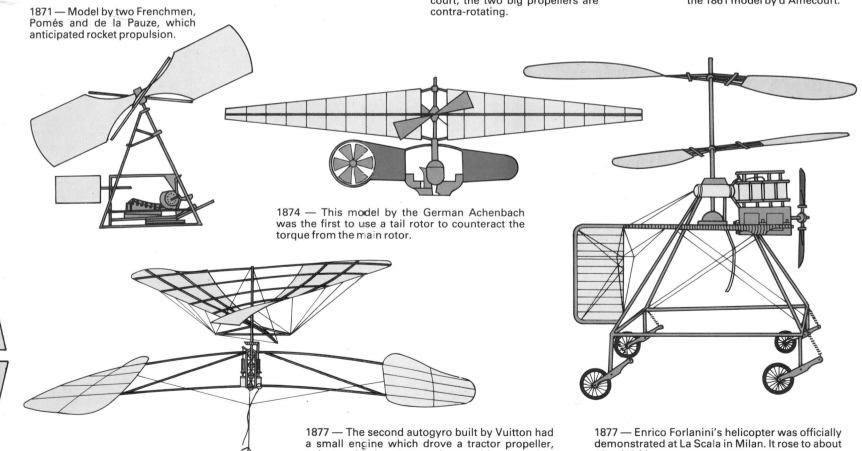

1874 — This model by the German Achenbach was the first to use a tail rotor to counteract the torque from the main rotor.

1877 — The second autogyro built by Vuitton had a small engine which drove a tractor propeller, twin two-blade rotors and a quadricycle undercarriage.

1877 — Enrico Forlanini's helicopter was officially demonstrated at La Scala in Milan. It rose to about 13 m (43 ft).

The Breguet-Richet craft had a 45 hp Antoinette engine and the rotors, only the rotation speed of which could be controlled, were 8 m (26 ft 3 in) in diameter. A year later, Gyroplane No. 2 appeared, with a more powerful 55 hp Renault engine and two forward-tilting two-blade rotors, of slightly smaller diameter than the main lifting surfaces, which provided the thrust for forward movement. In the late summer of 1908, this aircraft was badly damaged by a heavy landing, but was rebuilt and flew again next spring.

The Breguets were not alone, however, in that their record was challenged by Paul Cornu, a bicycle maker from Lisieux, whose machine, powered by a small 24 hp engine, could only have been called the "flying bicycle," consisting as it did of two large, spoked wheels on to which short, paddle-shaped wings were splined to form twin two-blade rotors about 6 m (19 ft 8 in) in diameter. The rotors were belt-driven and contra-rotating. The

central frame supported the engine, pilot seat and fuel tank, and the whole contraption weighed just over 250 kg (550 lbs). Various flights were made, including the notable occasion when Cornu succeeded in remaining airborne for about 20 seconds at a height of 30 cm (1 ft) on 13 November 1907. Thus it was he who was officially recognised as having made the first free flight.

At about that time, a name which was to play a vital role in the history of helicopters first appeared — Igor Ivanovich Sikorsky. He purchased a 25 hp three-cylinder Anzani engine on a visit to France and took it back to Russia where he built his first helicopter. However the prototype was too heavy for the capacity of the engine and did not succeed in becoming airborne; young Igor therefore turned his attention to fixed wing aircraft, only returning to helicopters some 30 years later.

In Great Britain, serious efforts to build a full scale rotary wing machine began in 1916, although design work on the Brennan Heli-

copter was initiated by Louis Brennan in 1884. Following discussions with the Ministry of Munitions and the Royal Aircraft Establishment at Farnborough, where the helicopter was to be built and tested, construction progressed in secrecy and on 22 December 1921 indoor tethered lift tests were carried out with the assistant engineer, Robert Graham, as pilot. The engine was a 230 hp Bentley B.R. 2 rotary. Outdoor tethered flights took place on 16 May 1924. A year later the Brennan Helicopter was making short flights of 18-27m (20-30 yards) at heights up to 1.5 m (5 ft), but on 2 October 1925 disaster struck — during the seventh small flight, the machine lurched at a height of about 1 m (3 ft) and the rotors struck the ground.

At this critical time in the helicopter's development Juan de la Cierva arrived in England with his promising "autogiro" and official interest in the Brennan Helicopter rapidly faded. Finally, in March 1926 funding ceased, and Louis Brennan, at the age of 74, moved on to other

inventions.

A machine which was less complex than Sikorsky's first prototype but equally heavy — almost a 1922 version of the famous Breguet No. 1 — was flown by a Russian émigré to the United States, de Bothezat, on 18 December of that year. The 1,600 kg (3,527 lb) vehicle, with a 220 hp engine, lifted itself to a height of 1.80 m (5 ft 10 in) and stayed in the air for one minute, 42 seconds. But the US Air Force was more interested in autogyros and blocked funds to de Bothezat, who was thus obliged to give up his experiments.

Autogyros were new machines, which were basically wingless airplanes in which the function of the wings was performed by an autorotating or windmilling rotor. They were invented in Spain in the early 1920s by the enterprising nobleman, Juan de la Cierva. Cierva's first attempts were unsuccessful. His odd-looking aircraft, based on existing airframes on to which a rotor was superimposed, seemed

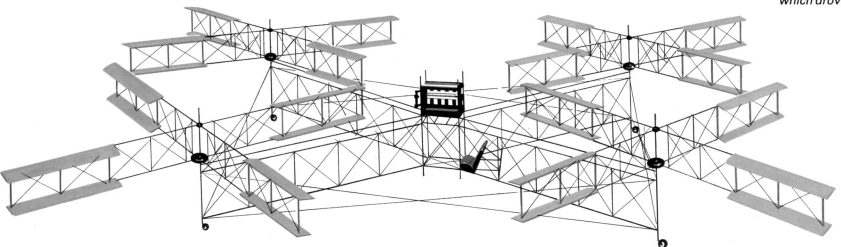

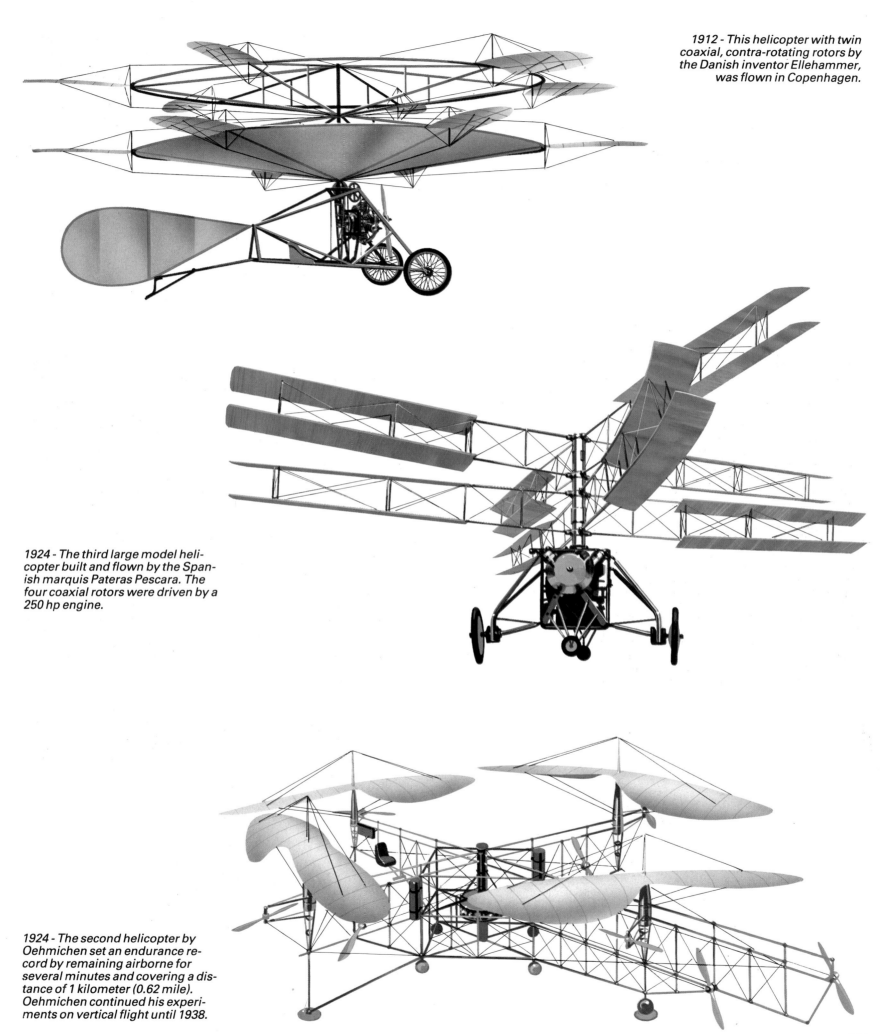

1912 - This helicopter with twin coaxial, contra-rotating rotors by the Danish inventor Ellehammer, was flown in Copenhagen.

1924 - The third large model helicopter built and flown by the Spanish marquis Pateras Pescara. The four coaxial rotors were driven by a 250 hp engine.

1924 - The second helicopter by Oehmichen set an endurance record by remaining airborne for several minutes and covering a distance of 1 kilometer (0.62 mile). Oehmichen continued his experiments on vertical flight until 1938.

11

1934 - The Cierva C-30 was the best-known autogyro prior to the Second World War. A. V. Roe built more than 100; another 40 were produced in Germany and about 100 more were built in France by Lioré and Olivier, under license from Cierva.

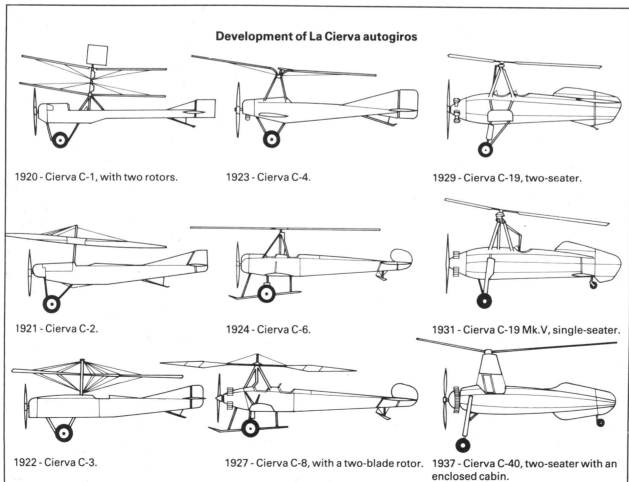

Development of La Cierva autogiros

1920 - Cierva C-1, with two rotors.

1923 - Cierva C-4.

1929 - Cierva C-19, two-seater.

1921 - Cierva C-2.

1924 - Cierva C-6.

1931 - Cierva C-19 Mk.V, single-seater.

1922 - Cierva C-3.

1927 - Cierva C-8, with a two-blade rotor.

1937 - Cierva C-40, two-seater with an enclosed cabin.

perfectly functional with the rotor at rest, but when set in motion they failed to take off and tipped over. Finally, towards the end of 1922, he developed a few flying models, with freely-flapping bamboo rotor blades which raised themselves against the relative wind as they advanced, thereby losing part of their lift, and lowered themselves as they retreated, thereby gaining lift. This sytem balanced out the gyroscopic torque which otherwise tended to turn the aircraft over. Hence Cierva was responsible for solving the problem of roll stability in single-engine rotorcraft — a fact which greatly contributed to the development of modern helicopters.

The first airworthy autogyro appeared in 1923. This was the Model C-4 which made its first flight near Madrid on 9 January. After a few days' trials, it could cover a 4 km (2.5 mile) closed circuit at an average of 60 km/h (37 mph). It had a four-blade rotor and a 110 hp le Rhône radial engine. The C-4 was followed shortly afterwards by the C-5, with a three-blade rotor, and the C-6 in 1924. The second example of the C-8 with an enlarged rotor made the first Channel crossing by a rotary wing craft on 18 September 1928, from the London airport of Croydon to Paris Le Bourget. After these successes, Cierva took up

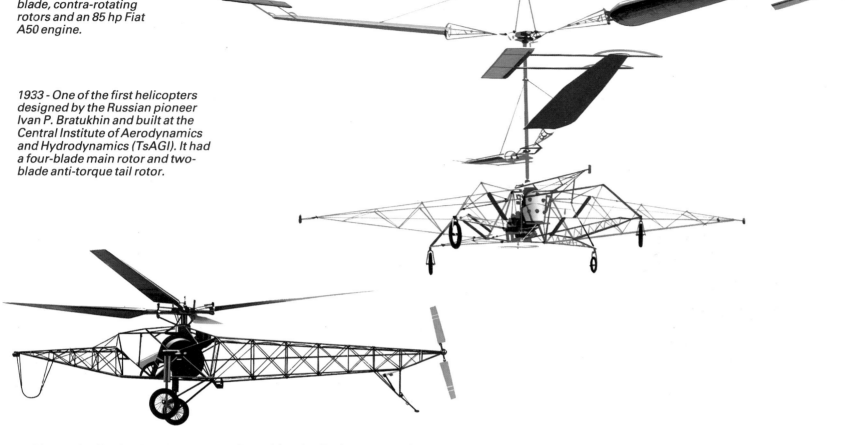

1930 - This Italian helicopter by Corradino D'Ascanio set altitude, distance and endurance records in 1930. It had twin two-blade, contra-rotating rotors and an 85 hp Fiat A50 engine.

1933 - One of the first helicopters designed by the Russian pioneer Ivan P. Bratukhin and built at the Central Institute of Aerodynamics and Hydrodynamics (TsAGI). It had a four-blade main rotor and two-blade anti-torque tail rotor.

residence in England, where he founded the Cierva Autogiro Company.

In the late 1920s and early 1930s a number of licenses were granted to develop the Cierva "autogiro." The companies concerned were mainly established aircraft manufacturers, such as Avro, de Havilland, Parnall and Westland, most of whom lost interest following Cierva's death in an airliner crash in 1936. One company was a marked exception. G & J Weir, a Scottish engineering company, formed an aircraft department at their Glasgow plant in 1932, with a view to developing small autogyros under license from Cierva.

The first efforts revolved around the single-seat Cierva C-28, redesignated the Weir W.1 and powered by a 40 hp Douglas Dryad engine. The W.1 first flew in May 1933 and was followed by the similar but improved W.2 in 1934, which tested a new "jump start" rotor system. The W.3 and W.4 autogyros further advanced the jump take-off principle, using a 50 hp Weir engine driving a two-blade rotor.

In 1937 the company decided to concentrate on helicopter development and this led to the first successful British helicopter, the W.5, a single-seat aircraft using the W.4 fuselage with side-by-side rotors in the layout already successfully

adopted by the Focke 61. The W.5 first flew at Dalrymple, Ayrshire on 7 June 1938, with cyclic but no collective pitch control, vertical movement being controlled by engine throttle to change rotor r.p.m.

The same principle was applied to the two-seat W.6 helicopter, which utilized a more powerful 205 hp de Havilland Gypsy Major engine and three-blade rotors 7.62 m (25 ft) in diameter, employing a hinge configuration identical to that later used by Sikorsky. The W.6 first flew in October 1939 but the outbreak of the Second World War led to development being virtually shelved in July 1940. During the war two further designs were proposed but were not pursued. These were the W.7, with folding outriggers for ship-board operations, and the W.8 with a tip-drive propulsion system. This was later developed into the W.9, which was built by a revitalized Cierva company in 1945.

The war also halted the work of Cierva's main rival in Great Britain, Raoul Hafner, who had left his native Austria in 1931 to seek British sponsorship; this he found in Major Coates, the cotton millionaire. Hafner's method of direct control of collective pitch and his rotor head design were an advance on Cierva's "jump start" rotor head, whilst his development of a torsional tie-bar for blade suspension on his AR III

autogyro eliminated the friction found with highly loaded pitch change bearings, and became commonly used on more modern helicopters.

In the United States the Pitcairn Autogiro Company was formed at Willowgrove PA in 1929 after its founder, Harold Pitcairn, had visited Juan de la Cierva in the United Kingdom and secured a license to develop the Cierva patents in the USA. This agreement led to a series of autogyros being produced under the Pitcairn name over the next decade before the company became the G & A Aircraft Division of Firestone.

The PCA-1, built in 1930, was based on the fuselage of an earlier Pitcairn Mailwing fixed wing airplane with the rotor system from a Cierva C-19 and the ability to pre-spin the rotor on the ground by deflecting the propeller slipstream. Only one PCA-1 was built but it led to the much improved PCA-2 of 1931, a two-seat autogyro powered by a 300 hp Wright J6-9 radial engine, which became the first autogyro to be commercially licensed in the United States and set up an official altitude record of 56,000 m (18,415 ft). Twenty-four PCA-2s were built, including several for the US Navy under the designation XOP-1 for shipboard trials.

Scaling down the PCA-2 led to the

PAA-1, powered by a 125 hp Kinner 3-5 engine with a four-blade rotor which could be inclined fore and aft to increase stability. Some 20 PAA-1s were built for the civil market and were followed by the PA-18, priced at $6,750 including pilot training, and powered by a 165 hp Kinner R-5 engine. Nineteen tandem-seat PA-18s were built between March 1932 and the end of 1933.

In October 1932 Pitcairn rolled out the largest autogyro built in America, the four-seat cabin PA-19, powered by a 420 hp Wright engine and featuring a four-blade rotor with a controllable trim. This was achieved by introducing a head which the pilot could tilt round an axis perpendicular to the axis of the aircraft, and preceded the direct-control head then being developed by Cierva in England. Continuing development by Pitcairn during the 1930s led to several further variants being built and tested, including the PA-20 (1932), PA-21 (1932), PA-22 (1933), PA-24 (1932), PA-33 (1935), PA-34 (1936), PA-35 (1937) and PA-36 (1938).

The PA-36 featured a 165 hp Warner Scarab engine mounted amidships in the streamlined all-metal cabin fuselage and a direct-control jump start rotorhead, which allowed the aircraft to take off vertically over a 9.10 m (30 ft) barrier and translate into normal flight without losing altitude.

The final autogyro built by Pitcairn was the PA-39, based on the earlier PA-18, with a direct control rotorhead. It was ordered by the British Air Commission in 1941 for shipboard antisubmarine trials. Seven PA-39s were built, but the loss of three during shipment to Europe and a decline in official interest in the helicopter led to the project being abandoned.

At the same time as Cierva and Pitcairn were developing the autogyro, the Americans Karman and Emile Berliner, Crocco, an Italian, and von Baumhauer, a Dutchman, were working on new machines. But the problems posed by helicopters in terms of aerodynamics, engineering, stability and vibrational control were so numerous and complex, that it is hardly surprising that the world records for altitude, distance and duration set on 8 October 1930 by the coaxial twin-rotor craft designed by the Italian engineer Corradino D'Ascanio, were only 18 m (59 ft), 1,078 m (3,537 ft) and 8 mins, 45 secs, respectively. D'Ascanio's helicopter was capable of flying with modest installed horsepower — an 85 hp Fiat A50

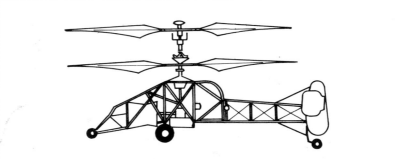

1933 - The experimental helicopter "Gyroplane Laboratoire" by Breguet and Dorand with an open-framework fuselage and coaxial, contra-rotating rotors.

engine — maintaining reasonable stability and good controllability.

Research into rotorcraft was particularly intense during this period in the Soviet Union, where another Italian, Vittorio Isacco, was involved. He had built his first helicopter in Great Britain in 1929 and subsequently moved to the USSR to join a recently formed team at the TsAGI (Central Institute of Aerodynamics & Hydrodynamics). It was there that he produced, in collaboration with Isakson, what was for years the world's largest helicopter. It had a 27.30 m (90 ft) rotor,

weighed 3,180 kg (7,000 lbs) and had five engines — four 120 hp for the main rotor and one 300 hp for the tractor propeller. The "helicogyre" was completed in 1935, but shortly afterwards Isacco left the USSR and continued his work in France. The prototype was abandoned without being flown.

In 1931 Cheremukhin flew the TsAGI-1 which had engines of various power ratings. It had cyclic pitch control and two anti-torque rotors, one at the back and one at the front. This was the formula chosen by another famous Russian

aircraft builder, Ivan P. Bratukhin.

Helicopter development was given new impetus when Louis Breguet actively resumed research into the stability of helicopters, between 1929 and 1930. He set up a company called the Syndicat d'Etudes du Gyroplane in 1931, together with René Dorand. An experimental helicopter was developed forthwith, the Gyroplane Laboratoire, which had an open-framework fuselage with plywood-covered tail surfaces and a wide-track tricycle undercarriage to improve stability. A 350 hp Hispano 9Q radial engine drove a pair of two-blade coaxial, contra-rotating rotors, with cyclic pitch control for movement in the horizontal plane and collective pitch control for movement in the vertical plane. In short, it was a modern helicopter in design and was completed in 1933. It made its first flight on 26 June 1936, and set a series of world records for helicopters: 158 m (518 ft) altitude; a flying time of 1 hour, 2 mins, 5 secs over a distance of 44 km (27.32 miles), with a speed in a straight line of 44.7 km/h (27.77 mph). During the war, this helicopter was destroyed, as was its hangar in Villacoublay.

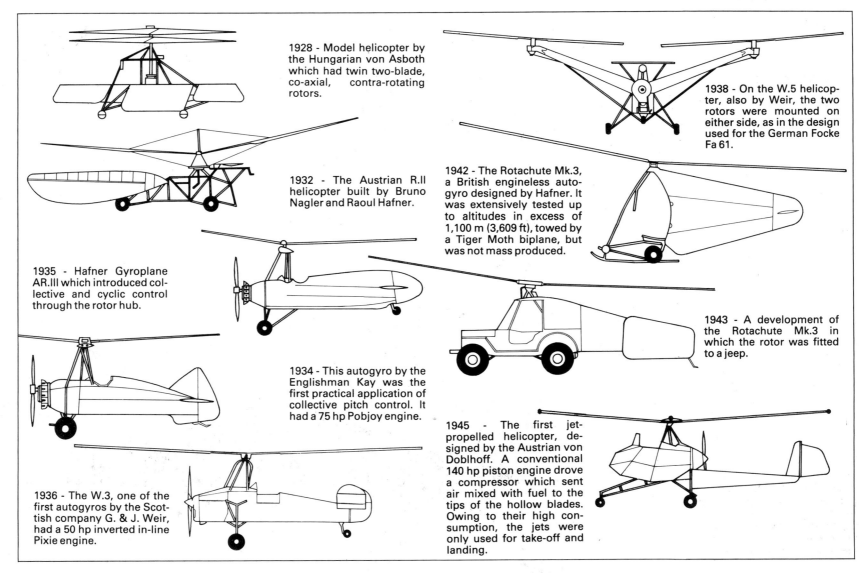

1928 - Model helicopter by the Hungarian von Asboth which had twin two-blade, co-axial, contra-rotating rotors.

1932 - The Austrian R.II helicopter built by Bruno Nagler and Raoul Hafner.

1935 - Hafner Gyroplane AR.III which introduced collective and cyclic control through the rotor hub.

1934 - This autogyro by the Englishman Kay was the first practical application of collective pitch control. It had a 75 hp Pobjoy engine.

1936 - The W.3, one of the first autogyros by the Scottish company G. & J. Weir, had a 50 hp inverted in-line Pixie engine.

1938 - On the W.5 helicopter, also by Weir, the two rotors were mounted on either side, as in the design used for the German Focke Fa 61.

1942 - The Rotachute Mk.3, a British engineless autogyro designed by Hafner. It was extensively tested up to altitudes in excess of 1,100 m (3,609 ft), towed by a Tiger Moth biplane, but was not mass produced.

1943 - A development of the Rotachute Mk.3 in which the rotor was fitted to a jeep.

1945 - The first jet-propelled helicopter, designed by the Austrian von Doblhoff. A conventional 140 hp piston engine drove a compressor which sent air mixed with fuel to the tips of the hollow blades. Owing to their high consumption, the jets were only used for take-off and landing.

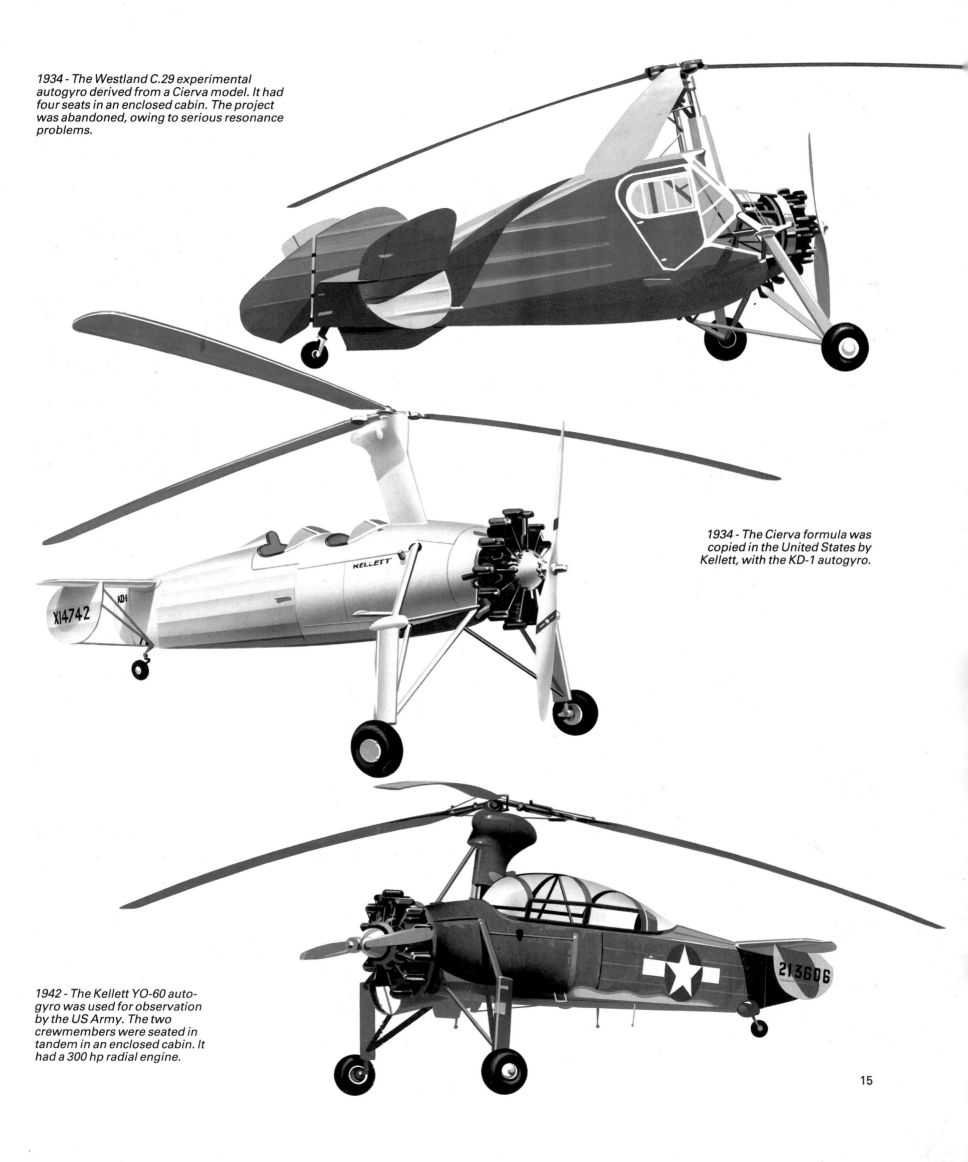

1934 - The Westland C.29 experimental autogyro derived from a Cierva model. It had four seats in an enclosed cabin. The project was abandoned, owing to serious resonance problems.

1934 - The Cierva formula was copied in the United States by Kellett, with the KD-1 autogyro.

1942 - The Kellett YO-60 auto-gyro was used for observation by the US Army. The two crewmembers were seated in tandem in an enclosed cabin. It had a 300 hp radial engine.

15

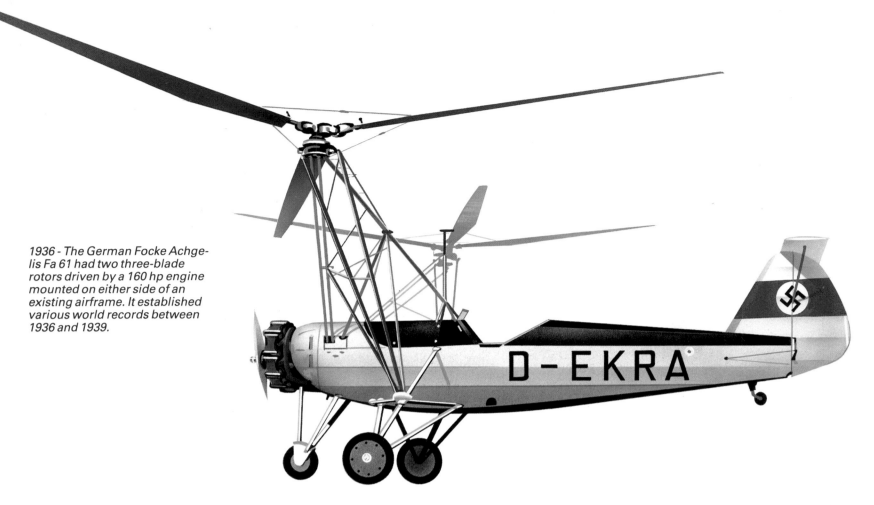

1936 - The German Focke Achgelis Fa 61 had two three-blade rotors driven by a 160 hp engine mounted on either side of an existing airframe. It established various world records between 1936 and 1939.

Technological advances in the field of autogyros led to a few extravagant models such as the C.24 built by de Havilland in 1932, which had a comfortable two-seat enclosed cabin, and the big four-seat Westland C.29 prototype which was, however, soon abandoned owing to excessive vibrations. In the meantime, Cierva had developed a system by which his "autogiro" could take off vertically and then make a rapid transition to translational flight, together with techniques for controlled vertical landings by means of autorotation, on one of the models mass produced for the RAF. They used about 30 Cierva C.30s named "Rota" for radar calibration and to train observers for the School of Army Cooperation. Apart from Avro in England, this type was also produced

by Lioré and Olivier in France under the designation C.301, powered by a 175 hp Salmson engine, and by Focke Wulf in Germany.

Kellett was the first to develop the Cierva "autogiro" under license in the United States when in 1934 he introduced the KD-1, a tandem two-seater with a folding three-blade rotor. A few years later, the KD-1 was transformed into a single-seater and made various demonstrational flights, mainly carrying mail in Washington and then Philadelphia, for a major air line company — Eastern Air Lines. A military version was also developed, designated the YO-60, with a 300 hp Jacobs R-915 engine and a bulged Plexiglass cockpit canopy. It was designed for air observation and several were built at the beginning of 1942. Copies of Kellett's auto-

gyros appeared in Japan, under the designation Kayaba Ka-1, with a 240 hp Kobe in-line engine manufactured under license from the German company Argus.

Germany seemed to have been some way behind on helicopter research compared with other European countries, but when the Focke Achgelis Fa 61 appeared in 1936, it was obvious that she had made up for lost time. Focke had developed a very practical design, using components supplied by Weir in Scotland and the airframe of an existing airplane, the Fw 44 Stieglitz. To the sides of this two long outriggers were fitted; each tip supported the hub of a three-blade rotor driven by the same 160 hp Siemens-Halske Sh 14 radial engine which powered the original trainer aircraft.

Because of its particular structural layout, the Fa 61 could have been mistaken for an autogyro, but it in fact had all the features of a helicopter. It moved forwards and sideways rapidly and easily, having a special device to facilitate movement by varying the pitch of the blades during their rotation.

Between 1936 and 1939, the Fa 61 established various world records, which were much publicized for political reasons. They give an idea of how far helicopters had developed at that time: 80 km (50 mile) closed circuit; 230 km (143 miles) non-stop; 1 hour, 20 mins, 49 secs endurance; 3,427 m (11,243 ft) altitude and a horizontal speed of 122.5 km/h (76 mph). In February 1938, the famous German woman aviator Hanna Reisch demonstrated the aircraft's excellent control by

1939 - The first helicopter designed and built by Igor Sikorsky in the United States, the VS-300. It had an open-framework fuselage, three-blade rotor and 100 hp Franklin engine.

1941 - The Fa 223, which was an enlarged version of the German Fa 61, had a 1,000 hp engine mounted at the center of the steel tube, fabric-covered fuselage. It could carry six and was intended for mass production.

flying it in the covered Deutschlandhall stadium in Berlin.

Although Lufthansa became interested in a six-seat commercial version, the war restricted development in Germany to military helicopters, and even these were given relatively low priority in the early stages.

Meanwhile, echoes of German successes had reached America, where Igor Sikorsky returned to his interest in vertical flight, producing the VS-300 in the summer of 1939. Designed to accept substantial modifications quite easily, it was not a good-looking aircraft, with an open-framework steel fuselage, a single pilot seat at the front, and tricycle landing gear. It was powered by a 100 hp Franklin engine. Igor Sikorsky tested it himself and made a number of flights before American armed forces commissions, who subjected it to further trials and were most impressed.

Much British rotary-wing know-how was sent to the United States during the war, to assist the work of Sikorsky and others. Britain concentrated on fighter and bomber production, but C. G. Pullin continued with some aerodynamic work, whilst Hafner led a team developing rotary wing alternatives to parachuting supplies and troops into battle zones. Initially this work involved several other established pioneers, including J.A. Bennett — who had continued Cierva's own work after his death — and Oliver Fitzwilliams from Weir. Their single-seat Rotachute led directly after the war to the American Ben-

1940 - The first in the Omega family of Russian helicopters inspired by the German Fa 61. It had two rotors driven by two independent engines mounted on outriggers at the sides of the fuselage.

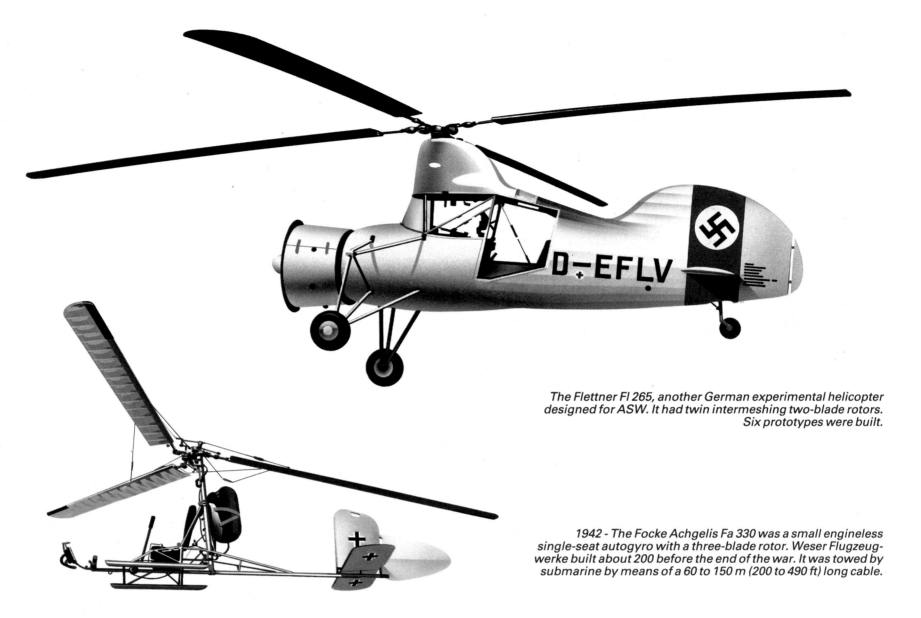

The Flettner Fl 265, another German experimental helicopter designed for ASW. It had twin intermeshing two-blade rotors. Six prototypes were built.

1942 - The Focke Achgelis Fa 330 was a small engineless single-seat autogyro with a three-blade rotor. Weser Flugzeug-werke built about 200 before the end of the war. It was towed by submarine by means of a 60 to 150 m (200 to 490 ft) long cable.

sen series of light gyroplanes and other modern derivatives.

With the progress of the war in Germany, the helicopter's status improved considerably, and an underground factory near Berlin was built to produce a large number of Fa 223s — the military designation given to a much enlarged version of the Fa 61, powered by a 1,000 hp Bramo 323Q-3 radial engine installed at the center of the fuselage. Of the 100 ordered by the German Army in 1942, only 17 were completed and many of these were destroyed on the factory airfield before the end of the war. One of them was captured by the British; another was put together in France in 1948 from parts captured in Germany, with the designation SNCASE SE3000; two ended up in Czechoslovakia and several went to the Soviet Union, where the formula was put to good use by Bratukhin's design bureau.

The 1944 Omega II was in fact directly derived from the German helicopter. At first it was equipped with American Pratt & Whitney engines and then with "domestic" 500

hp Ivchenko AI-26 engines and bigger rotors.

One of the few American projects inspired by the German Focke Achgelis was the Platt LePage XR-1A presented to the American armed forces in 1941. Larger than the German aircraft, weighing 2,300 kg (5,070 lbs), it had a 450 hp Pratt & Whitney engine at the center of the fuselage, which was very similar to that of an airplane and fitted with broad tail surfaces. The pilot and observer sat in two extensively-glazed cockpits and the two outriggers supporting the 9.30 m (30 ft 6 in) diameter three-blade rotors were carefully streamlined.

One of the protagonists of the transformation of autogyros into modern helicopters was the German, Anton Flettner, whose first rotary wing craft flew in 1932. Through various stages, Flettner had developed a machine which, in 1939, aroused the interest of the German Navy, who planned to use it for antisubmarine patrol. Accordingly, 30 prototypes of the new, two-seat Fl 282 Kolibri were ordered immediately, plus 15 assessment

craft. The first Fl 282 flew towards the end of 1941. The cabin was enclosed by a type of multi-faceted Plexiglass bubble, although to save time, most of the prototypes had open cockpits and unskinned fuselages. By 1942, the Kolibri was operational on warships with suitable platforms, escorting convoys in the Baltic, Mediterranean and Aegean and was thus effectively the first military helicopter in the world.

As the Allies advanced into Normandy in 1944, the Fl 282s were destroyed to prevent capture, but at least a couple fell into Allied hands. By that time, plans were already completed for the improved Fl 285 model which could carry two small depth charges and for the Fl 339 transport, which still had the characteristic intermeshing rotors, and was copied immediately after the war by Kellett and subsequently by Kaman.

A jet helicopter also appeared in Germany during the Second World War, built by Friedrich von Doblhoff who flew the prototype, the WNF 342, in 1942. The rotor had three hollow blades through which the

fuel/air mixture was compressed to burn through nozzles at the blade tips. It was intended for the German Navy, for its ocean-going submarines — the very lightweight helicopter could be housed in a bay let into the submarine's turret. The jet propulsion system — which consumed an enormous amount of fuel — was used for take-off, hovering and vertical landing, whilst during translational flight the rotor autorotated and thrust was provided by a propeller at the rear, driven by a 140 hp Siemens-Halske engine. However the Doblhoff aircraft was never mass produced and the last of the four prototypes was captured by the Americans.

The interest of the American armed forces in helicopters was confirmed in 1941 when, following the success of Sikorsky's VS-300, they decided to order an experimental helicopter designated XR-4 from the Vought Sikorsky Company. It had a fabric-covered fuselage of steel tubing, with a glazed cockpit and 185 hp Warner R.550 radial engine. The XR-4 flew on 13 January 1942 and proved so

1941 - The German Flettner Fl 282 Kolibri designed for anti-submarine patrol. In 1942 it was deployed on some warships in the Baltic and Mediterranean.

1942 - After the successful test flights of the VS-300, Sikorsky built the R-4 two-seater, of which 130 were produced during the war. An 185 hp Warner R-550-I radial engine was installed in the fuselage.

1943 - The R-6 was a redesigned version of the R-5 with a more streamlined fuselage and a more powerful 235 hp Franklin opposed cylinder engine; 225 were built.

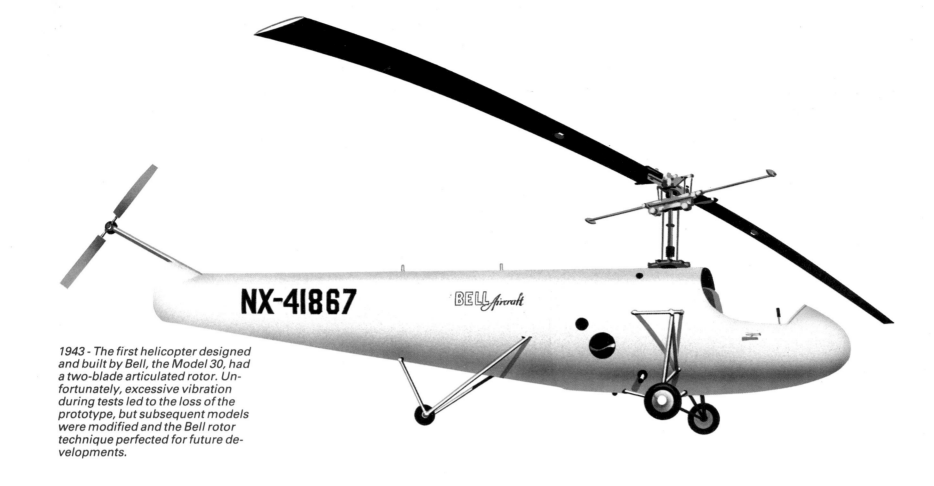

1943 - The first helicopter designed and built by Bell, the Model 30, had a two-blade articulated rotor. Unfortunately, excessive vibration during tests led to the loss of the prototype, but subsequent models were modified and the Bell rotor technique perfected for future developments.

1944 - The XR-8 experimental helicopter was radically different from other projects by Kellett. It had two intermeshing rotors and was nicknamed "the egg whisk."

reliable that after only 20 hours' testing, it was flown to the Wright airfield, covering the 1,100 km (684 mile) journey in 11 laps, at an average of 90 km/h (56 mph).

Following the success of the XR-4, Sikorsky set to work simultaneously on two other projects — one of them a direct development, the VS-316B/R-6, which had a redesigned fuselage but identical mechanical parts to those of the R-4. The XR-6 prototype first flew on 15 October 1943 and on 2 March 1944 it established world distance, duration, and altitude records by flying from Washington to Dayton: 623 km (387 miles), 4 hours, 53 mins and 1,524 m (5,000 ft) respectively. The R-6 also went into full-scale production and all 193 models ordered were built by Nash, since Sikorsky was engaged on the VS-327, a two-seat observation helicopter. The prototype, the XR-5, flew on 18 August 1943. It was larger than its predecessors, but still on classic Sikorsky lines, with a three-blade main rotor and anti-torque rotor. After five prototypes, the US Army Air Force ordered 24 pre-production YR-5As and 100 R-5As.

Meanwhile, Bell Aircraft, who were then producing the P-39 Airacobra and P-63 Kingcobra fighter aircraft, had also entered the helicopter field. The first Bell helicopter,

the Model 30, appeared in late 1942; it was powered by a 165 hp Franklin engine, and had a covered fuselage but an open cockpit and tailwheel landing gear. The two-blade rotor with stabilizer bar was also interesting, and was to remain a feature of Bell helicopters for many years.

Towards the end of 1943, Frank Nicholas Piasecki also appeared on the scene. He had previously been involved in development of the Platt LePage XR-1 and had undertaken a small-scale project of his own. The PV-2 weighed just under 500 kg (1,102 lbs) and was powered by a 90 hp Franklin. It had a three-blade articulated rotor with folding blades. He flew the aircraft several times in public, creating a sensation, but it was then dropped because Piasecki turned his attention to the more ambitious field of large military helicopters; with the PV-3 he returned to the twin-rotor formula which had given rise to his earlier experiment.

Another pioneer working in America in 1944 was Stanley Hiller who, at the age of only 18, flew the first American helicopter with coaxial, contra-rotating rotors, the Hillercopter. However Hiller was interested in developing a straightforward, economical helicopter and accordingly turned his attention a year later to a project in the same category as the Bell 47.

1943 - The single-seat PV-2 designed by Frank Piasecki had a three-blade rotor which could be folded for stowage in an ordinary car port. It was demonstrated several times in public, creating a sensation.

1944 - The Hillercopter, the first American helicopter with coaxial, contra-rotating rotors, was tested personally by its designer Stanley Hiller Jnr.

1944 - One of the last projects of the Cierva company in Britain, the W.9, used an experimental tail air jet system to counter the torque from the three-blade main rotor.

CIVIL AND MILITARY HELICOPTERS

At the beginning of the 1950s there were only 11 major companies building helicopters in the West: five in the United States, three in Great Britain and three in France. There were also a number of smaller manufacturers who made interesting advances. A typical example of the research devoted to simplifying the construction of light helicopters was the Dutch Kolibrie, which introduced ram-jets. Spain also developed some ingenious projects which have never been launched on the commercial market. Two Eastern European countries have made a substantial contribution: the Czech state industries have produced some interesting original models, and Poland, with experience gained through constructing civil and military helicopters under license for the USSR, has recently undertaken successful designs of its own. Sporadic activity in the field of helicopter construction has also occurred in Canada and South America.

The 1960s saw a boom in the helicopter industry in Europe. In France the industry was in disarray after the Second World War, but was revitalized by Louis Breguet when he resumed his helicopter research. Major developments were the formation of Aérospatiale from Sud-Aviation (resulting in turn from the merger of Sud-Est and Sud-Ouest), and the use of turbines as a light, very powerful means of propulsion, largely as a result of the tremendous technological advances achieved by the then comparatively small engine company, Turboméca.

Aérospatiale's name is now almost synonymous with French helicopter development and construction — the company has been able to draw on 30 years' combined expertise, as a result of the mergers from which it was formed. The first Alouette helicopters were built in 1951 and in 1953 the jet-powered Djinn (the first production helicopter to employ "cold-jet" propulsion) appeared. When Sud-Est and Sud-Ouest merged in March 1957, the two types of rotorcraft were developed under the aegis of the new company and the Djinn was soon joined by the new, improved Alouette II and the Alouette III. Several hundred were produced, most of which were bought by military users all over the world.

In 1967 Westland partnered Aérospatiale in developing and building the new generation Puma and Gazelle helicopters. These projects marked the introduction of some interesting new technological advances, one of which was the *fenestron* — a shrouded tail rotor (which actually looks more like a ducted fan) reducing the danger of the blades striking a person or object on the ground. Another step forward was the use of composite materials for the rotor blades and of titanium for the rotorhead. At the same time Aérospatiale did not neglect the heavy-duty helicopter market, and its Super Frelon has been as successful as the smaller aircraft. The simplicity, reliability and performance of their helicopters has consistently been outstanding. Today Aérospatiale is the world's second largest helicopter producer. It has recently concentrated more of its attention on the commercial sector. The result of this is two helicopters which have been well-received worldwide: a light helicopter, the Ecureuil, and the medium, twin-engine Dauphin.

German constructors made pioneering advances during the war; the extremely significant work of Friedrich von Doblhoff, Focke-Achgelis and Anton Flettner — who designed the first helicopter to become fully operational — was to be exploited by the Americans and the Russians in the postwar era. Von Doblhoff continued his work from 1945 onwards in the United States.

Resumption of helicopter research and development in Germany was marked by the maiden flight of the experimental Bolkow Bo.46; despite its complexity, it incorporated some significant technical innovations, in particular the high-speed rotor system with five articulated fiberglass blades. Helicopter output has been fairly modest in spite of the fact that the German armed forces make wide use of helicopters: both the German Army and Air Force use American helicopters constructed under license. The standard helicopter is the Bell 205 produced by Dornier, while the CH-53G, built by VFW-Fokker, again under license, is in service for troop transport.

The one helicopter wholly produced in Germany is the Bo.105, developed by MBB (Messerschmitt-Bölkow-Blohm) initially for the civil sector although military versions were subsequently introduced. The Bo.105 has proved very effective, being highly manoeuvrable and with considerable aerobatic potential, due to its rigid unarticulated main rotor with folding fiberglass reinforced plastic blades. Based on the experience gained during construction of the Bo.105, a new helicopter, the BK-117 has been developed as a joint venture with the Japanese company, Kawasaki, and represents the point of departure from which both the German and Japanese helicopter industries will develop new products for the civil market.

British pioneers of rotary wing craft began to regroup towards the end of the Second World War. Hafner became chief helicopter designer for the Bristol Aeroplane Co., which first produced the lightweight Model 171, followed by the larger Type 173 twin-rotor transport; Bennett took up a similar position with Fairey Aviation to continue with the pre-war Cierva "Gyrodyne" concept (later taken to the United States); Fitzwilliams joined Westland to lead their newly established helicopter activities, and Pullin became managing director of a new Cierva company formed by G. & J. Weir. Later this company was taken over by Saunders Roe, whose first helicopter, the Skeeter, retained the Weir legacy in its W.14 designation. Two notable projects by Fairey were the tiny Gyrodyne and the Rotodyne, an example of a "compound" helicopter designed for intercity passenger services.

In 1959-60 government policy forced a realignment of the

industry under the Westland banner. The real helicopter revolution occurred with the introduction of turbine engines and Westland, who held the license to manufacture Sikorsky aircraft in Britain, pioneered the conversion of these machines from reciprocating to turbine engines, starting with the license-built Sikorsky S-55, whose radial engine was considered inadequate in terms of reliability, maintenance and consumption.

First the Whirlwind and then the Wessex were for years standard aircraft for both the RAF and Royal Navy, and both were a major market success, being exported in large numbers to various parts of the world. The lighter Scout and corresponding Wasp for the Navy also covered a wide range of uses, from observation to air rescue and liaison, and are only now being replaced by more modern machines. This success story continues with the latest additions to the Westland family. The Lynx, which was also the first helicopter wholly designed by Westland, answers the need for a multirole land and naval machine, while the larger Westland 30 is now available for the civil and military transport markets.

After the first experiments by D'Ascanio in 1930, no further progress was made in the helicopter industry in Italy until just after the war. In 1949 the Ministry of Agriculture purchased two Bell 47s which were used in anti-mosquito operations in Sardinia. The arrival of American helicopters in Italy marked the beginning of a positive interest in rotary wing craft, with the result that Agusta, then a medium-sized Italian company, agreed to negotiate with Bell for a production license. Agusta's cooperation with the main American companies was so successful that, within the space of a few years, this company was among the leaders in the rotary wing sector.

While Agusta continued manufacturing helicopters on an industrial scale for the Italian armed forces, police, and fire brigade, there were isolated attempts by other Italian manufacturers at producing rotary wing craft, such as the Aer Lualdi 55, the original Fiat 7002 with a new, cold-jet propulsion system, and the small, but efficient and economical Silvercraft SH-4. However the history of the Italian helicopter industry is essentially that of Agusta (apart from the production of Hughes helicopters by Breda-Nardi). In addition to manufacturing aircraft under license (this now includes aircraft by Sikorsky and Boeing-Vertol as well as Bell), Agusta has developed some interesting original designs, one of the latest being the modern A.109 twin turboshaft, a comfortable and reliable aircraft.

In the United States the emergence of Bell and Sikorsky in a depleted post-war market discouraged one of the most important early pioneers, the Pitcairn Autogiro Company, from continuing the helicopter development undertaken in the early 1940s. At the end of the war, Harold Pitcairn and his company held 164 patents on rotary-wing devices, including helicopters, and when the US government failed to honour royalty payments on infringements by Bell, Sikorsky and other helicopter manufacturers (who themselves had been indemnified), Pitcairn sued and was eventually awarded $32.4 million in damages.

On 8 December 1945, only a few months after the end of the war, the first Bell 47 took to the air. This simple, versatile helicopter was highly successful and was the first development which led to Bell becoming the world's largest helicopter company.

In the space of a few years, the Americans developed new and increasingly advanced types of helicopters, from the lightweight Hiller UH-12 and the Hughes 269, the medium Sikorsky S-55 and S-58, to the distinctive "flying bananas" by Piasecki. These were all produced in large numbers and licenses to build them were granted to various companies. They proved thoroughly suitable for both civil and military operation and were largely responsible for the confidence in rotary wing craft established among civil operators and the armed forces in the fifties. A good example is the long and successful career of the Bell 204 and 205. As has been mentioned, turbine engines were soon also installed on models originally powered by piston engines, such as the Sikorsky S-55/58.

The big transport helicopters appeared in the sixties, from the tandem rotor Vertols, which were a development of the Piasecki design, to the classic formula of the single main rotor Sikorsky S-64. They were all essentially designed to meet military requirements but proved invaluable for other roles as well. The Cobra family of high-speed combat helicopters, on the other hand, are purely for military use. They were widely used in South-East Asia during the Vietnam War, and experience there led to the specification for the first real American attack helicopter, the Hughes AH-64.

A large number of Chinooks — the US Army's standard tactical transport helicopter — were also present in Vietnam. This highly successful machine is now available in a civil version. Indeed the American helicopter industry has more recently concentrated on the civil market, which until a few years ago was considered unready for rotary wing craft. Together with the Bell 222 twin turbine, which arrived on the scene a little late compared with the competition, the Sikorsky S-76 is taking a good share of the corporate market. Designed from the outset as a civil aircraft with full IFR capability, it is also proving popular as a medium-range transport, especially for offshore oil support.

The Soviet Union has been less prolific in the rotary wing field than in other sectors, largely confining its output to transport aircraft and carrier-based antisubmarine helicopters. However, as the civil airline Aeroflot uses the same equipment as the armed forces, in case of an emergency, a large number of reserve aircraft are available which do not need extensive modification before use.

Compared with America, the Soviet helicopter industry has placed more emphasis on helicopters as logistic vehicles for ferrying troops and supplies to the battlefield, rather than as armed assault craft (the only example of which appears to be the Mil Mi-24). The series of troop transports designed by Mikhail Mil is very extensive, beginning in 1947 with the Mi-1, which was also built in Poland, followed by the Mi-2 and Mi-4. Early examples were modelled on American aircraft, while the Mi-6 and Mi-10 heavy lift helicopters are a substantial departure from this pattern. Although designed for a military role, their outstanding payload capacity clearly suits them to a number of other tasks as well.

The Russians have also produced the world's largest helicopter, the Mil-12. The naval sector is well represented by Kamov helicopters, the most important of which is the Ka-25 (in the same category as the American SH-3D and French Super Frelon). Apart from its odd structural formula, its performance seems to be inferior to that of Western counterparts and in any case, it does not appear to have been developed for ASW to the same extent.

An idea of the outstanding progress made by the helicopter in terms of performance levels may be seen from the impressive current distance, altitude and speed records: 3,561.55 km (2,213 miles), 12,442 m (40,820 ft), 355.845 km/h (221.111 mph) respectively. Nonetheless these figures are well below the records set by the airplane, 40 years after its first flight. As a result it is not surprising that engineers have tried to develop hybrid machines by combining some characteristics of helicopters with others of airplanes, to produce what are appropriately called compound aircraft.

However, airplanes and helicopters have characteristics which are not easily reconciled. For instance, winged helicopters must have conventional control surfaces at the tail in addition to a lifting surface. There is also the very difficult problem of controllability, particularly during the transition flight regime, and finally that of the mechanical complexity of the helicopter, which gives compound aircraft a substantial weight and aerodynamic penalty. A number of aircraft manufacturers have devoted themselves to compound helicopters, but while the results they have produced are undoubtedly interesting, their efforts have often been doomed to failure.

A number of highly original machines have been invented in the VTOL (Vertical Take-Off and Landing) category, including those in which the conventional rotor is replaced by a ducted propeller, usually with several blades of relatively small diameter, turning inside a close-fitting ring. However of all the variations tested, undoubtedly it is the "tilt rotor" which shows greatest promise. This is basically a fixed wing aircraft, the propellors of which are replaced by twin rotors; complete with their powerplants, they can swivel from the vertical to the horizontal position in flight. The tilt rotor is set to break the traditional helicopter mould, and by the year 2000 could well be in commercial and military service.

Scale views of selected civil and military helicopters

Gyrodyne Rotorcycle (USA)

Dornier Do.32 (D)

Wallis WA-116F (USA)

Bensen B-8M (USA)

NHI H-3 Kolibrie (NL)

Fairey Ultra Light (GB)

Avian 2/180 Gyroplane (CDN)

SO.1221 Djinn (F)

Fairey Gyrodyne (GB)

Robinson R-22 (USA)

Umbaugh Model 18 (USA)

Nord 500 (F)

AISA Autogiro GN (E)

Hughes Model 300 (USA)

Hughes Model 500D (USA)

Kamov Ka-18 (USSR)

SO.1110 Ariel (F)

Brantly B-305 (USA)

Silvercraft SH-4 (I)

Kaman HH-43B Huskie (USA)

Kamov Ka-26 (USSR)

Aerotecnica AC-14 (E)

Z-35 (CS)

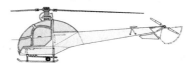

Bratukhin Omega (USSR)

HC-102 Helibaby (CS)

Hiller H-23D (USA)

Bölkow Bo.105C (D)

Agusta A.106 (I)

Fairchild Hiller Model FH-1100 (USA)

Westland Scout AH Mk.I (GB)

Spitfire Mk.II (USA)

Bell XV-3 (USA)

SA.341C Gazelle (F)

Bell Model 47G-3B (USA)

SE.3130 Alouette II (F)

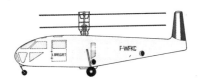

Breguet G.IIE Gyroplane (F)

Piasecki H-25A (USA)

Kamov Ka-25K (USSR)

MBB-Kawasaki BK-117 (D)

Bell Model 206A JetRanger (USA)

Kawasaki KH-4 (J)

SA.315B Lama (F)

SA.319 B Alouette III (F)

AS.350 Ecureuil I (F)

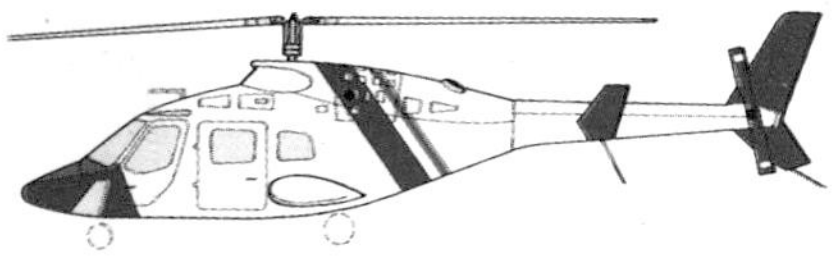

Bell Model 222 (USA)

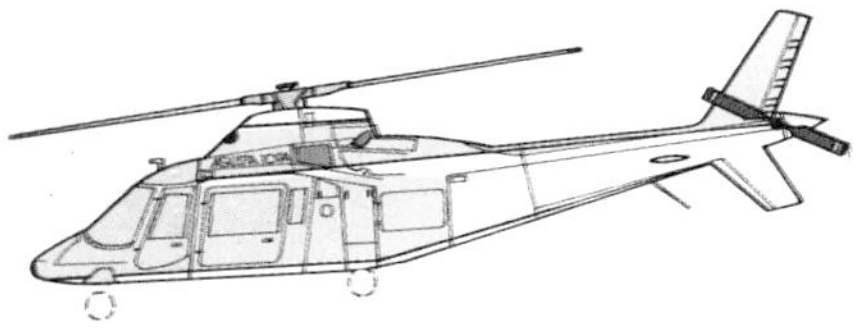

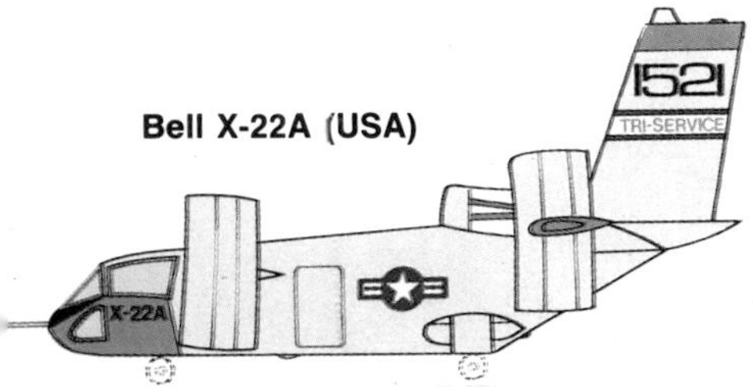

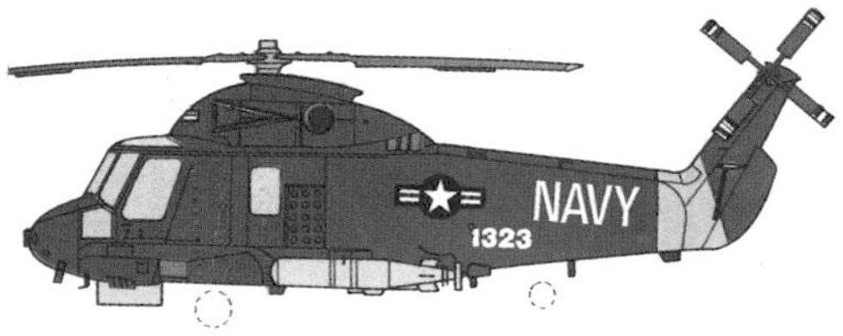

Kaman SH-2F Seasprite (USA)

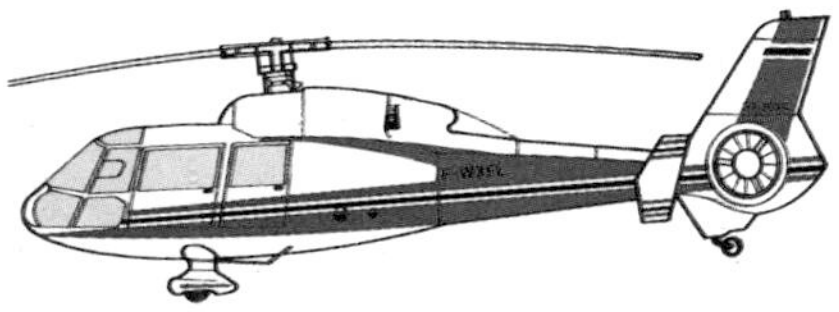

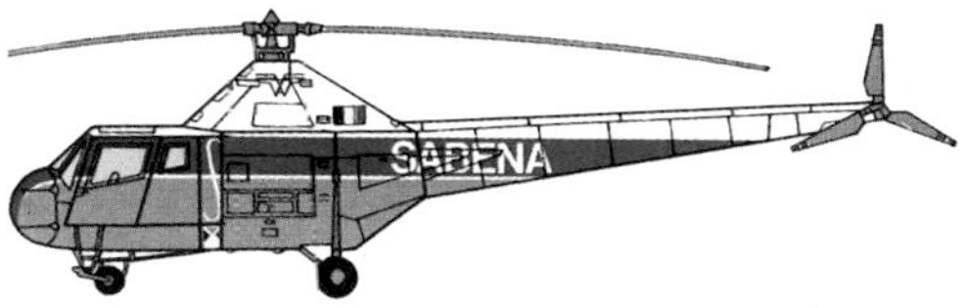

Bell HU-1A (USA)

Agusta A.109A (I)

Westland Widgeon (GB)

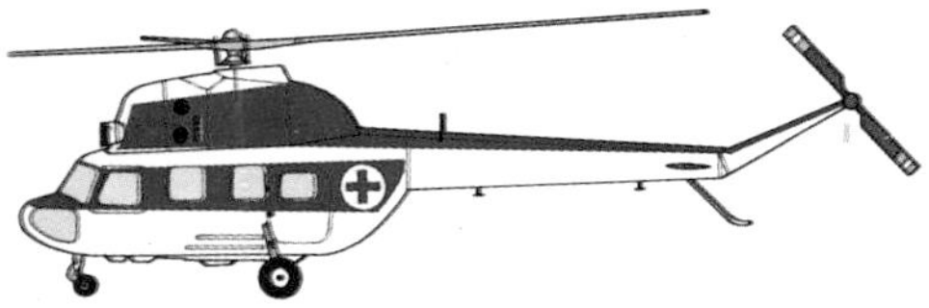

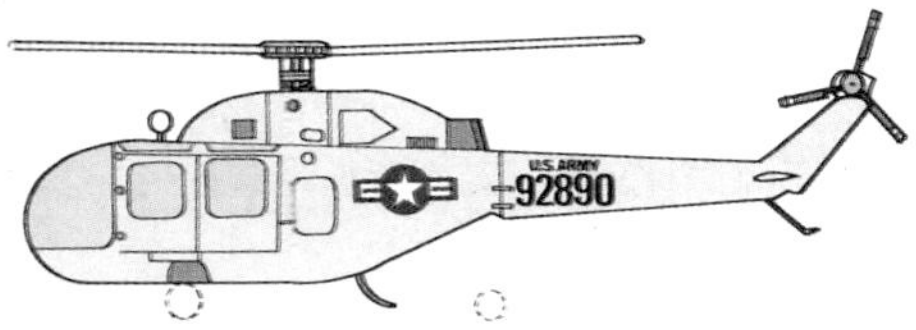

Curtiss-Wright X-19 (USA)

SA.365C Dauphin 2 (F)

Sikorsky S-51 (USA)

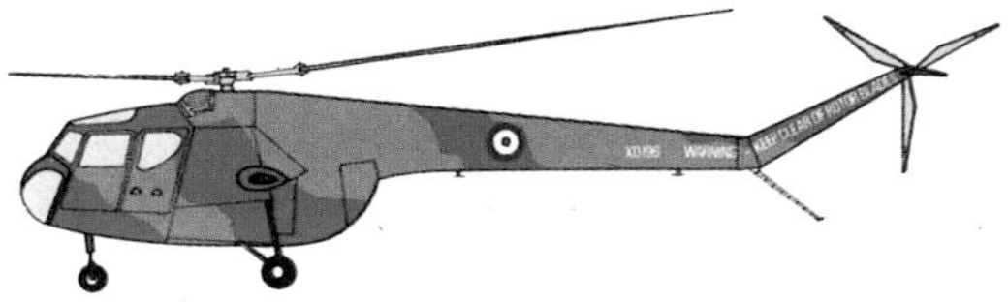

Bristol 171 Mk.13 Sycamore (GB)

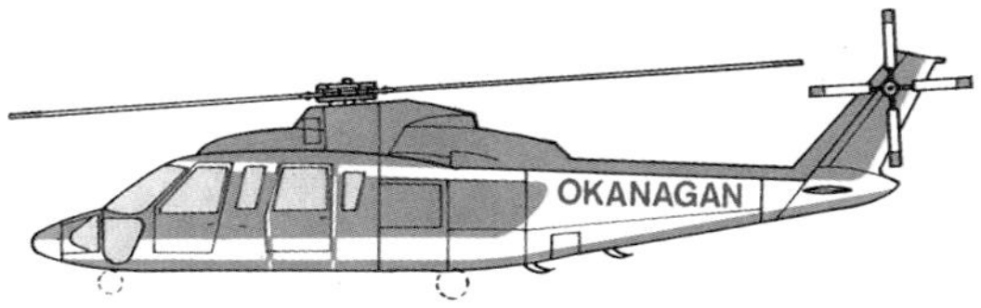

Westland Lynx Mk.25 (GB)

Agusta A.102 (I)

Sikorsky S-76 (USA)

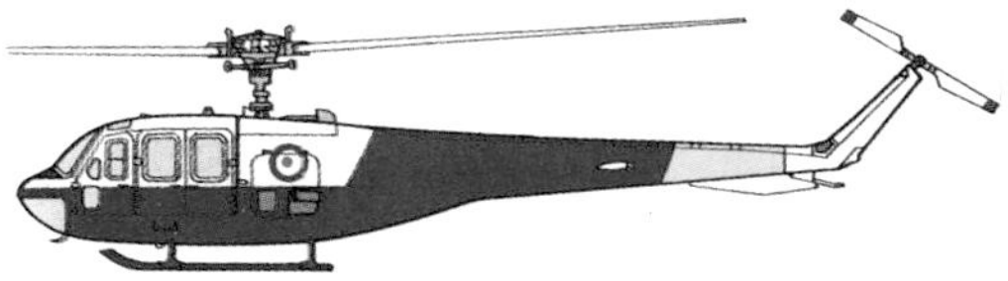

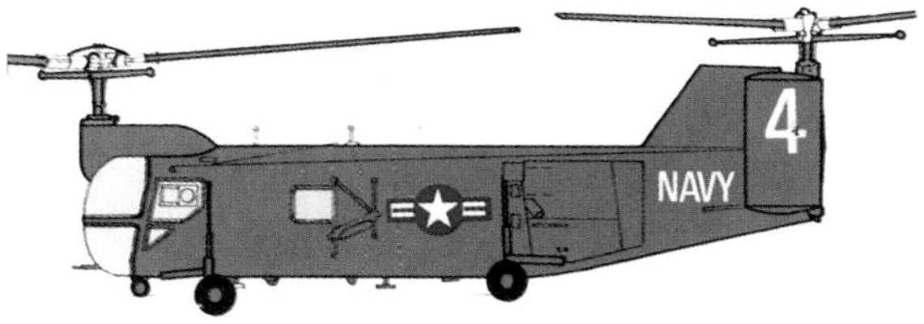

Mil Mi-2 (USSR)

Bell HSL-1 (USA)

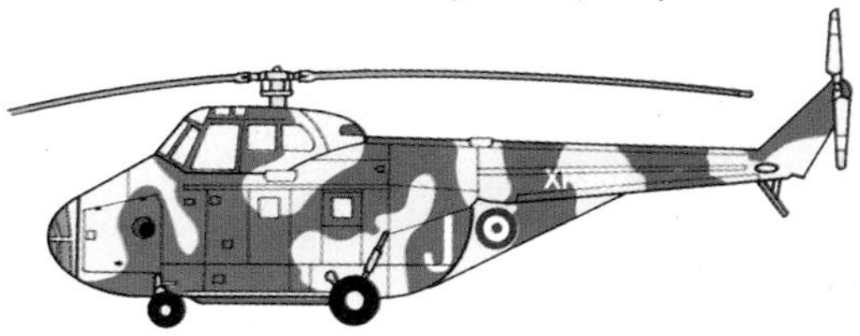

Westland Whirlwind HC Mk.10 (GB)

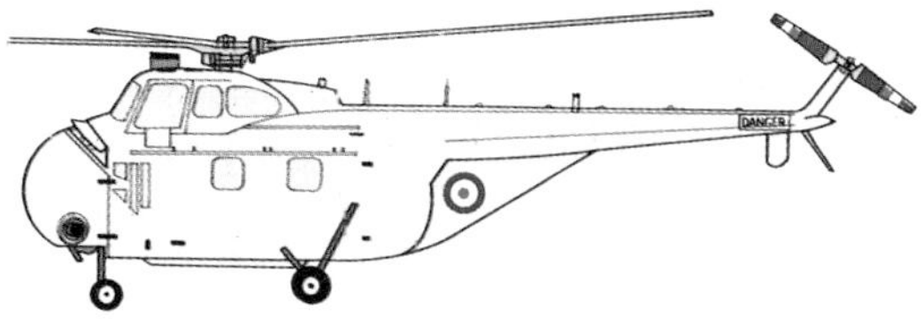

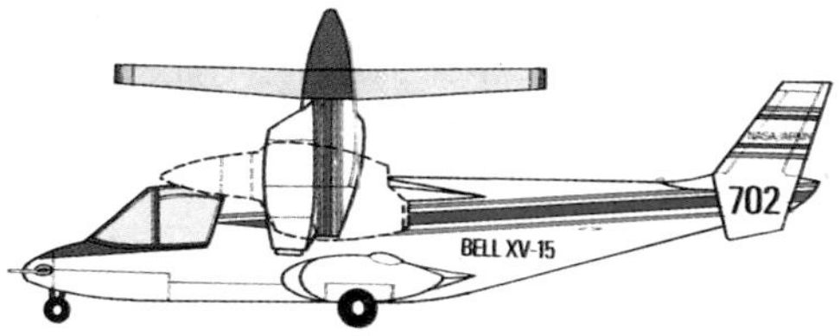

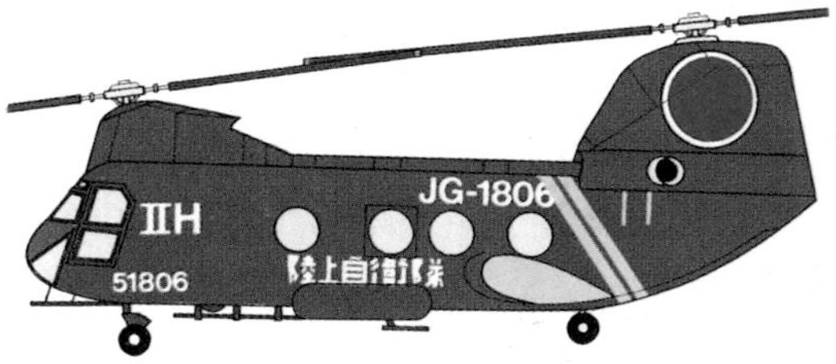

Sikorsky S-59 (USA)

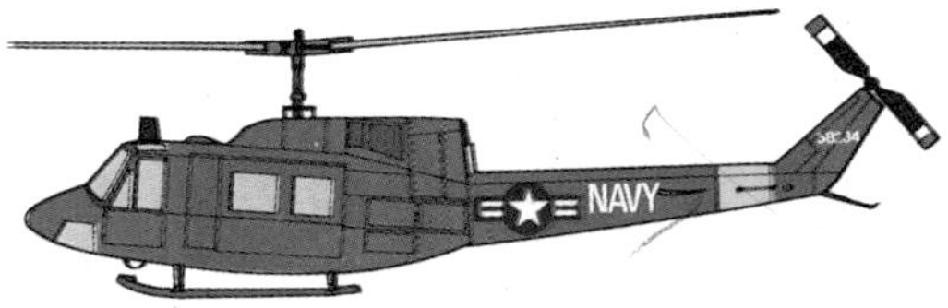

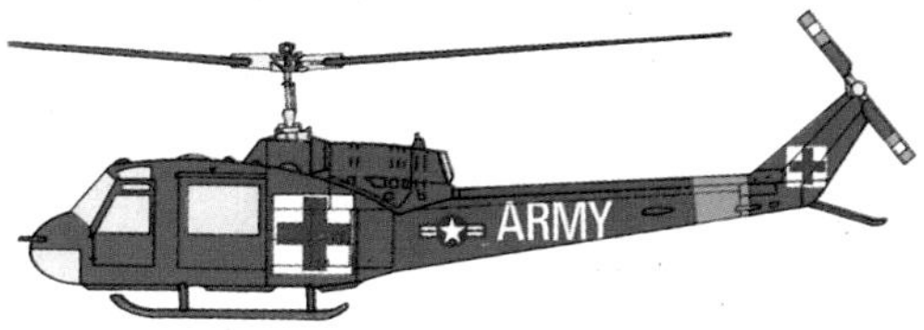

Bell UH-1D (USA)

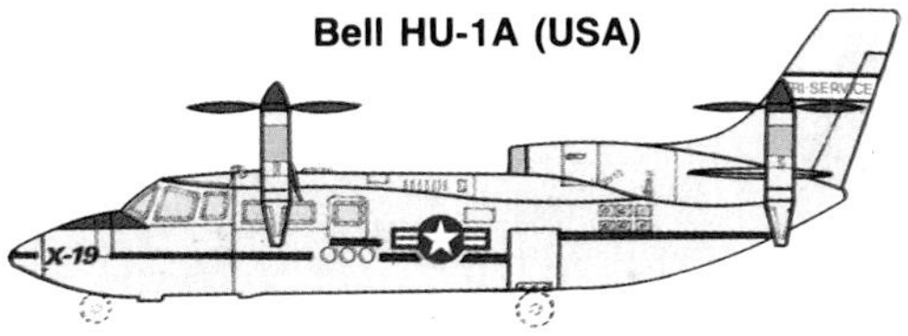

Boeing Vertol CH-46A (USA)

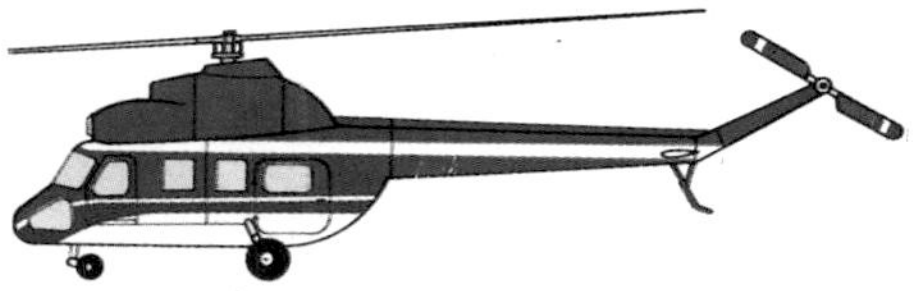

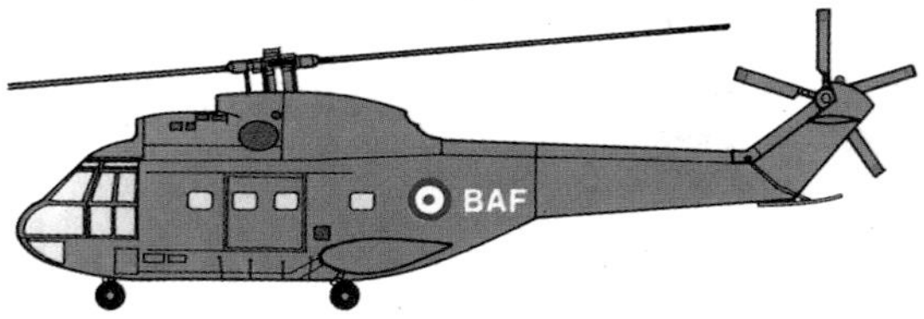

WSK-PZL Kania/Kitty Hawk (PL)

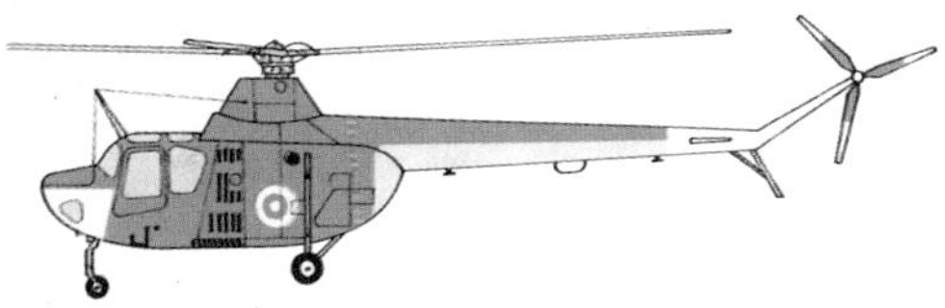

Sikorsky H-19C (USA)

SA.330H Puma (F)

Mil Mi-1 (USSR)

Bell XV-15 (USA)

Bell AH-1J SeaCobra (USA)

Bell UH-1N (USA)

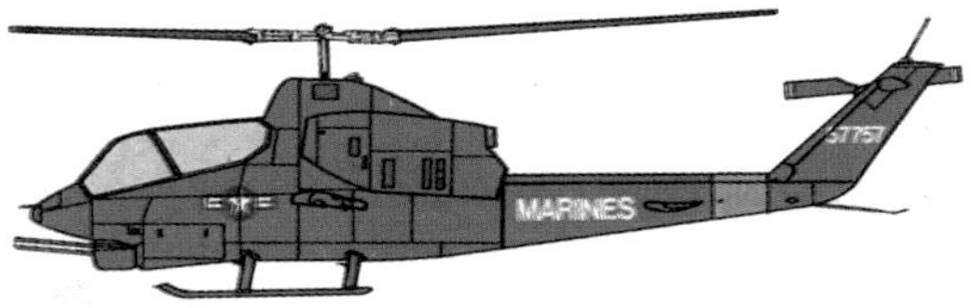

Sikorsky S-58 (USA)

Bell X-22A (USA)

25

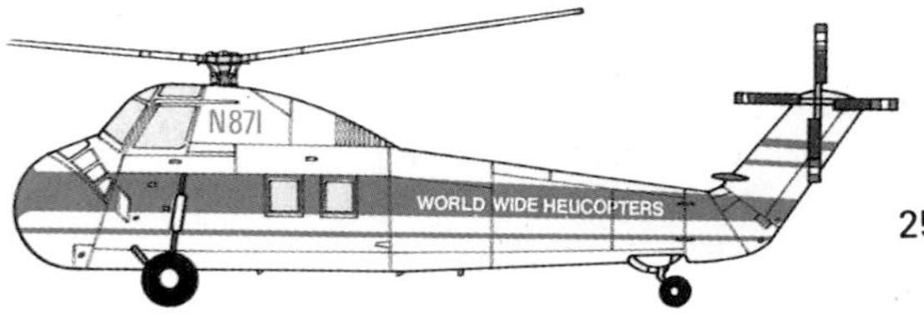

Scale views of selected civil and military helicopters

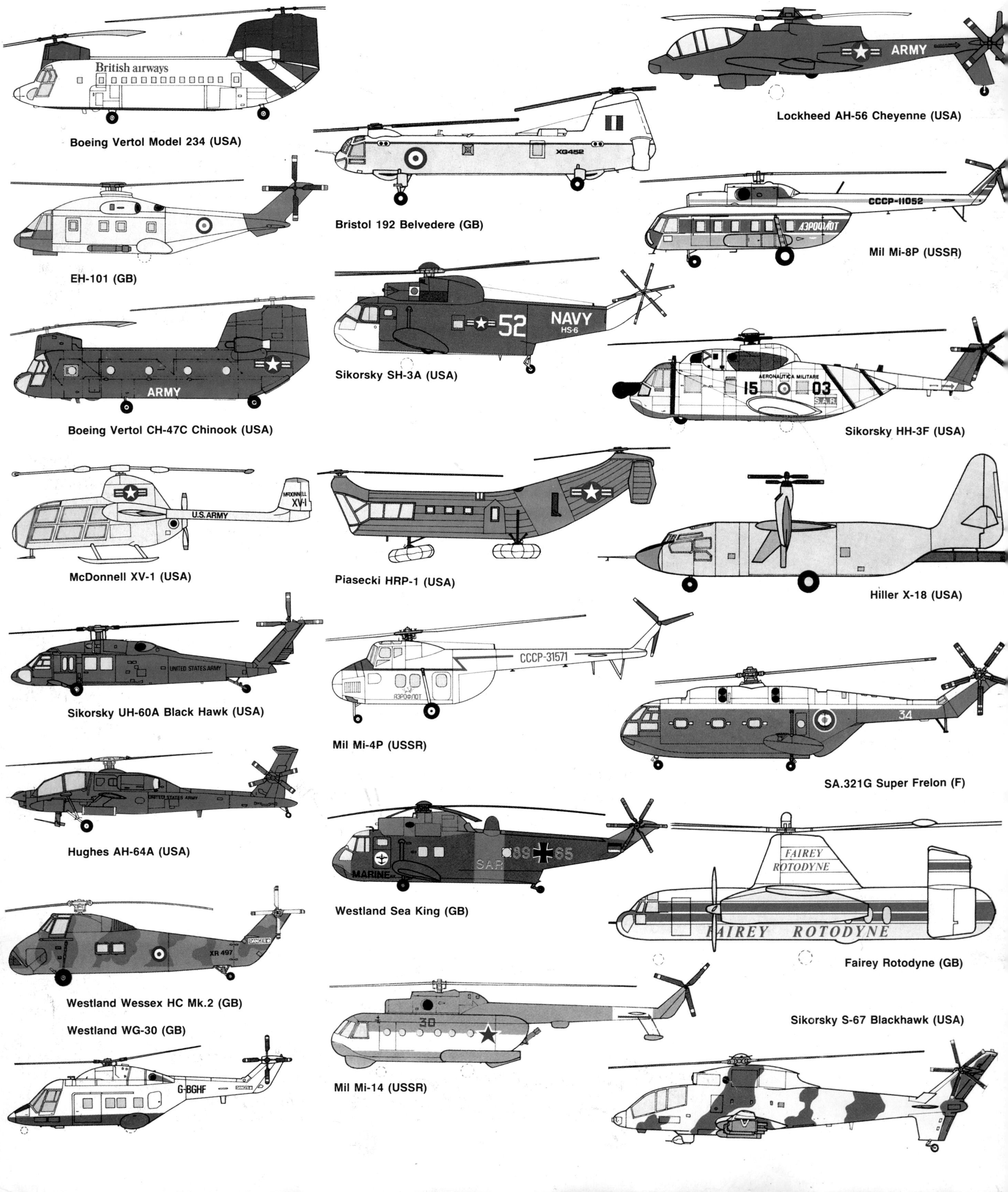

Boeing Vertol Model 234 (USA)

Bristol 192 Belvedere (GB)

Lockheed AH-56 Cheyenne (USA)

EH-101 (GB)

Mil Mi-8P (USSR)

Boeing Vertol CH-47C Chinook (USA)

Sikorsky SH-3A (USA)

Sikorsky HH-3F (USA)

McDonnell XV-1 (USA)

Piasecki HRP-1 (USA)

Hiller X-18 (USA)

Sikorsky UH-60A Black Hawk (USA)

Mil Mi-4P (USSR)

SA.321G Super Frelon (F)

Hughes AH-64A (USA)

Westland Sea King (GB)

Fairey Rotodyne (GB)

Westland Wessex HC Mk.2 (GB)

Westland WG-30 (GB)

Sikorsky S-67 Blackhawk (USA)

Mil Mi-14 (USSR)

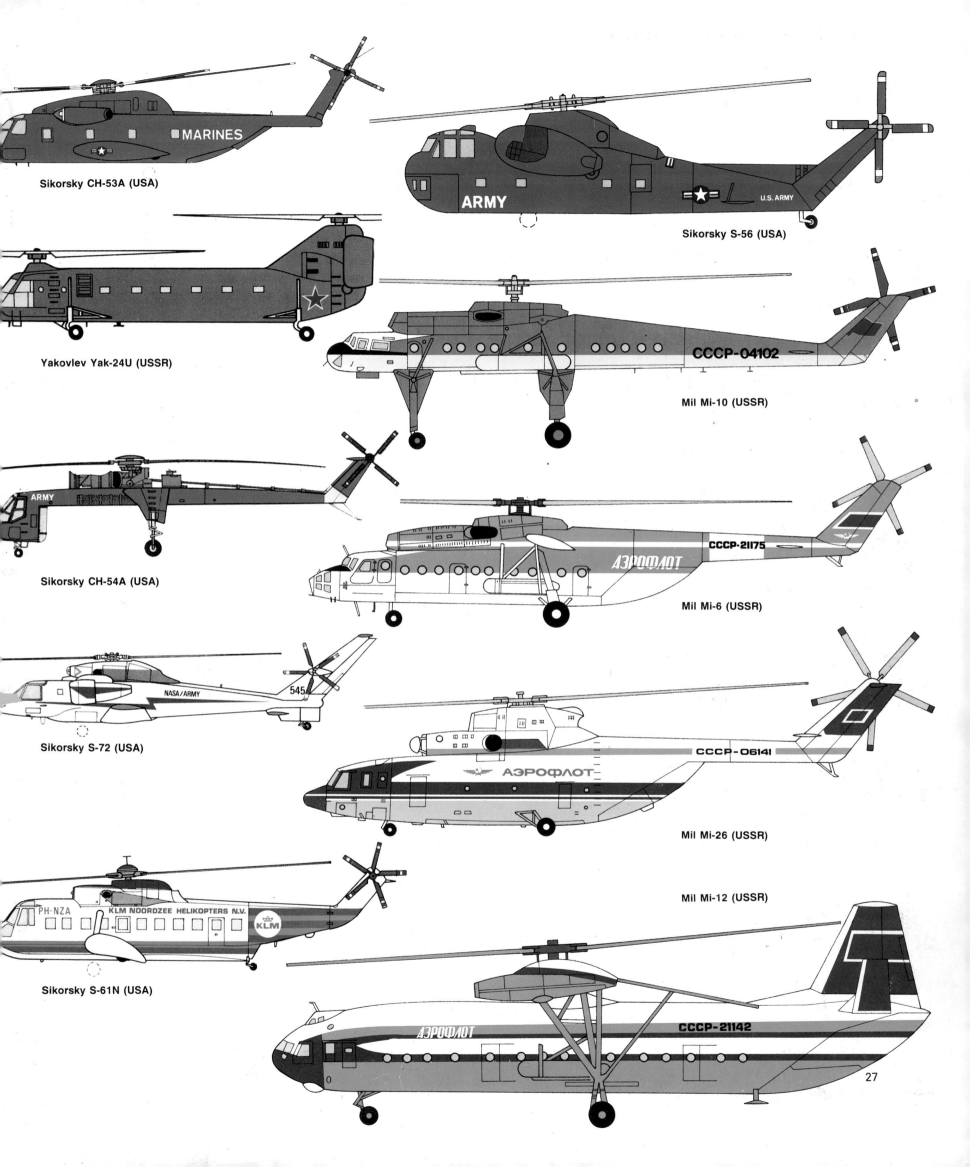

Sikorsky CH-53A (USA)

Sikorsky S-56 (USA)

Yakovlev Yak-24U (USSR)

Mil Mi-10 (USSR)

CCCP-04102

Sikorsky CH-54A (USA)

Mil Mi-6 (USSR)

CCCP-21175

АЭРОФЛОТ

Sikorsky S-72 (USA)

Mil Mi-26 (USSR)

CCCP-06141

АЭРОФЛОТ

Mil Mi-12 (USSR)

Sikorsky S-61N (USA)

PH-NZA KLM NOORDZEE HELIKOPTERS N.V.

CCCP-21142

АЭРОФЛОТ

27

Some of the most important civil and military helicopters 1947-57

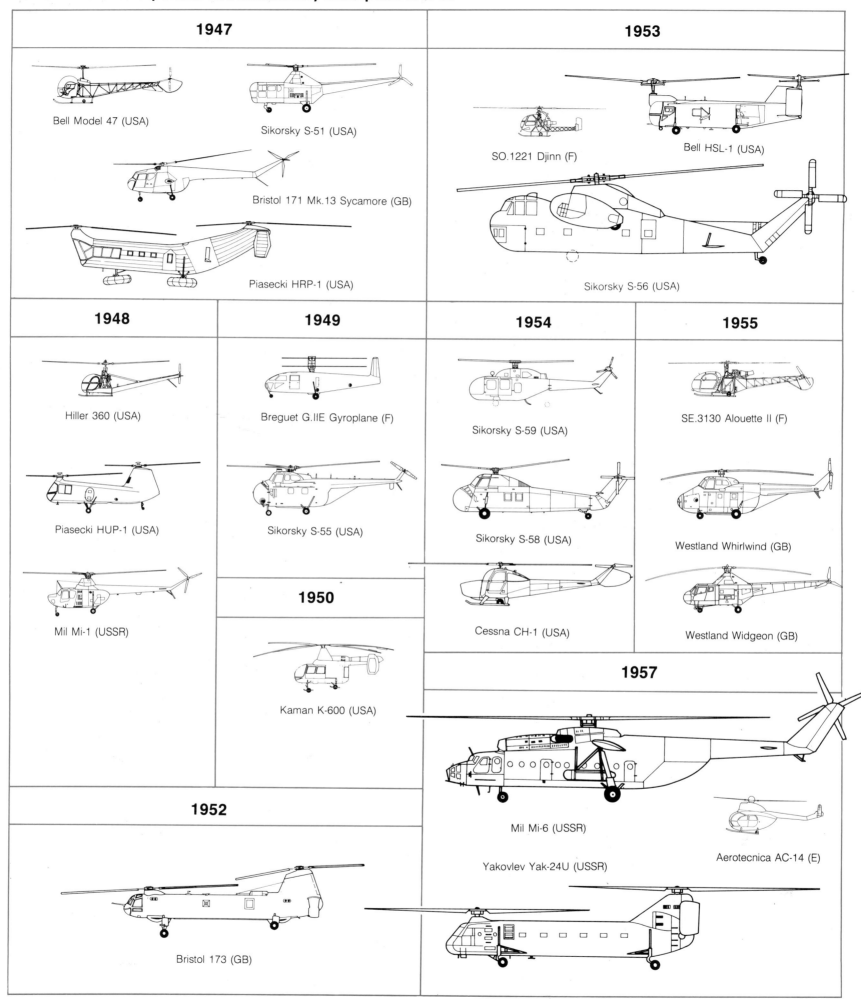

1947

Bell Model 47 (USA)

Sikorsky S-51 (USA)

Bristol 171 Mk.13 Sycamore (GB)

Piasecki HRP-1 (USA)

1948

Hiller 360 (USA)

Piasecki HUP-1 (USA)

Mil Mi-1 (USSR)

1949

Breguet G.IIE Gyroplane (F)

Sikorsky S-55 (USA)

1950

Kaman K-600 (USA)

1952

Bristol 173 (GB)

1953

SO.1221 Djinn (F)

Bell HSL-1 (USA)

Sikorsky S-56 (USA)

1954

Sikorsky S-59 (USA)

Sikorsky S-58 (USA)

Cessna CH-1 (USA)

1955

SE.3130 Alouette II (F)

Westland Whirlwind (GB)

Westland Widgeon (GB)

1957

Mil Mi-6 (USSR)

Yakovlev Yak-24U (USSR)

Aerotecnica AC-14 (E)

Some of the most important civil and military helicopters 1958-64

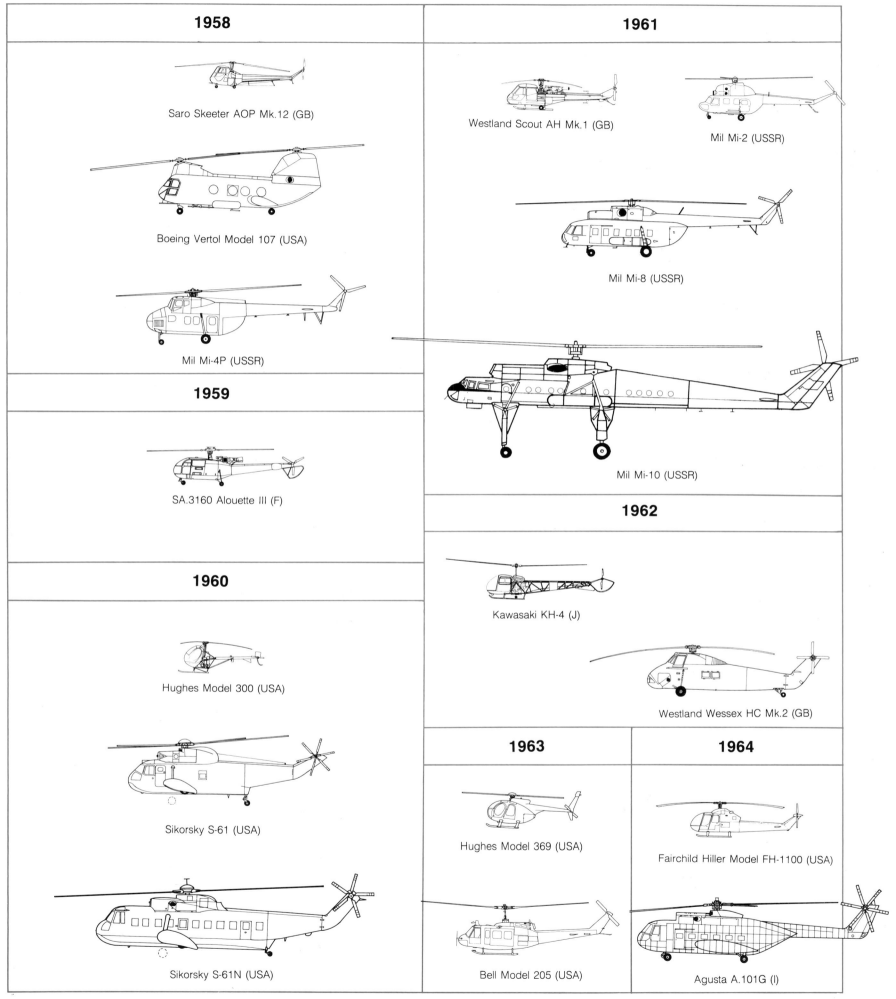

1958

Saro Skeeter AOP Mk.12 (GB)

Boeing Vertol Model 107 (USA)

Mil Mi-4P (USSR)

1959

SA.3160 Alouette III (F)

1960

Hughes Model 300 (USA)

Sikorsky S-61 (USA)

Sikorsky S-61N (USA)

1961

Westland Scout AH Mk.1 (GB)

Mil Mi-2 (USSR)

Mil Mi-8 (USSR)

Mil Mi-10 (USSR)

1962

Kawasaki KH-4 (J)

Westland Wessex HC Mk.2 (GB)

1963

Hughes Model 369 (USA)

Bell Model 205 (USA)

1964

Fairchild Hiller Model FH-1100 (USA)

Agusta A.101G (I)

Some of the most important civil and military helicopters 1965-69

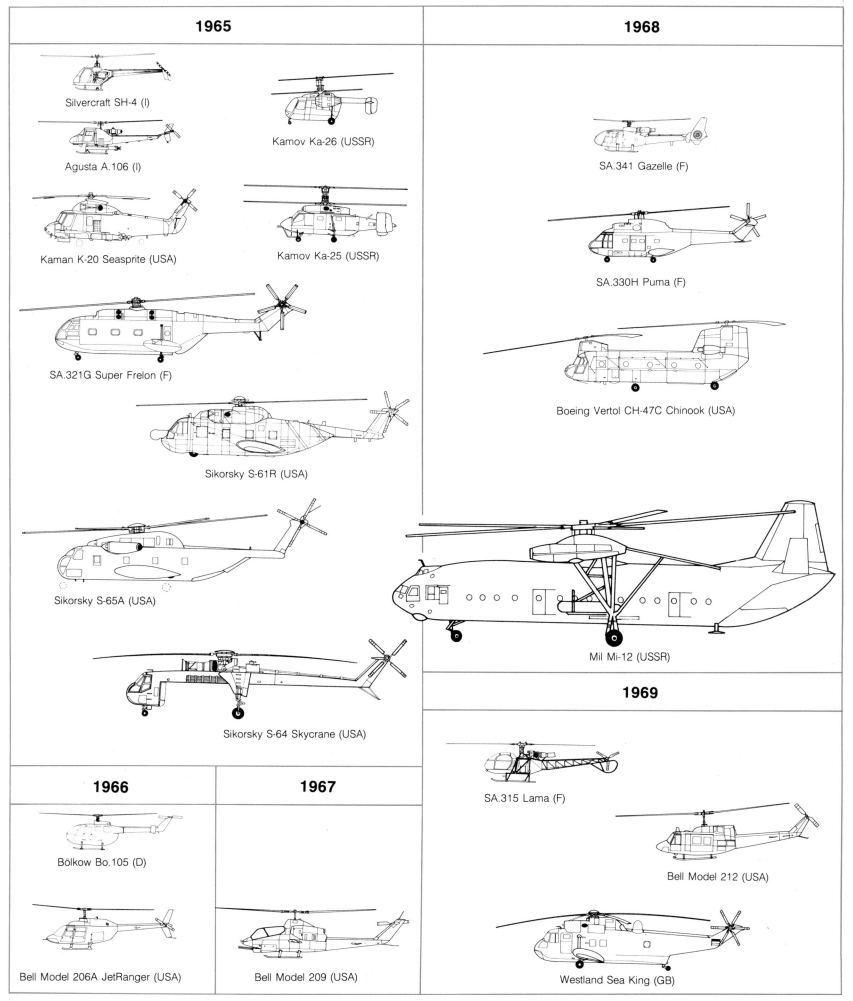

1965	1968

Silvercraft SH-4 (I)

Kamov Ka-26 (USSR)

Agusta A.106 (I)

SA.341 Gazelle (F)

Kaman K-20 Seasprite (USA)

Kamov Ka-25 (USSR)

SA.330H Puma (F)

SA.321G Super Frelon (F)

Boeing Vertol CH-47C Chinook (USA)

Sikorsky S-61R (USA)

Sikorsky S-65A (USA)

Mil Mi-12 (USSR)

| | 1969 |

Sikorsky S-64 Skycrane (USA)

SA.315 Lama (F)

1966	1967

Bölkow Bo.105 (D)

Bell Model 212 (USA)

Bell Model 206A JetRanger (USA)

Bell Model 209 (USA)

Westland Sea King (GB)

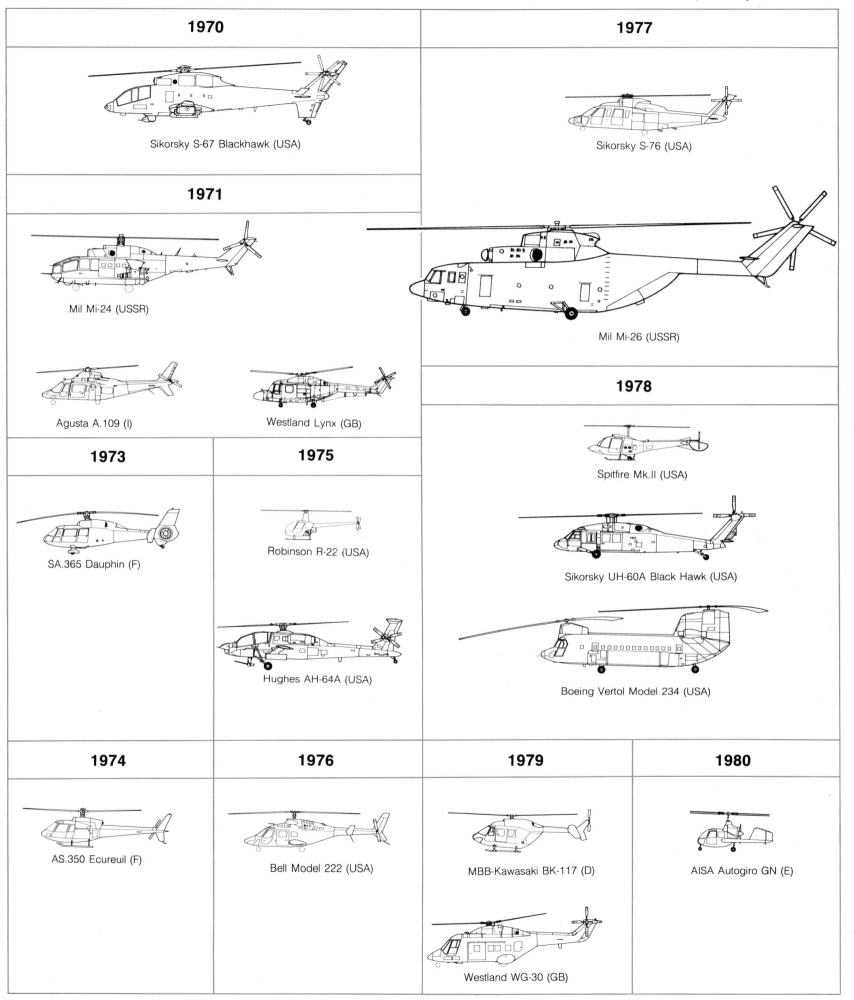

1970	1977

Sikorsky S-67 Blackhawk (USA)

Sikorsky S-76 (USA)

1971

Mil Mi-24 (USSR)

Mil Mi-26 (USSR)

Agusta A.109 (I)

Westland Lynx (GB)

1978

1973	1975

Spitfire Mk.II (USA)

SA.365 Dauphin (F)

Robinson R-22 (USA)

Sikorsky UH-60A Black Hawk (USA)

Hughes AH-64A (USA)

Boeing Vertol Model 234 (USA)

1974	1976	1979	1980

AS.350 Ecureuil (F)

Bell Model 222 (USA)

MBB-Kawasaki BK-117 (D)

AISA Autogiro GN (E)

Westland WG-30 (GB)

Comparative speeds of helicopters from 1944 to the present day

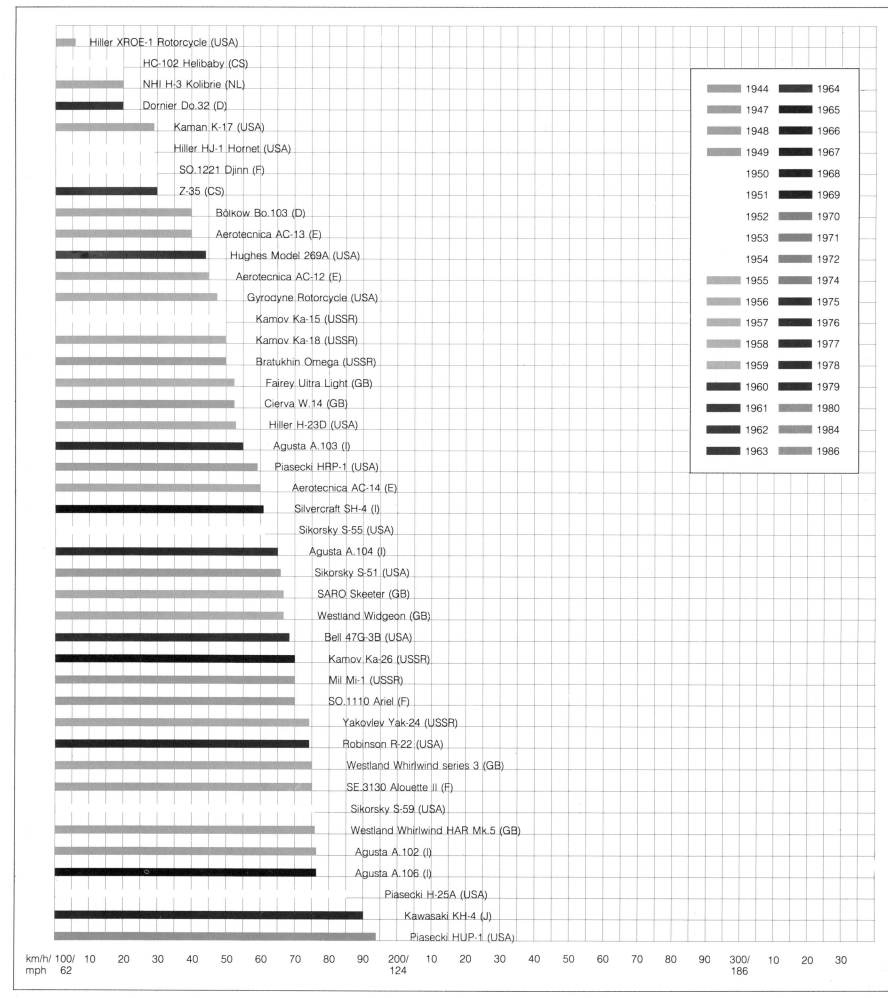

	1944		1964
	1947		1965
	1948		1966
	1949		1967
	1950		1968
	1951		1969
	1952		1970
	1953		1971
	1954		1972
	1955		1974
	1956		1975
	1957		1976
	1958		1977
	1959		1978
	1960		1979
	1961		1980
	1962		1984
	1963		1986

Hiller XROE-1 Rotorcycle (USA)
HC-102 Helibaby (CS)
NHI H-3 Kolibrie (NL)
Dornier Do.32 (D)
Kaman K-17 (USA)
Hiller HJ-1 Hornet (USA)
SO.1221 Djinn (F)
Z-35 (CS)
Bölkow Bo.103 (D)
Aerotecnica AC-13 (E)
Hughes Model 269A (USA)
Aerotecnica AC-12 (E)
Gyrodyne Rotorcycle (USA)
Kamov Ka-15 (USSR)
Kamov Ka-18 (USSR)
Bratukhin Omega (USSR)
Fairey Ultra Light (GB)
Cierva W.14 (GB)
Hiller H-23D (USA)
Agusta A.103 (I)
Piasecki HRP-1 (USA)
Aerotecnica AC-14 (E)
Silvercraft SH-4 (I)
Sikorsky S-55 (USA)
Agusta A.104 (I)
Sikorsky S-51 (USA)
SARO Skeeter (GB)
Westland Widgeon (GB)
Bell 47G-3B (USA)
Kamov Ka-26 (USSR)
Mil Mi-1 (USSR)
SO.1110 Ariel (F)
Yakovlev Yak-24 (USSR)
Robinson R-22 (USA)
Westland Whirlwind series 3 (GB)
SE.3130 Alouette II (F)
Sikorsky S-59 (USA)
Westland Whirlwind HAR Mk.5 (GB)
Agusta A.102 (I)
Agusta A.106 (I)
Piasecki H-25A (USA)
Kawasaki KH-4 (J)
Piasecki HUP-1 (USA)

km/h/ 100/ 10 20 30 40 50 60 70 80 90 200/ 10 20 30 40 50 60 70 80 90 300/ 10 20 30
mph 62   124   186

Kaman H-43B Huskie (USA)
Avian 2/180 Gyroplane (CDN)
Brantly B-305 (USA)
Enstrom F-280 (USA)
Westland Wasp HAS Mk.1 (GB)
Bristol 171 Sycamore (GB)
Westland Wessex (GB)
Cessna CH-1B (USA)
Sikorsky S-58 (USA)
Fairey Gyrodyne (GB)
Mil Mi-10 (USSR)
Sikorsky S-64 Skycrane (USA)
Bell Model 212 (USA)
Fairchild Hiller Model FH-1100 (USA)
Sikorsky S-56 (USA)
Agusta A.105 (I)
Mil Mi-2 (USSR)
Mil Mi-4 (USSR)
SA.315B Lama (F)
SA.3160 Alouette III (F)
Westland Scout AH Mk.1 (GB)
Westland Sea King Mk.41 (GB)
Piasecki H-21C Workhorse (USA)
Breguet G.IIE Gyroplane (F)
Bell HSL-1 (USA)
Spitfire Mk.II (USA)
Kamov Ka-25K (USSR)
Bell Model 206A JetRanger (USA)
SA.319B Alouette III (F)
Bell UH-1D (USA)
Bell UH-1H (USA)
Bristol 192 Belvedere (GB)
Hughes Model 385 (USA)
Cierva W.11 (GB)
Mil Mi-8 (USSR)
Mil Mi-14 (USSR)
Piasecki YH-16 (USA)
Bell Model 204 (USA)
AISA Autogiro GN (E)
Agusta A.101G (I)
Bell Model 206L-1 LongRanger (USA)
Sikorsky S-61N (USA)
Hughes Model 500D (USA)

km/h 100/ 10 20 30 40 50 60 70 80 90 200/ 10 20 30 40 50 60 70 80 90 300/ 10 20 30
mph 62   124   186

Comparative speeds of helicopters from 1944 to the present day

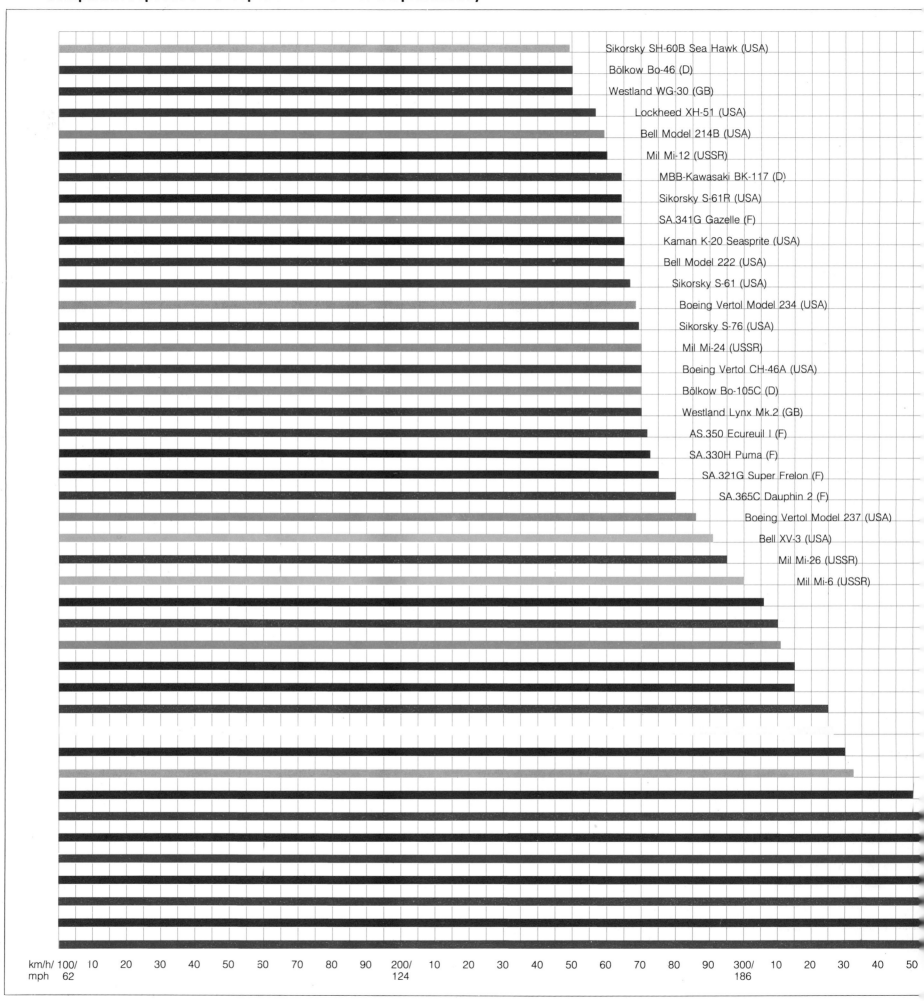

Sikorsky SH-60B Sea Hawk (USA)
Bölkow Bo-46 (D)
Westland WG-30 (GB)
Lockheed XH-51 (USA)
Bell Model 214B (USA)
Mil Mi-12 (USSR)
MBB-Kawasaki BK-117 (D)
Sikorsky S-61R (USA)
SA.341G Gazelle (F)
Kaman K-20 Seasprite (USA)
Bell Model 222 (USA)
Sikorsky S-61 (USA)
Boeing Vertol Model 234 (USA)
Sikorsky S-76 (USA)
Mil Mi-24 (USSR)
Boeing Vertol CH-46A (USA)
Bölkow Bo-105C (D)
Westland Lynx Mk.2 (GB)
AS.350 Ecureuil I (F)
SA.330H Puma (F)
SA.321G Super Frelon (F)
SA.365C Dauphin 2 (F)
Boeing Vertol Model 237 (USA)
Bell XV-3 (USA)
Mil Mi-26 (USSR)
Mil Mi-6 (USSR)

| km/h | 100/ | 10 | 20 | 30 | 40 | 50 | 60 | 70 | 80 | 90 | 200/ | 10 | 20 | 30 | 40 | 50 | 60 | 70 | 80 | 90 | 300/ | 10 | 20 | 30 | 40 | 50 |
| mph | 62 | | | | | | | | | | 124 | | | | | | | | | | 186 | | | | | |

34

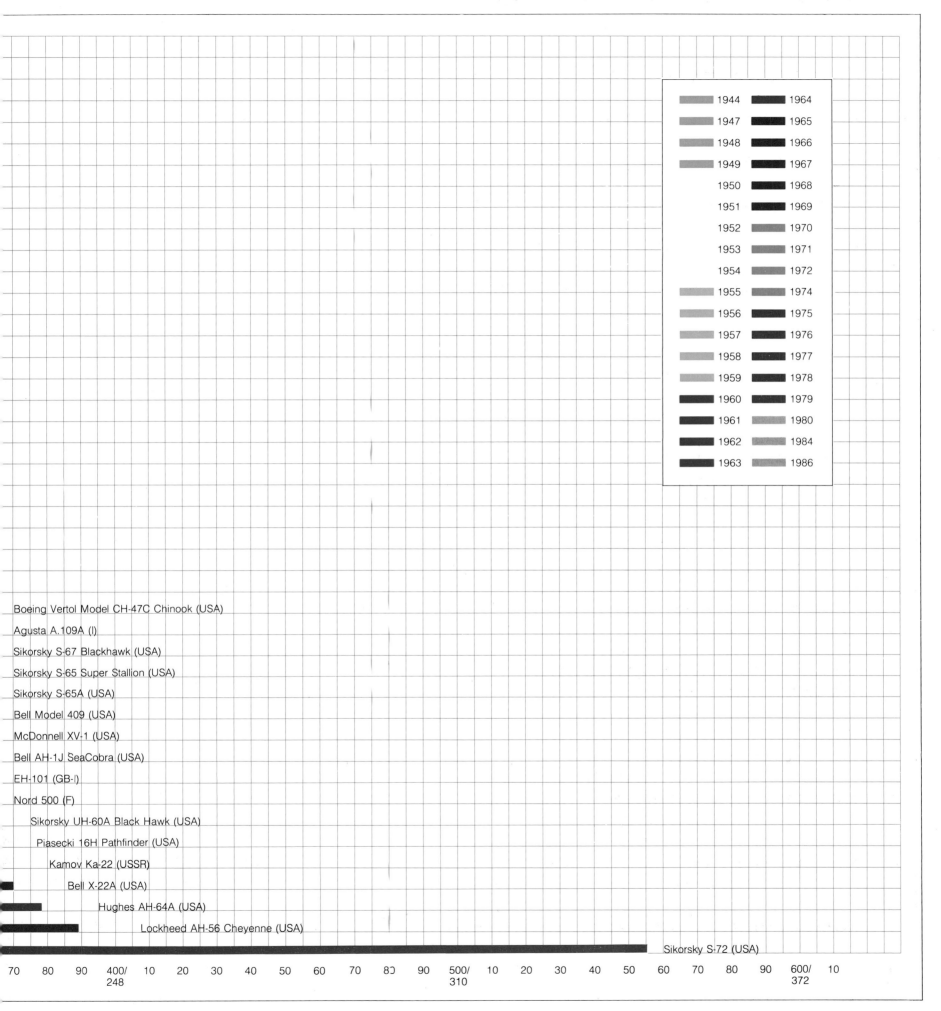

Boeing Vertol Model CH-47C Chinook (USA)

Agusta A.109A (I)

Sikorsky S-67 Blackhawk (USA)

Sikorsky S-65 Super Stallion (USA)

Sikorsky S-65A (USA)

Bell Model 409 (USA)

McDonnell XV-1 (USA)

Bell AH-1J SeaCobra (USA)

EH-101 (GB-I)

Nord 500 (F)

Sikorsky UH-60A Black Hawk (USA)

Piasecki 16H Pathfinder (USA)

Kamov Ka-22 (USSR)

Bell X-22A (USA)

Hughes AH-64A (USA)

Lockheed AH-56 Cheyenne (USA)

Sikorsky S-72 (USA)

1944	1964
1947	1965
1948	1966
1949	1967
1950	1968
1951	1969
1952	1970
1953	1971
1954	1972
1955	1974
1956	1975
1957	1976
1958	1977
1959	1978
1960	1979
1961	1980
1962	1984
1963	1986

70 80 90 400/248 10 20 30 40 50 60 70 80 90 500/310 10 20 30 40 50 60 70 80 90 600/372 10

Comparative ranges of helicopters from 1944 to the present day

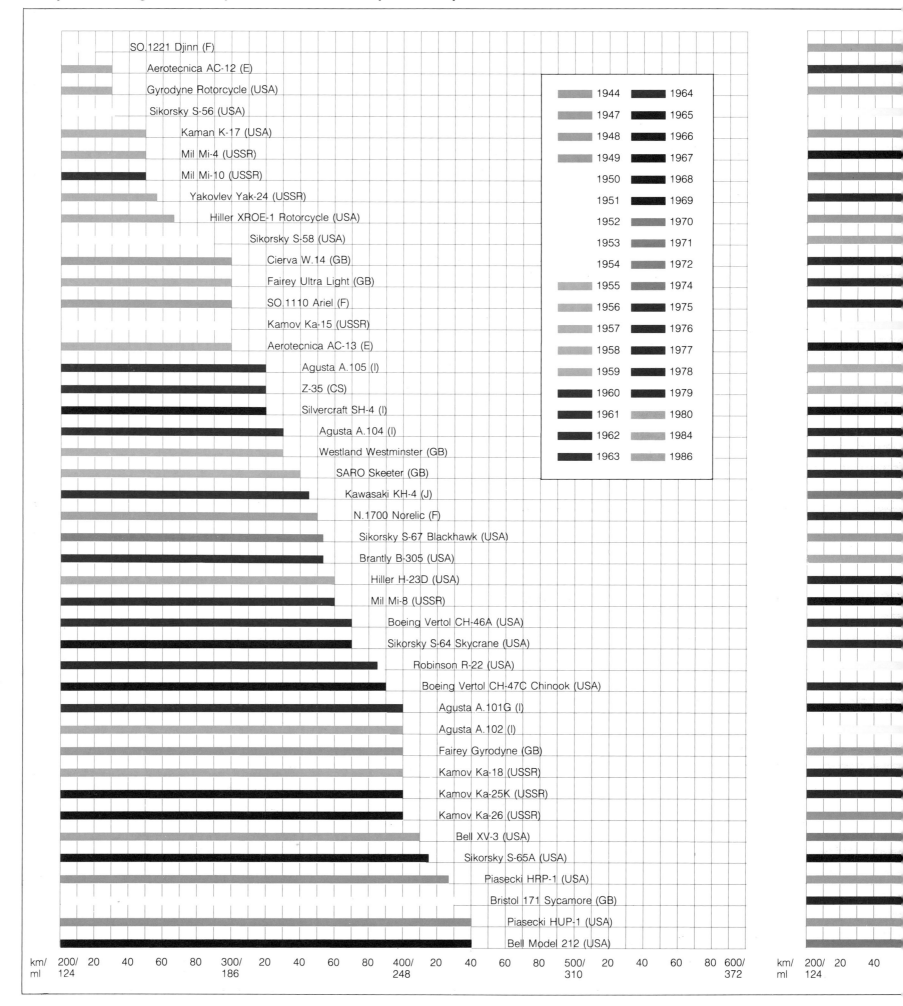

SO.1221 Djinn (F)
Aerotecnica AC-12 (E)
Gyrodyne Rotorcycle (USA)
Sikorsky S-56 (USA)
Kaman K-17 (USA)
Mil Mi-4 (USSR)
Mil Mi-10 (USSR)
Yakovlev Yak-24 (USSR)
Hiller XROE-1 Rotorcycle (USA)
Sikorsky S-58 (USA)
Cierva W.14 (GB)
Fairey Ultra Light (GB)
SO.1110 Ariel (F)
Kamov Ka-15 (USSR)
Aerotecnica AC-13 (E)
Agusta A.105 (I)
Z-35 (CS)
Silvercraft SH-4 (I)
Agusta A.104 (I)
Westland Westminster (GB)
SARO Skeeter (GB)
Kawasaki KH-4 (J)
N.1700 Norelic (F)
Sikorsky S-67 Blackhawk (USA)
Brantly B-305 (USA)
Hiller H-23D (USA)
Mil Mi-8 (USSR)
Boeing Vertol CH-46A (USA)
Sikorsky S-64 Skycrane (USA)
Robinson R-22 (USA)
Boeing Vertol CH-47C Chinook (USA)
Agusta A.101G (I)
Agusta A.102 (I)
Fairey Gyrodyne (GB)
Kamov Ka-18 (USSR)
Kamov Ka-25K (USSR)
Kamov Ka-26 (USSR)
Bell XV-3 (USA)
Sikorsky S-65A (USA)
Piasecki HRP-1 (USA)
Bristol 171 Sycamore (GB)
Piasecki HUP-1 (USA)
Bell Model 212 (USA)

1944	1964
1947	1965
1948	1966
1949	1967
1950	1968
1951	1969
1952	1970
1953	1971
1954	1972
1955	1974
1956	1975
1957	1976
1958	1977
1959	1978
1960	1979
1961	1980
1962	1984
1963	1986

km/ml 200/124 20 40 60 80 300/186 20 40 60 80 400/248 20 40 60 80 500/310 20 40 60 80 600/372

km/ml 200/124 20 40

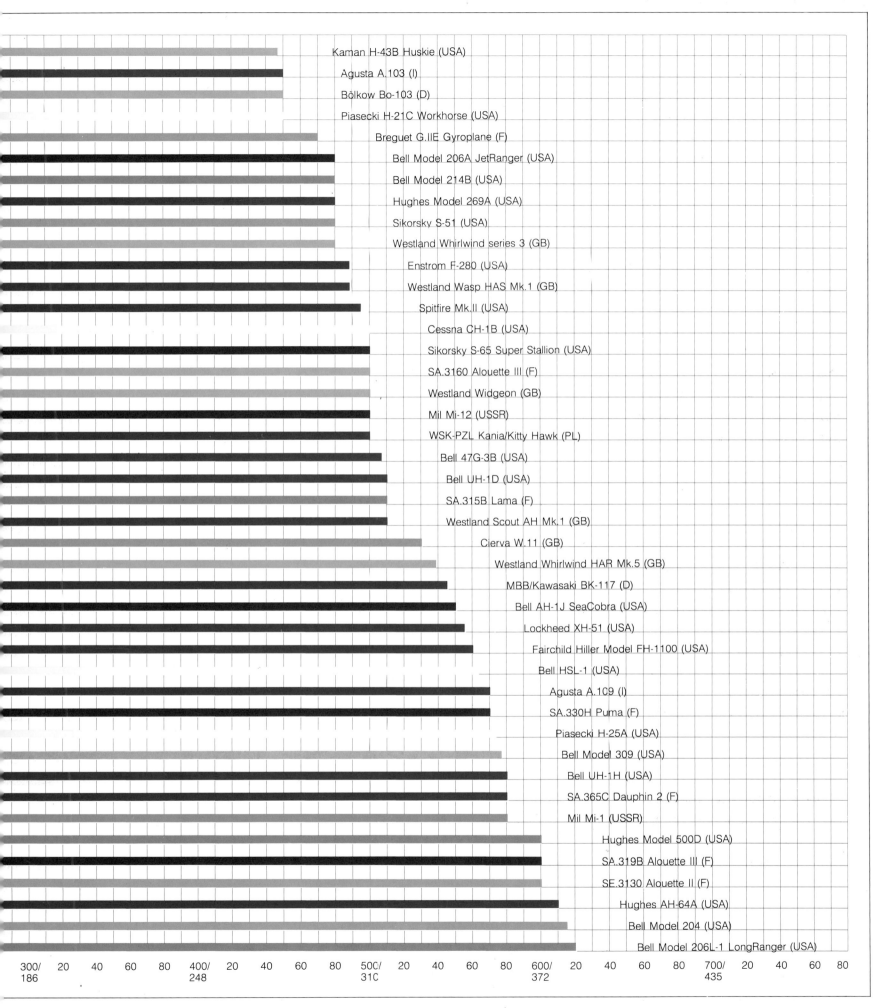

Kaman H-43B Huskie (USA)

Agusta A.103 (I)

Bölkow Bo-103 (D)

Piasecki H-21C Workhorse (USA)

Breguet G.IIE Gyroplane (F)

Bell Model 206A JetRanger (USA)

Bell Model 214B (USA)

Hughes Model 269A (USA)

Sikorsky S-51 (USA)

Westland Whirlwind series 3 (GB)

Enstrom F-280 (USA)

Westland Wasp HAS Mk.1 (GB)

Spitfire Mk.II (USA)

Cessna CH-1B (USA)

Sikorsky S-65 Super Stallion (USA)

SA.3160 Alouette III (F)

Westland Widgeon (GB)

Mil Mi-12 (USSR)

WSK-PZL Kania/Kitty Hawk (PL)

Bell 47G-3B (USA)

Bell UH-1D (USA)

SA.315B Lama (F)

Westland Scout AH Mk.1 (GB)

Cierva W.11 (GB)

Westland Whirlwind HAR Mk.5 (GB)

MBB/Kawasaki BK-117 (D)

Bell AH-1J SeaCobra (USA)

Lockheed XH-51 (USA)

Fairchild Hiller Model FH-1100 (USA)

Bell HSL-1 (USA)

Agusta A.109 (I)

SA.330H Puma (F)

Piasecki H-25A (USA)

Bell Model 309 (USA)

Bell UH-1H (USA)

SA.365C Dauphin 2 (F)

Mil Mi-1 (USSR)

Hughes Model 500D (USA)

SA.319B Alouette III (F)

SE.3130 Alouette II (F)

Hughes AH-64A (USA)

Bell Model 204 (USA)

Bell Model 206L-1 LongRanger (USA)

| 300/
186 | 20 | 40 | 60 | 80 | 400/
248 | 20 | 40 | 60 | 80 | 500/
310 | 20 | 40 | 60 | 80 | 600/
372 | 20 | 40 | 60 | 80 | 700/
435 | 20 | 40 | 60 | 80 |

km/ml	200/124	20	40	60	80	300/186	20	40	60	80	400/248	20	40	60	80	500/310	20	40	60	80	600/372	20	40	60	80	700/435

km/ml	200/124	20	40	60	80	300/186	20	40	60	80	400/248	20	40	60	80	500/310	20	40	60	80	600/372	20	40	60	80	700/435

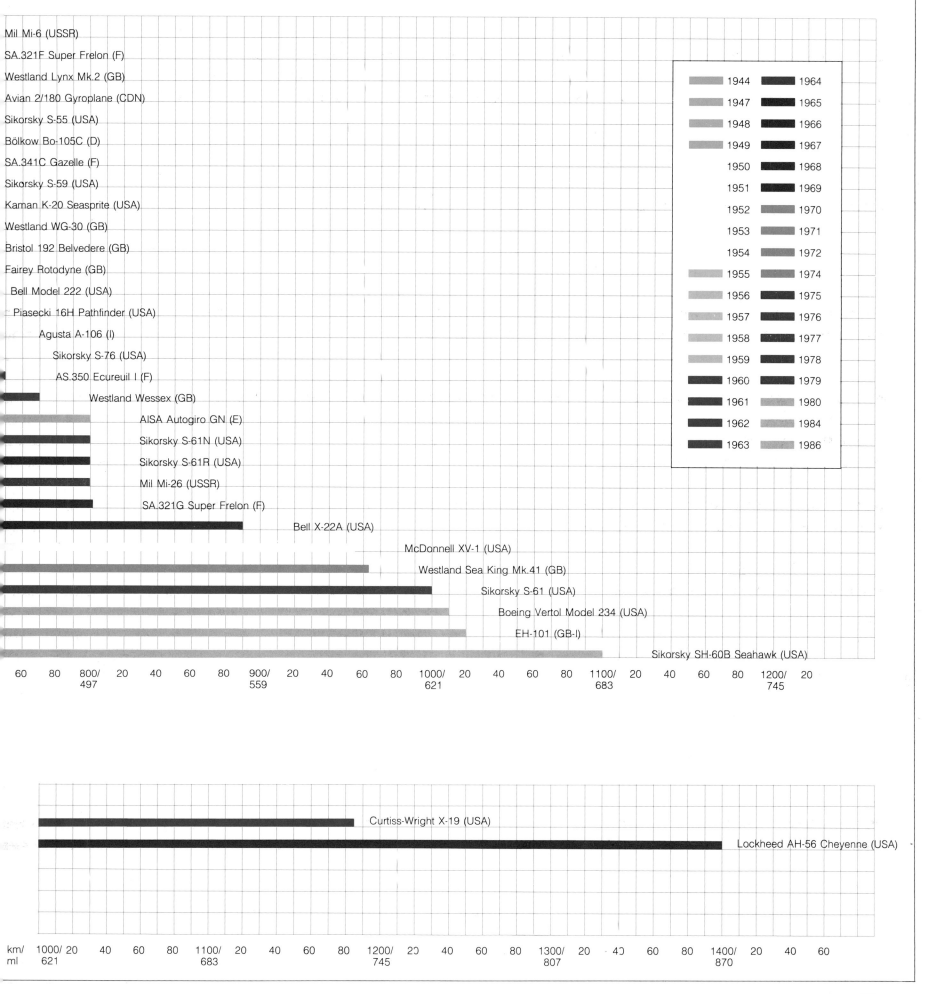

Mil Mi-6 (USSR)
SA.321F Super Frelon (F)
Westland Lynx Mk.2 (GB)
Avian 2/180 Gyroplane (CDN)
Sikorsky S-55 (USA)
Bölkow Bo-105C (D)
SA.341C Gazelle (F)
Sikorsky S-59 (USA)
Kaman K-20 Seasprite (USA)
Westland WG-30 (GB)
Bristol 192 Belvedere (GB)
Fairey Rotodyne (GB)
Bell Model 222 (USA)
Piasecki 16H Pathfinder (USA)
Agusta A-106 (I)
Sikorsky S-76 (USA)
AS.350 Ecureuil I (F)
Westland Wessex (GB)
AISA Autogiro GN (E)
Sikorsky S-61N (USA)
Sikorsky S-61R (USA)
Mil Mi-26 (USSR)
SA.321G Super Frelon (F)
Bell X-22A (USA)
McDonnell XV-1 (USA)
Westland Sea King Mk.41 (GB)
Sikorsky S-61 (USA)
Boeing Vertol Model 234 (USA)
EH-101 (GB-I)
Sikorsky SH-60B Seahawk (USA)

1944	1964
1947	1965
1948	1966
1949	1967
1950	1968
1951	1969
1952	1970
1953	1971
1954	1972
1955	1974
1956	1975
1957	1976
1958	1977
1959	1978
1960	1979
1961	1980
1962	1984
1963	1986

60   80   800/   20   40   60   80   900/   20   40   60   80   1000/   20   40   60   80   1100/   20   40   60   80   1200/   20
              497   559   621   683   745

Curtiss-Wright X-19 (USA)
Lockheed AH-56 Cheyenne (USA)

km/   1000/   20   40   60   80   1100/   20   40   60   80   1200/   20   40   60   80   1300/   20   40   60   80   1400/   20   40   60
ml   621   683   745   807   870

39

A

Aérospatiale, see p. 93
American Helicopter XH-26 Jet Jeep, see p. 121

AEROTECNICA
Aerotecnica S.A. (Spain)

This company was set up in Spain in order to pursue the design studies into rotorcraft begun in 1952 by Jean Cantinieau for the French company, Matra. The Spanish government purchased the construction rights for the Cantinieau helicopters and the contract was awarded to Aerotecnica.

Aerotecnica AC-12/13/14

The Spanish company Aerotecnica began designing and building rotary wing craft in 1955, developing a project conceived by the French engineer Cantinieau. The Spanish Air Force sponsored the construction of two prototypes of the Model AC-12 and subsequently bought 12. The powerplant of this helicopter was installed on the cabin roof and it had automobile-type transmission with a reduction gear. The three-blade metal rotor had duralumin spars, ribs and leading edges with a part fiberglass skin. The tail rotor was also three-bladed and of metal construction. The two-seat cabin was provided with dual controls. A turbine-powered variant of the AC-12 was under development when Aerotecnica closed down in 1962.

In the AC-13 variant, the Lycoming engine was replaced by a Turboméca Artouste turbine, and the antitorque rotor was abolished, its work being done by the exhaust gases from the turbine, which were ducted along the tail boom to a nozzle at the tip. One of the prototypes of the AC-13 was taken to France for research purposes and designated Nord 1750 Norelfe.

The AC-14, derived from one of the two AC-13 prototypes, had a much bigger fuselage and cabin space for a pilot and four passengers seated on two bench seats behind. As with the AC-12, the 400 shp Turboméca Artouste IIB1 engine was installed above the cabin

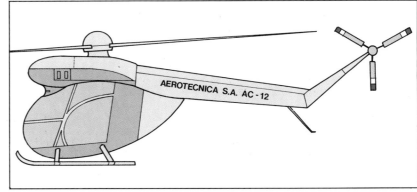

Helicopter: **AC-12**
Manufacturer: **Aerotecnica S.A.**
Type: **liaison**
Year: **1956**
Engine: **168 hp Lycoming O-360-B2A**
Rotor diameter: **8.50 m (27 ft 11 in)**
Fuselage length: **7.55 m (24 ft 9 in)**
Overall length: —
Height: **2.75 m (9 ft)**
Empty weight: **500 kg (1,102 lbs)**
Gross weight: **820 kg (1,808 lbs)**
Maximum speed: **145 km/h (90 mph)**
Hovering ceiling IGE*: **2,400 m (7,874 ft)**
Service ceiling: **4,000 m (13,125 ft)**
Range: **230 km (143 miles)**
Capacity: **1 pilot + 1 observer**
*in ground effect

Helicopter: **AC-13**
Manufacturer: **Aerotecnica S.A.**
Type: **liaison**
Year: **1957**
Engine: **260 shp Turboméca Artouste I**
Rotor diameter: **9.37 m (30 ft 9 in)**
Fuselage length: **7.48 m (24 ft 6 in)**
Height: **2.75 m (9 ft)**
Empty weight: **574 kg (1,265 lbs)**
Gross weight: **880 kg (1,940 lbs)**
Maximum speed: **140 km/h (87 mph)**
Hovering ceiling IGE: **2,650 m (8,694 ft)**
Service ceiling: **6,065 m (19,900 ft)**
Range: **300 km (186 miles)**
Capacity: **1 pilot + 1 observer**

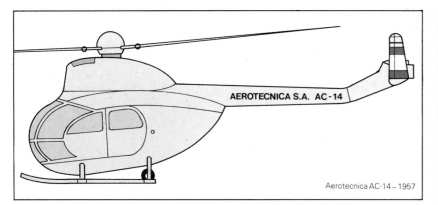

Aerotecnica AC-14 – 1957

Helicopter: AC-14
Manufacturer: **Aerotecnica S.A.**
Type: **liaison/light transport**
Year: **1957**
Engine: **400 shp Turboméca Artouste IIB**
Rotor diameter: **9.67 m (31 ft 8 in)**
Fuselage length: **8.02 m (26 ft 4 in)**
Height: **3.10 m (10 ft 2 in)**
Empty weight: **620 kg (1,366 lbs)**
Gross weight: **1,200 kg (2,645 lbs)**
Maximum speed: **160 km/h (100 mph)**
Hovering ceiling IGE: **4,900 m (16,075 ft)**
Service ceiling: **6,800 m (22,310 ft)**
Capacity: **1 pilot + 4 passengers**

and the exhaust gases (ducted along the tail boom) were used instead of a tail rotor for directional control at low speed, control in fast flight being provided by two small fins. The AC-14 also had skid landing gear. Ten were built for the Spanish Air Force, with the designation EC-XZ-4. Further developments of these aircraft were halted by closure of the company.

AGUSTA
Costruzioni Aeronautiche Giovanni Agusta S.p.A. (Italy)

Giovanni Agusta started building airplanes when very young and flew his first plane in 1910 at Capua outside Naples. When the First World War was over he founded the aircraft company at Cascina Costa which still bears his name. In addition to his factory at Malpensa airport, near Milan, he opened two new factories in 1923, at Tripoli and Benghazi.

During the twenties the company built a succession of very small sporting and competition aircraft, one of which was the Ag.3, powered by a 15 hp Anzani engine. Giovanni Agusta died in 1927, leaving his wife, Giuseppina, in charge of the business.

After the war aircraft construction was not resumed at Cascina Costa until 1950. In 1952 an agreement was entered into with Bell Aircraft for the construction and marketing of its helicopters in Europe. The first helicopter to take to the air at Cascina Costa was the two-seat Agusta Bell 47. By 1958 Agusta had already gained enough expertise to undertake its own projects, such as the A.101G, the A.102, the A.104 and the A.105 but none of these helicopters progressed beyond the prototype stage.

In 1965 the company commenced construction of the Bell 205, followed the next year by the AB-206 JetRanger light helicopter. Agusta then acquired the Italian rights to manufacture the twin-engine Sikorsky SH-3D under license, and those for the twin-rotor tandem Boeing Vertol CH-47, through its associated company, Elicotteri Meridionali.

The twin-turbine Agusta Bell 212 went into production at the same time as the AS-61R search and rescue helicopter and the AB-212 ASW antisubmarine and antiship helicopter. From the latter Agusta derived its own design, the A.109. In 1973 a cooperation agreement was signed with the EFIM government finance agency. During its lengthy and varied career in the aviation business, Agusta has produced over 4,400 civil and military helicopters.

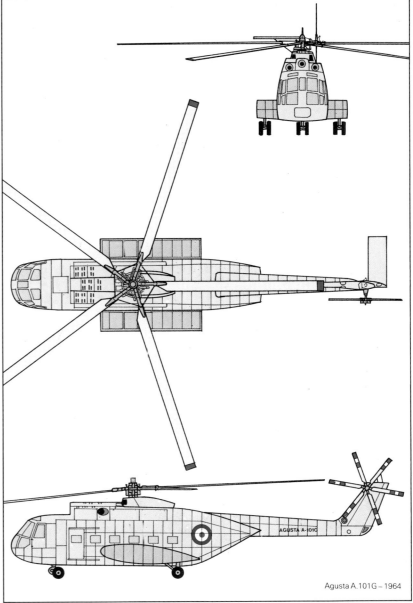

Agusta A.101G – 1964

Helicopter: A.101G
Manufacturer: **Costruzioni Aeronautiche G. Agusta**
Type: **military transport**
Year: **1964**
Engines: **3 × 1,400 shp Rolls-Royce Bristol Gnome H-1400**
Rotor diameter: **20.40 m (66 ft 11 in)**
Fuselage length:—
Overall length: **20.15 m (66 ft 1 in)**
Height: **6.56 m (21 ft 6 in)**
Empty weight: **6,855 kg (15,112 lbs)**
Gross weight: **12,912 kg (28,466 lbs)**
Maximum speed: **241 km/h (150 mph)**
Hovering ceiling IGE: **3,450 m (11,319 ft)**
Service ceiling: **4,600 m (15,090 ft)**
Range: **400 km (248 miles)**
Capacity: **37 troops or 5,000 kg (11,020 lbs)**

Agusta A.101

Filippo Zappata's Agusta A.101D project was introduced at the Milan Trade Fair in April 1958, in the form of a somewhat rudimentary model. During 1959, this ambitious Italian helicopter began to take shape, but progress was slow, owing to heavy production programmes at the Cascina Costa plant. It was first flown on 19 October 1964 by top test pilot Ottorino Lancia. A lengthy develop-

ment period ensued under the direction of engineers Bellavita and Lovera, involving over 400 flying hours in addition to those on the rotor test rig.

The A.101's performance was inferior to that of the contemporary French Super Frelon, but it was more stable, had less vibration and a more capacious fuselage. The powerplant was new, consisting of three turbine engines. The single prototype of the Agusta helicopter underwent visible external modifications during development — it was fitted with a twin nosewheel assembly and longer fairings on each side of the fuselage, which had also been extended by grafting in a new section. The helicopter performed service trials involving rapid embarkation and disembarkation through the two lateral sliding doors and tail ramp. It could carry two pilots and 35 equipped troops, or a 5,000 kg (11,020 lbs) load.

The A.101 was examined by interested foreign parties visiting Cascina Costa and was displayed at the Turin Air Show in June 1966, where it stood out from other Agusta models simply on account of its size. By autumn 1966 the aircraft was ready for large-scale production, but a further two years were lost awaiting a decision by the authorities. In 1968 the helicopter reappeared at the Turin Air Show in camouflage finish and was tested at an all-up weight of 13,500 kg (29,762 lbs). At the end of autumn 1968 the A.101G was transferred to Pratica di Mare, the military airport outside Rome, for a series of trials which were completed in summer 1971. The aircraft made a few more flights, but by that time was hopelessly out-of-date.

Meanwhile, Agusta had reworked the A.101H by redesigning the fuselage and a few basic dynamic components. The fuselage was extended by 3 m (9 ft 10 in), while the rotor remained the same, and more powerful General Electric T58 turbine engines were installed. However this programme was also cancelled in favour of production under license of foreign aircraft whose reliability had been proven, such as Sikorsky and Boeing-Vertol helicopters.

Agusta A.102

From an old Bell Model 48 sent to Italy in 1956, Agusta developed a helicopter using the same mechanical components, powerplant and dimensions, but an entirely new fuselage. Behind the two pilot seats, there was room for two-three passengers plus a bench seat for another four-five in the fuselage, which was over 2.7 m (8 ft 10 in) wide. The original quadricycle landing gear was replaced by skids.

The prototype of the A.102 flew on 3 February 1959, and was displayed in military colours at that year's Paris Air Show. But Agusta also intended the A.102 for the civil market, which was growing in Italy, and indeed Elivie, the company which was already running flights with AB-47J helicopters between Naples and the islands, took delivery of a couple of A.102s in spring 1961, to operate a regular service between the center of Turin and Milan airports. The availability of new turbine-powered helicopters, however, soon rendered the A.102 obsolete.

Agusta A.105

After the A.102, Agusta tackled other original designs and at the beginning of the sixties, the single-seat A.103 and two-seat A.104 were produced by the Cascina Costa works with a powerplant which was also original — the 140 hp Agusta 1MV.

A few days after the first flight of the big A.101G, another original helicopter took to the air — the A.105, a light two-seater incorporating modern technical features designed to simplify construction enormously. The A.105 had a Turboméca-Agusta TA-230 turbine engine with a reduction gear designed and built by Agusta. The helicopter was intended for liaison, aerial photography and high-speed transport. The four-seat variant of the same helicopter, the A.105B, was also displayed at the 1965 Paris Air Show. It had the same mechanical and structural parts as the two-seater, but a bigger cabin. Both models remained at the prototype stage.

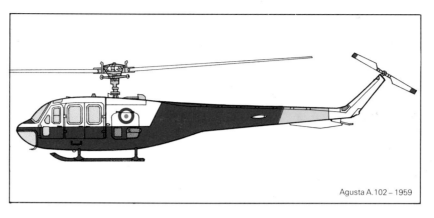

Agusta A.102 – 1959

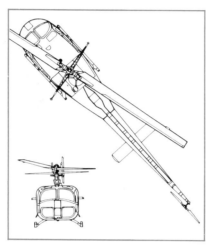

Helicopter: **A.102**
Manufacturer: **Costruzioni Aeronautiche G. Agusta**
Type: **light transport**
Year: **1959**
Engine: **600 hp Pratt & Whitney R-1340**
Rotor diameter: **14.50 m (47 ft 7 in)**
Fuselage length: **12.60 m (41 ft 4 in)**
Overall length: **17.92 m (58 ft 9 in)**
Height: **3.23 m (10 ft 7 in)**
Empty weight: **1,800 kg (3,968 lbs)**
Gross weight: **2,725 kg (6,007 lbs)**
Maximum speed: **177 km/h (110 mph)**
Cruise speed: **160 km/h (100 mph)**
Service ceiling: **3,900 m (12,795 ft)**
Range: **400 km (248 miles)**

Helicopter: **Agusta A.105**
Manufacturer: **Construzioni Aeronautiche G. Agusta**
Type: **light transport/liaison**
Year: **1964**
Engine: **350 shp Turboméca-Agusta TA-230**
Rotor diameter: **9.00 m (29 ft 6 in)**
Fuselage length: **—**
Overall length: **—**
Height: **2.60 m (8 ft 6 in)**
Empty weight: **485 kg (1,069 lbs)**
Gross weight: **1,000 kg (2,205 lbs)**
Maximum speed: **210 km/h (130 mph)**
Hovering ceiling IGE: **—**
Service ceiling: **4,750 m (15,585 ft)**
Range: **320 km (200 miles)**
Capacity: **1 pilot + 1 passenger**

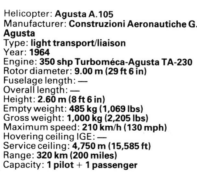

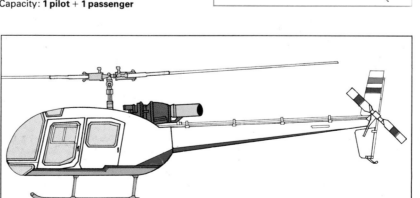

Agusta A.105 – 1964

Agusta A.106

The A.106 made its first flight in November 1965. It was developed to meet a somewhat ambitious Italian naval specification for a single-seat helicopter which could fit into the hangars of smaller vessels such as frigates. In designing it, Agusta drew upon the experience acquired with the A.103, A.104 and A.105 light helicopters. The little single-seater had a Turboméca-Agusta TAA-230 turbine behind the very compact cockpit, and landing skids with auxiliary flotation gear (but provision for two inflated pontoons). The two-blade light alloy rotor could be folded back. Systems included an autostabilizing device, an acoustic submarine detector and armament of two Mk.44 torpedoes. The Italian Navy ordered two prototypes and five production aircraft, but construction of the latter was suspended in 1973.

Agusta A.109

Agusta began taking an interest in light turbine-powered helicopters in 1959 and developed a series of prototypes culminating in the A.105. Feasibility studies for a medium-capacity helicopter to succeed it — the A.109 — began in 1969, when many different designs were examined and the most promising subjected to thorough research. Wind tunnel tests, lasting almost a year, enabled the characteristics of the new helicopter to be greatly refined. Once the basic project had been drawn up, final design work of parts and equipment began in spring 1970, and in the summer detailed construction work was started.

The A.109 was originally intended to have a Turboméca Astazou or UACL PT6B turbine engine, delivering about 700 shp, but the A.109C (civil) version had the same four-blade rotor but a completely new fuselage, with clean, elegant lines. The powerplant was changed to twin 370 shp Allison 250-C14 turbines and a retractable undercarriage was fitted.

The new aircraft was assembled in spring 1971; ground tests then took place, and the prototype made its first flight on 4 August 1971 from the Cascina Costa plant. It was piloted by Ottorino Lancia accompanied by Paolo Bellavita, who had developed the aircraft together with Bruno Lovera. Owing to a minor accident, testing was resumed some time later, in 1972, using the second prototype, as well as a special static test rig for the dynamic

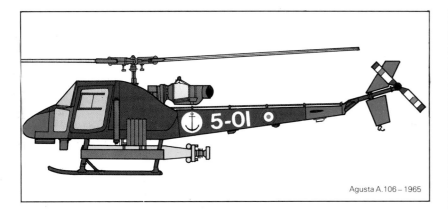

Agusta A.106 – 1965

components. In 1973 a third prototype in military configuration was developed, together with a fourth model for civil use and an airframe for static tests.

The A.109 high-speed civil helicopter is in a class mid-way between the AB-206 and the Bell 212. It has a conventional configuration with a classic, four-blade articulated rotor, especially designed for fast flight. The rotor blades are of conventional honeycomb structure with a light alloy skin and extensive structural bonding. The carefully streamlined, compact fuselage consists of a broad, ventral shell in metal honeycomb with thin, light alloy panels designed to withstand the stresses from the cabin loads and shocks from the landing gear. The cabin can have various internal layouts, with pilot and crew seated side-by-side, two bench seats for two-three people, and a baggage compartment. Behind the cabin is the rear fuselage section which carries the landing gear units and fuel tanks. The retractable tricycle landing gear ensures optimum mobility on the ground and offers advantages in terms of reduced drag in fast flight. The fuel is distributed by electric pumps from two tanks with a total capacity of 550 liters (121 gallons). The two turbine engines are mounted side-by-side but are fully independent; breakdown of one does not affect the output of the other.

The five prototypes of the A.109 were certified in summer 1975. In fact, the Italian Aeronautical Register granted type approval to the A.109, the first twin-engine helicopter to be designed, developed and built wholly in Italy, on 30 May, shortly before the opening of the 31st Paris Aeronautical and Space Show. American approval followed two days later. In the meantime, production had already begun with five aircraft for evaluation by the Italian Army. Atlantic Aviation, then the American distributors of the Agusta 109, took out an option on 100 aircraft for the civil market at the same time.

More recently, Agusta has intro-

Helicopter: **Agusta A.106**
Manufacturer: **Costruzioni Aeronautiche G. Agusta**
Type: **shipboard antisubmarine**
Year: **1965**
Engine: **350 shp Turboméca-Agusta TAA-230 turbine**
Rotor diameter: **9.50 m (31 ft 2 in)**
Fuselage length: **8.70 m (28 ft 6 in)**
Overall length: **10.97 m (36 ft)**
Height: **2.50 m (8 ft 2 in)**
Empty weight: **690 kg (1,521 lbs)**
Gross weight: **1,340 kg (2,954 lbs)**
Maximum speed: **177 km/h (110 mph)**
Hovering ceiling IGE: **2,545 m (8,350 ft)**
Range: **740 km (466 miles)**
Armament: **2 Mk.44 torpedoes**

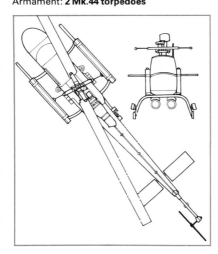

Helicopter: **Agusta A.109A**
Manufacturer: **Costruzioni Aeronautiche G. Agusta**
Type: **light transport**
Year: **1977**
Engines: **2 × 420 shp Allison 250-C20B**
Rotor diameter: **11.00 m (36 ft 1 in)**
Fuselage length: **11.16 m (36 ft 7in)**
Overall length: **13.08 m (42 ft 11 in)**
Height: **3.32 m (10 ft 11 in)**
Empty weight: **1,360 kg (3,000 lbs)**
Gross weight: **2,450 kg (5,400 lbs)**
Maximum speed: **310 km/h (193 mph)**
Hovering ceiling IGE: **3,050 m (10,000 ft)**
Service ceiling: **4,572 m (15,000 ft)**
Range: **570 km (354 miles)**
Capacity: **2 crew + 5/6 passengers**

duced the Model A.109A Mk. II derivative, which has been substantially modified in the light of the flying experience of customers from 15 countries in all parts of the world. As a result engine-out performance has been improved at high altitudes, and in hot climates.

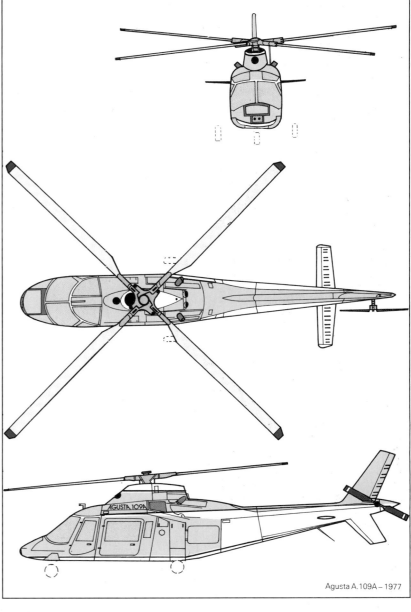

Agusta A.109A – 1977

Agusta A.129 Mangusta

The latest original design to appear from the Agusta stable, the A.129 Mangusta (Mongoose) is a day/ night military scout/antiarmour helicopter, which is expected to enter service with Italian Army Aviation squadrons in early 1986. Preliminary design of the A.129 began in 1978, and the first of four flying prototypes made its initial flight on 15 September 1983.

The A.129 uses a fully-articulated four-blade main rotor system with elastomeric bearings and low-noise profile tips. The fiberglass blades are designed to have a ballistic tolerance against hits from 12.7 mm ammunition and considerable tolerance against 23 mm hits. The transmission has a run-dry capability. A Harris digital integrated multiplex system controls communication, navigation, engine, armament,

Helicopter: **Agusta A.129**
Manufacturer: **Costruzioni Aeronautiche G. Agusta**
Type: **light scout/antiarmour helicopter**
Year: **1983**
Engines: **2 × 915 shp Rolls-Royce Gem 2 Mk. 1004D**
Rotor diameter: **11.90 m (39 ft ½ in)**
Fuselage length: **12.275 m (40 ft 3¼ in)**
Overall length: **14.29 m (46 ft 10½ in)**
Height: **3.35 m (11 ft)**
Empty weight: **2,529 kg (5,575 lbs)**
Gross weight: **3,700 kg (8,157 lbs)**
Maximum speed: **270 km/h (168 mph)**
Hovering ceiling IGE: **3,290 m (10,800 ft)**
Service ceiling: **2,390 m (7,850 ft)**
Range: **750 km (465 miles)**
Capacity: **2 crew**

power distribution and utility systems. The avionics include active and passive self-protection systems, and the 70 per cent composite-built airframe is resistant to 12.7 mm ammunition and meets the latest crashworthiness standards. The two crew are seated

in a tandem cockpit, fitted with a low-glint canopy and with a small frontal area to minimize visual and radar detection. The powerplant is two Rolls-Royce Gem 2 turbines, license-built in Italy by Piaggio.

A variety of offensive armament can be carried by the A.129 on four stub-wing attachment points, the inner pair being stressed for loads up to 300 kg (661 lbs). All four pylons can be elevated 3° and depressed 12°. Typical antiarmour weaponry which can be carried includes eight Hughes TOW or Euromissile HOT missiles, using a telescopic sight with laser range finder and FLIR for target acquisition, or six Rockwell Hellfires, using a mast-mounted sight, pilot's night vision equipment and integrated helmet and display sighting system.

A total of 66 A.129s had been ordered by the Italian Army by early 1984, when Agusta was also anticipating future orders from the Middle East and South America.

The twin-turbine A.109 by Agusta, first seen at the Paris Air Show in 1977.

AISA
Aeronautica Industrial S.A. (Spain)

Founded in 1923 by Jorge Loring Martinez in premises at the Madrid airport of Cuatro Vientos. The company's business entailed the construction, overhaul and servicing of aircraft and helicopters as well as the construction of Fokker transports under license. Since the end of the Second World War AISA has concentrated its efforts on designing and building aircraft and helicopters.

AISA Autogyro GN

At the end of the seventies, the Spanish company AISA, with past experience of building Cierva autogyros, developed a design of its own intended for the civil market, with larger capacity than that of contemporary autogyros produced in Great Britain and the United States. The GN autogyro, powered by a 300 shp Lycoming LO-540 engine driving a two-blade, constant-speed pusher propeller, seats four in an enclosed cabin, with access doors on either side. The four-blade articulated rotor has a brake, and a stub wing supports twin tail booms with twin fins. The semi-monocoque fuselage is of light alloy and the rest of the structure is also metal, with fixed nose-wheel landing gear.

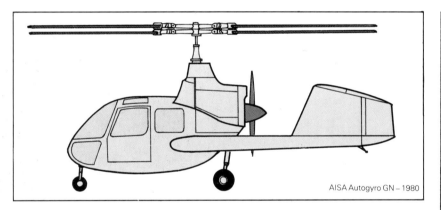

AISA Autogyro GN – 1980

Aircraft: **AISA Autogyro GN**
Manufacturer: **Aeronautica Industrial S.A.**
Type: **autogyro**
Year: **1980**
Engine: **300 shp Lycoming LO-540**
Rotor diameter: **12.80 m (42 ft)**
Fuselage length: **6.50 m (21 ft 4 in)**
Wingspan: **2.60 m (8 ft 6 in)**
Height: **3.20 m (10 ft 6 in)**
Empty weight: **708 kg (1,560 lbs)**
Gross weight: **1,200 kg (2,645 lbs)**
Maximum speed: **240 km/h (150 mph)**
Rate of climb: **390 m/min (1,280 ft/min)**
Range: **800 km (500 miles)**

Aircraft: **Avian 2/180 Gyroplane**
Manufacturer: **Avian Aircraft Ltd.**
Type: **two-seat compound**
Year: **1961**
Engine: **200 hp Lycoming LO-360**
Rotor diameter: **11.28 m (37 ft)**
Fuselage length: **4.92 m (16 ft 2 in)**
Height: **2.95 m (9 ft 8 in)**
Empty weight: **590 kg (1,300 lbs)**
Gross weight: **862 kg (1,900 lbs)**
Maximum speed: **193 km/h (120 mph)**
Hovering ceiling IGE: **—**
Service ceiling: **4,280 m (14,042 ft)**
Range: **640 km (398 miles)**

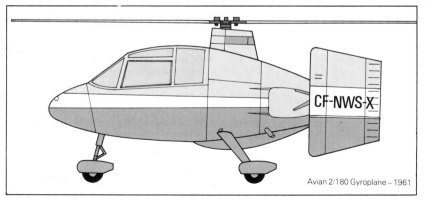

Avian 2/180 Gyroplane – 1961

AVIAN
Avian Aircraft Ltd. (Canada)

The company was founded in 1959 by Peter Payne, together with a small group of fellow designers and engineers, who had left Avro Canada once the contract for the Arrow interceptor was completed. This Canadian company has its headquarters at Georgetown, Ontario, and from its inception concentrated on the design and construction of helicopters and autogyros.

Avian 2/180 Gyroplane

This little two-seat Gyroplane was a compound aircraft flew in spring 1960 as an experimental machine, and a small production run followed. After the rotor had been set in motion for vertical take-off, movement was transferred to a four-blade, ducted pusher propeller at the tail. The Avian 2/180 underwent various modifications and improvements before being granted approval as a civil aircraft in 1967. The engine was a 200 hp Lycoming LO-360 which enabled it to fly at 193 km/h (120 mph). In spite of its good performance, high costs prevented further development.

B

BELL
Bell Helicopter Company — Textron Inc. (USA)

Lawrence Dane Bell was born in 1894 in Indiana, and in 1935 founded the Bell Aircraft Corporation in Buffalo, remaining chief executive of the company until the Second World War. During its early years the company depended mainly on subcontracts for its income, but in July 1937 it completed its first original project, the XFM-1, a twin-engine long-range escort fighter with pusher propellers and impressive armament consisting of two 37 mm cannons and four 12.7 mm machine guns. The next project was the construction of the P-39 Airacobra single-seat fighter, an interesting feature of which was the siting of the engine in the center of the fuselage behind the pilot. This was followed by the P-63 Kingcobra single-seat fighter-bomber. Bell also built the first American jet aircraft, the P-59 Airacomet which made its maiden flight in October 1942.

One of Bell's most exciting and impressive post-war achievements was the construction of the first supersonic aircraft as part of a joint programme sponsored by the USAF and NACA (later to become NASA). This was a piloted, rocket-motor propelled experimental aircraft with thin-section straight wings. The X-1 started tests in 1946 and became the first airplane to exceed the speed of sound in October 1947. During their experimental flights subsequent models in the X-1 series reached a maximum speed of mach 2.44 and an altitude of over 27,000 m (88,590 ft). As the 1950s progressed Bell constructed several other experimental aircraft, among them the X-5 variable geometry wing plane and a vertical take-off aircraft, the X-14. The company also continued to work with NASA on investigating the problems of supersonic flight.

Bell became involved in helicopter design immediately after the United States entered the Second World War, and after two years of tests and trials brought a private venture of its own to fruition without any government support: its Model 30 experimental helicopter flew in 1943. One of the main achievements of this programme was that Bell had perfected the rotor system, later used to such good effect in one of the company's most successful helicopters, the Model 47.

In March 1952 Bell's helicopter activities were hived off into a separate division from Bell Aircraft and a completely new factory complex and offices were built at Fort Worth, Texas. This was known as the Bell Helicopter Division and, from 1957 onwards, as the Bell Helicopter Corporation. During the fifties the company entered into cooperation agreements with Kawasaki in Japan, Westland in Great Britain, and Agusta in Italy for the construction under license of its helicopters. Fixed wing activities remained concentrated at Niagara Frontier, which specialized in aircraft production, avionics and meeting military hardware requirements.

In July 1960 Bell, by this time renamed the Bell Aerospace Corporation, became part of the Textron Inc. industrial conglomerate. It was then re-organised into three divisions: Bell Aerosystem Company (which corresponded to the Niagara Frontier Division), Bell Helicopter Company, and the Hydraulic Research and Manufacturing Company (Burbank, California). Bell Aerosystems remained responsible for fixed-wing aircraft construction, powerplant, electronics and defense systems (among other contracts the company carried out experimental vertical flights with the tilting-duct VTOL X-22 it had built), while all work on rotorcraft continued to be carried out by Bell Helicopter at Fort Worth. Over a period of 30 years a total of more than 14,000 civil and military helicopters have left the assembly lines of the enormous Texas plant. The factory at Fort Worth also has an experimental unit based at the Arlington municipal airport and a logistical center at Hurst Airport.

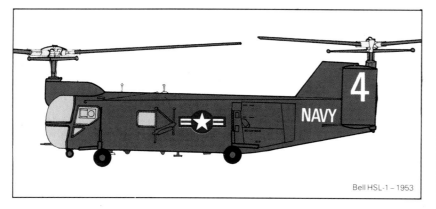

Bell HSL-1 – 1953

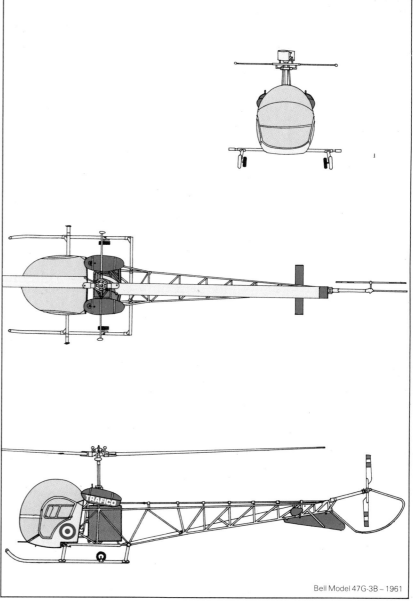

Bell Model 47G-3B – 1961

Bell HSL-1

The only invasion by Bell into Piasecki's province of heavy tandem-rotor helicopters was the HSL-1 (Bell 61). This was a nine-tonne aircraft with typical Bell two-blade rotors in a tandem layout, powered by a single 1,900 hp Pratt & Whitney double radial located at the rear of the fuselage. The helicopter won a US Navy design competition for a submarine hunter-killer.

After a three-year development period, the prototype flew on 4 March 1953. With two pilots and two sonar operators on board, it could carry 800 kg (1,764 lbs) of depth charges or two Petrel air-to-underwater missiles. However, trials showed that it created too much noise for effective ASW operation, and the ending of the Korean War led to cancellation of the

order for 96 HSL-1s for the US Navy and 18 for the Royal Navy. Only 50 were delivered to the US Navy.

Bell Model 47

The founder member of a family of helicopters which is still going strong made its first flight in spring 1943. The Bell Model 30 introduced to the helicopter world a two-blade rotor of fairly wide chord, forming an integral unit, hinged at the center like a balance, based on what was appropriately called the "seesaw" formula. Below it was a bar, also hinged on the rotor axis, with two streamlined counterweights at the tips which acted as gyroscopic stabilizers, connected to the cyclic pitch control mechanism. This was operated by tilting the plane of the two blades in relation to the vertical axis by means of the seesaw suspension. This layout was to characterize all Bell helicopters for nearly 40 years.

The first Bell helicopter had a 150 hp six-cylinder opposed Franklin engine. The open-framework welded steel tube fuselage was only covered at the front. The YR-13, a two-seater which was compact for helicopters of that period with a car-type enclosed cabin, retained this open structure; the civil version was designated the Bell 47B. Almost contemporary with this was the Model 42 with five seats, which did not get beyond the prototype stage.

The first Bell helicopter mass produced for military use was the Model 47D, developed in 1947 (designated H-13D and H-13E for the US Army and HTL-4 for the US Navy), in which the cabin was replaced by a "goldfish bowl" Plexiglass canopy; 490 were built.

From the 47D, two main types were derived, the 47G, and the 47J Ranger with a covered fuselage. The Bell 47G (OH-13G) was a fully redesigned version, which had a 200 hp Franklin 6V4-200-C32 engine. Its main characteristics were the linking of the horizontal plane

with the rotor angle and the inclusion of two dorsal fuel tanks. From 1953, 265 were built, all assigned to the US Army. The model 47G-2 was identical except for the adoption of a 250 hp Lycoming TVO-435 engine. The US Army took over 400 (H-13H), while a small number of a similar model (H-13J) went to the USAF.

Another long-running series was the 47G-3 which remained in production in the United States and overseas for many years. The US Army commissioned 283 Bell 47G-3Bs (OH-13S) in addition to which 274 pilot trainers (TH-13T) were built, equipped with VOR, ADF, ILS and marker beacons. Other versions of the 47G were the G-4, with a 305 hp Lycoming TVO-540 engine, the G-3B-2, with a 270 hp Lycoming TVO-435 (with turbo-charger), designed for use at high altitudes, and the G-5, a simplified version for civil use. The 47G-3B-2A version for hot climates and high altitudes, which

Helicopter: Bell HSL-1
Manufacturer: **Bell Helicopter Company**
Type: **antisubmarine**
Year: **1953**
Engine: **1,900 hp Pratt & Whitney R-2800-50**
Rotor diameter: **15.70 m (51 ft 6 in)**
Fuselage length: **12.70 m (41 ft 8 in)**
Overall length: **—**
Height: **4.40 m (14 ft 5 in)**
Empty weight: **5,652 kg (12,460 lbs)**
Gross weight: **9,080 kg (20,018 lbs)**
Maximum speed: **217 km/h (135 mph)**
Hovering ceiling IGE: **3,017 m (9,900 ft)**
Service ceiling: **4,725 m (15,500 ft)**
Range: **563 km (350 miles)**
Armament: **2 torpedoes or 800 kg (1,764 lbs) of bombs**

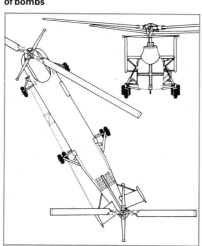

Helicopter: Bell 47G-3B
Manufacturer: **Bell Helicopter Company**
Type: **observation/liaison**
Year: **1961**
Engine: **270 hp Lycoming TVO-435**
Rotor diameter: **11.35 m (37 ft 3 in)**
Fuselage length: **9.62 m (31 ft 7 in)**
Overall length: **13.17 m (43 ft 2 in)**
Height: **2.83 m (9 ft 3 in)**
Empty weight: **814 kg (1,795 lbs)**
Gross weight: **1,340 kg (2,954 lbs)**
Maximum speed: **169 km/h (105 mph)**
Hovering ceiling IGE: **6,100 m (20,013 ft)**
Service ceiling: **5,330 m (17,487 ft)**
Range: **507 km (315 miles)**
Capacity: **1 pilot + 2 passengers**

was suitable for both civil and military operation, remained in production in the USA until 1970, as did the 47G-5A, which had a cabin about 30 cm (1 ft) wider, mainly intended for agricultural and similar tasks.

One Bell Model 47G was fitted experimentally with a Turboméca Artouste turbine built under license by Continental as the Model 200-T51T-3; it delivered 425 shp. As the XH-13F, it was built at the beginning of 1955 to test some components

46

for the Bell 204. Another 47G airframe was also fitted with wings for a special research programme.

The Bell 47 was a major success abroad, thanks to the sizeable numbers built under license by Agusta in Italy, where it remained in production until the beginning of the seventies. Until the appearance of more modern aircraft, the small AB-47 formed the backbone of Italy's helicopter units. Her Army Air Corps ordered a total of 75, in the AB-47G-2 and 47G-3B versions. A few went to the Navy and no fewer than 70 served with the Italian carabinieri, police, customs and fire brigade. Another 50 were supplied to the British Army Air Corps before Westland began producing them under license. Hundreds of the Italian AB-47 were supplied to operators all over the world, the last examples going to Zambia.

The model 47J was fully redesigned, with a covered fuselage like that of the commercial 47H-1, and a longer cabin to make room for a bench seat for three. The Bell 47J Ranger was supplied to the US Navy (HTL-7), the US Coast Guard and Marine Corps. Like its predecessors, the Ranger was also built by Agusta who developed an anti-submarine version (the first helicopter of this type to be carried on Italian naval vessels). However problems with stability, all-weather capability and weapon load detracted from the suitability of the Super Ranger as an ASW craft. Agusta built over 1,100 AB-47G/Js.

Bell Model 204

The Bell Model 204 was designed in 1954 to meet a US Army specification for a military helicopter for casualty evacuation, troop carrying, and pilot training. The US Army ordered three XH-40 prototypes, the first of which flew at Fort Worth on 22 October 1956, piloted by Floyd Carlson, less than 16 months after the project had begun. It was the first turbine-powered aircraft adopted by the Army.

The prototypes were followed by six YH-40 pre-production aircraft, delivered in August 1958 for evaluation. The YH-40 was different in some respects, notably in that the cabin was 30 cm (1 ft) longer. Other modifications included 10 cm (4 in) higher landing skids, a wider access door and changes to the controls, whilst the original 700 shp Lycoming T53 turbine was replaced by a new 770 shp version. The helicopter followed the Bell formula of using a two-blade rotor and stabilization system with a two-blade anti-torque tail rotor. The turbine, installed on the cabin roof, could operate on all the main types of fuel, including petrol, kerosene and JP4, and 1,000 hours could elapse between overhauls. The spacious cabin could accommodate two crew and eight troops or four stretchers.

After a series of intensive trials in various climatic conditions, the US Army decided to order a further batch of nine, which were known as HU-1 (Helicopter Utility) under the Army Air Forces' new, independent system of aircraft designation. The first HU-1 left the factory in September 1958 and was delivered to an experimental base in Alaska for cold weather trials. In October 1959,

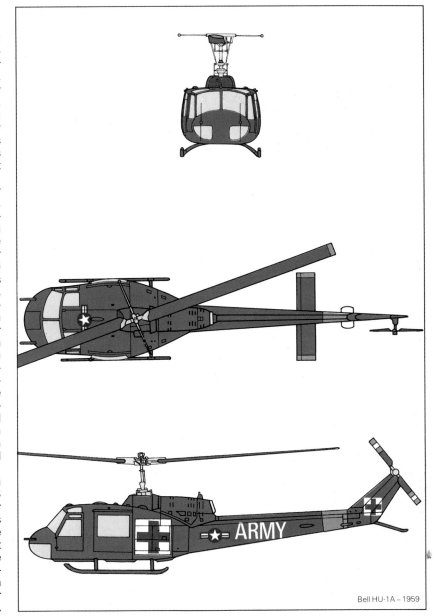

Bell HU-1A – 1959

it was sent to Fort Rucker for tests with Nord SS11 missiles.

As the Iroquois, the HU-1A was the first version to be ordered in large numbers, in March 1959. Delivery of the first batch of 100 (which were known by the unofficial name of "Huey") was not completed until June 1961; from spring 1960, the Iroquois was also assigned to light aviation units overseas (in Korea and Europe). Fourteen were fitted with IFR avionics and were assigned to the Army Aviation School. Various weapons fits were then tested on the HU-1A, including six Nord AGM-22A wire-guided missiles, four Emerson M73 7.62 mm machine guns or a General Electric automatic grenade launcher, as well as 70 mm rockets. The armed HU-1As went into action in Vietnam in October 1962 equipped with two 7.62 mm guns and 16 air-to-ground rockets.

Development of the HU-1's suc-

Helicopter: **Bell Model 204 (HU-1A)**
Manufacturer: **Bell Helicopter Company**
Type: **utility/transport**
Year: **1959**
Engine: **860 shp Lycoming T53-L-1A**
Rotor diameter: **13.40 m (44 ft)**
Fuselage length: **12.98 m (42 ft 7 in)**
Overall length: **13.59 m (44 ft 7 in)**
Height: **3.87 m (12 ft 8 in)**
Empty weight: **2,050 kg (4,520 lbs)**
Gross weight: **3,856 kg (8,500 lbs)**
Maximum speed: **238 km/h (148 mph)**
Hovering ceiling IGE: **3,230 m (10,600 ft)**
Service ceiling: **3,500 m (11,483 ft)**
Range: **615 km (382 miles)**
Capacity: **2 pilots + 8 troops**
Armament: **2 × 7.62 mm machine guns**

cessor, the Model 204B, began in June 1959, when the US Army ordered four YHU-1B prototypes. These had more powerful Lycoming engines and wider chord, honeycomb-structure, rotor blades. The first prototype flew in 1960 and delivery of production HU-1Bs began in December of that year. Various weapons fits were adopted, similar to those on the earlier model; the HU-1Bs which went into

The prototype of the Bell Model 47J. Unlike the Model 47G, it had a covered fuselage and the cabin capacity was increased from three to four seats. The 47J was produced in large numbers for civil and military operators.

operation in Vietnam in the late autumn of 1962 carried four 7.62 mm M60 machine guns and two containers for air-to-ground rockets. The last HU-1Bs (which from 1962 were given the new interforces designation of UH-1B) were built with 1,115 shp T53-L-11 turbines, and in 1965 the UH-1C version, which had a new "door-hinge" type rotor with 69 cm (27 inch) chord blades, went into production.

One Model 204B was converted into a Model 533, using a much modified YHU-1B airframe to improve streamlining. By adding two Continental J69T-9 turbojets delivering 420 kg (926 lbs) thrust, it became a compound helicopter, the first to exceed a speed of 380 km/h (236 mph).

The UH-1B was delivered to various allies of the United States including Australia, New Zealand, Indonesia, South Vietnam, Thailand, Norway and Colombia. It was manufactured abroad by Agusta in Italy and Fuji in Japan. The first Agusta Bell 204B flew in Italy on 10 May 1961, fitted initially with a Bristol Siddeley Gnome turbine engine. The AB-204B has been supplied to the Italian armed forces (109 aircraft) and to various countries including Sweden, Holland, Saudi Arabia and Turkey.

The antisubmarine version developed in Italy was especially interesting; 30 were built for the Italian Navy and two for the Spanish Navy. It was a shipboard helicopter with an automatic stabilization system, Ekco search radar and two Mk.44 torpedoes.

Bell Model 205

The UH-1D has for many years been the US Army's standard tactical helicopter. Originally known as the Bell 205, it had a longer cabin than its predecessor, the Bell 204, with a different internal layout to accommodate ten-12 troops or six stretchers and a medical attendant.

The production models were preceded by seven prototype UH-1Ds, the first of which flew on 16 August 1961. The same powerplant was used: the T53-L-11, capable of delivering a maximum of 1,419 shp but with a maximum continuous power of 1,100 shp. As with the previous aircraft, the fuselage was built in two parts: the cabin section and the tail boom section. The cabin was particularly spacious with an internal capacity of 6.2 cu.m (219 cu.ft), representing an increase of 75 per cent compared to the volume of the earlier UH-1 series models. All the available space could be made use of, thanks to sliding doors giving access to the entire floor. A wide range of cabin configurations was possible; with the two crew seats at the front, this could vary from the high density version with a total capacity of 15 seats, to a five-seat VIP version. The classic Bell skid landing gear was of the high energy attenuation type.

All the flight controls of the Bell 205 are servo-assisted and the helicopter can be flown by a single pilot, seated on the right. A cargo hook is installed at the exact center of gravity, and the helicopter's stability and manoeuvrability are un-

affected even by a slung load. The 205's versatility is further increased by a wide range of optional equipment, provision for which is included in the standard configuration: dual controls, rotor brake, stretchers (six), fixed flotation gear, emergency flotation gear, skis, pods for external stores, and universal attachment points.

The first UH-1Ds that went into service, in August 1963, were assigned to the 11th Air Assault Division of the US Army. They were sent shortly afterwards to Vietnam, where they were mainly used for landing operations. Only rarely were they armed. American-built UH-1Ds went into service in Australia, Chile, Canada, Thailand, Laos, New Zealand, Peru and Turkey, while 352 aircraft ordered by the German armed forces were built under license by Dornier. The German company carried out the production programme in three phases, from straightforward assembly to manufacture of the entire aircraft, with the exception of a few dynamic components.

For Agusta, purchase of the license to produce the Bell 205 in Italy was a logical step, given their excellent sales and export record with the earlier AB-204B. Agusta began producing the 205 in 1963, first with a T53-L-11 turbine, then with the 1,400 shp T53-L-13 (with the AB-205A corresponding to the American UH-1H) and finally they produced a commercial version, the AB-205A-1. Agusta also designed and built two versions of its own: the AB-205TA with two 800 shp

Turboméca Astazou XII and the AB-205 Bi-Gnome with two 1,250 shp Rolls-Royce Gnome engines. Development of these two interesting machines was not pursued, as Agusta acquired instead the license to build the Bell Model 212 twin turboshaft. Several hundred AB-205s have been built for the armed forces of various countries including Italy, Iran, Kuwait, Abu Dhabi, Morocco, Saudi Arabia, Israel, Spain, Turkey, Greece, Zambia, and the sultanate of Oman.

Bell Model 206

In 1960 the US Department of Defense issued a specification for a Light Observation Helicopter (LOH) capable of performing economically the tasks normally allotted to at least three different types of helicopter: transport of personnel and cargo, casualty evacuation, light ground attack, artillery observation and photoreconnaissance. Of the dozen or so entrants, three finalists were selected: a project by Bell, one by Hiller and one by Hughes. Five prototypes of the respective models were ordered in spring 1961: the OH-4A, OH-5A and OH-6A. The first to be eliminated was the Bell project, but from the five government-financed OH-4A prototypes, a highly successful aircraft was later evolved: the Bell 206A JetRanger.

The specification called for an extensively-glazed four-seat aircraft with an Allison T63-A-5 turbine, a 360 kg (794 lb) payload and a max-

One of the 60 Bell 204s built under license by Agusta (AB-204B), in service with the Italian Air Force from 1963.

*One of the Bell Model 205s built by
Agusta, in service with the Air Force
of the sultanate of Muscat and
Oman in the seventies.*

imum speed of 250 km/h (155 mph).
The result was a machine with a
quadrangular cabin, a turbine on
the roof and a normal tail boom.
The main rotor was the classic Bell
type with a two-blade tail rotor on
the left-hand side of the fuselage.

Evaluation of the Bell model, originally designated D-250, ended on
30 June 1964 and, after the failure of
their military project, the Texan
company appeared at first to aban-
don any attempts at further development. Then, in order to be able
to compete on the civil market with
the other loser of the LOH contest,
the Fairchild Hiller FH-1100, Bell
began redesigning the Model 206 in
1965, to make it more attractive and
less military. The result was a very
fine design with elegant lines,
which won the approval of the civil
market and easily outclassed its
rival. The JetRanger had the same
dynamic components as the military prototype, but used all the power produced by the 317 shp Allison
250-C18 turbine. The prototype flew
on 10 January 1966 and was certified by the FAA on 20 October of
that year.

The Bell aircraft was an immediate market success, and by mid
1968 300 had been sold. Its performance was so outstanding that,
several years after its elimination
from the LOH contest, the interest of
the American armed forces was
rekindled. Although the capabilities
of the Hughes OH-6A were better (at
least on paper), its cost was higher

than foreseen. The US Army consequently went back on its decision, in
spite of the fact that the Allison 250
turbine fitted to the JetRanger was
giving some trouble at high speeds,
and on 8 March 1968 ordered no
less than 2,200 of the Model 206A,
renamed the OH-58 Kiowa. For its
part, the US Navy had already
ordered 40 trainers, which were
designated TH-57A SeaRanger.

Production of the OH-58 eventually ended with the completion of
2,200 army models in July 1973.
The first was delivered to the US

Helicopter: **Bell Model 205 (UH-1D)**
Manufacturer: **Bell Helicopter Company**
Type: **general purpose**
Year: **1963**
Engine: **1,100 shp Lycoming T53-L-11**
Rotor diameter: **14.63 m (48 ft)**
Fuselage length: **12.77 m (41 ft 10 in)**
Overall length: **17.40 m (57 ft)**
Height: **4.42 m (14 ft 6 in)**
Empty weight: **2,240 kg (4,938 lbs)**
Gross weight: **4,310 kg (9,500 lbs)**
Maximum speed: **222 km/h (138 mph)**
Hovering ceiling IGE: **5,550 m (18,210 ft)**
Service ceiling: **6,700 m (21,980 ft)**
Range: **510 km (317 miles)**
Capacity: **2 pilots + 10-12 troops**

Helicopter: **Bell Model 205 (UH-1H)**
Manufacturer: **Bell Helicopter Company**
Type: **general purpose**
Year: **1963**
Engine: **1,400 shp Lycoming T53-L-13**
Rotor diameter: **14.63 m (48 ft)**
Fuselage length: **12.77 m (41 ft 10 in)**
Overall length: **17.40 m (57 ft)**
Height: **4.42 m (14 ft 6 in)**
Empty weight: **2,177 kg (4,800 lbs)**
Gross weight: **4,310 kg (9,500 lbs)**
Maximum speed: **222 km/h (138 mph)**
Hovering ceiling IGE: **4,145 m (13,600 ft)**
Service ceiling: **6,700 m (21,980 ft)**
Range: **580 km (360 miles)**
Capacity: **2 pilots + 11-14 troops**

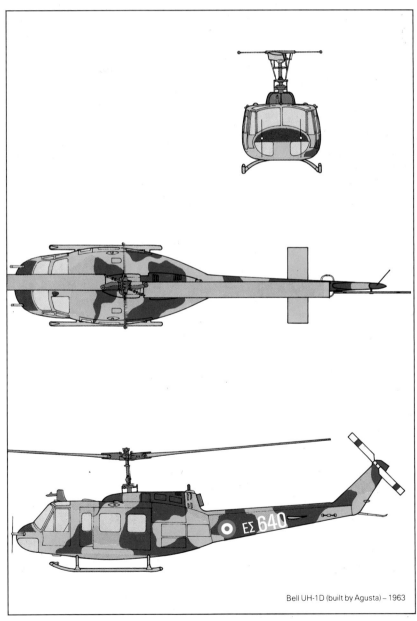

Bell UH-1D (built by Agusta) – 1963

49

Army on 23 May 1969, and in November of that year the type joined the Hughes OH-6A Cayuse in Vietnam, in the difficult task of replacing the old H-13 Sioux and H-23 Raven. To help meet the large number of orders, Bell subcontracted production of the fuselage to Beechcraft.

The military version of the Model 206A JetRanger also did well abroad, largely as a result of it being licensed to Agusta, who began producing it towards the end of 1967. Many aircraft were delivered to the armed forces of Italy, Iran, Spain, Sweden, Turkey, Austria, Abu Dhabi and Saudi Arabia.

The AB-206A-1 JetRanger (also called JetRanger I to distinguish it from the subsequent version) appeared to be somewhat underpowered (270 shp continuous), and was followed by the AB-206B-1 JetRanger II, with an Allison 250-C20 turbine delivering 400 shp and 317 shp on take-off. This was needed in particular by the Italian Army for work in the mountains and by the Iranian Army, often involved in missions at over 1,000 m (3,280 ft) in torrid heat. Initially, a modification was provided in the form of an injection system which could be retrofitted to existing aircraft, but introduction of the new, more powerful turbine provided a permanent solution to the problem. The Italian Army acquired 39 of the AB-206A-1 and 41 of the AB-206B-1; the Iranian Army ordered 43 and 27 respectively, and 30 were fitted with high skids for rough ground. The AB-206 continues to be used by the Italian Army Air Corps in many roles, notably observation and liaison. From spring 1971, Bell also built the JetRanger II, whilst 585 OH-58As were converted and fitted with the more powerful turbine and another 75 sent to Australia.

The most recent OH-58 variant is the updated OH-58D AHIP (Army Helicopter Improvement Program), under test in 1983 as a near-term scout helicopter for the US Army. Its configuration includes a mast-mounted sight, a new four-blade main rotor and a Sperry cockpit control and display system. At least 578 early-model OH-58s are expected to be converted to AHIP configuration between 1985-91.

The JetRanger has also been a big success on the civil market, which has absorbed over 220. In January 1976 the helicopter, equipped with a system developed by Collins, was also approved for instrument flight. In February 1977 the new JetRanger III was added to the family, the main innovation being the adoption of a 420 shp Allison 250-C20B turbine, giving a further improvement in flying performance at high altitudes and

temperatures. Meanwhile, the Bell 206L LongRanger was also introduced with a fuselage extended by 63 cm (2 ft 1 in) to make room for two more passengers (five seats plus the crew of two).

Bell TwinRanger

The Model 400 TwinRanger was announced in February 1983 as the first in a new family of Bell helicopters designed to maintain the company's leading position in the light/medium weight class. First flown in the spring of 1984 the initial Model 400 employs the four-blade soft in-plane main rotor already introduced on the OH-58D AHIP, with composite blades and hub, an advanced technology transmission with run-dry capability and twin Allison 250-C20P turboshaft engines. The fuselage is based on that

of the highly successful JetRanger, but deepened to provide extra fuel tankage, and terminates in a new ring fin tail assembly featuring a guarded tail rotor.

Production of the TwinRanger will begin in 1986 at a new Bell plant in Montreal, Canada, where development of two new variants, the 400A and 440 will be undertaken during the late 1980s. The Model 400A will introduce a new 937 shp Pratt & Whitney PW209T powerplant and the Model 440 will feature a larger fuselage, made possible by

Helicopter: **Bell Model 400 TwinRanger**
Manufacturer: **Bell Helicopter Company**
Type: **light transport**
Year: **1984**
Engine: **2 × 420 shp Allison 250-C20P**
Rotor diameter: **10.60 m (35 ft)**
Empty weight: **1,400 kg (3,075 lbs)**
Gross weight: **2,495 kg (5,500 lbs)**
Maximum speed: **278 km/h (172 mph)**
Hovering ceiling IGE: **—**
Service ceiling: **—**
Range: **760 km (450 miles)**
Capacity: **2 pilots + 5 passengers**

Bell Model 206A JetRanger – 1966

Helicopter: **Bell Model 206A JetRanger**
Manufacturer: **Bell Helicopter Company**
Type: **observation and light transport**
Year: **1966**
Engine: **317 shp Allison 250-C18**
Rotor diameter: **10.77 m (35 ft 4 in)**
Fuselage length: **9.93 m (32 ft 6 in)**
Overall length: **12.49 m (41 ft)**
Height: **2.91 m (9 ft 6 in)**
Empty weight: **664 kg (1,464 lbs)**
Gross weight: **1,049 kg (2,313 lbs)**
Maximum speed: **220 km/h (137 mph)**
Hovering ceiling IGE: **4,115 m (13,500 ft)**
Service ceiling: **5,760 m (18,900 ft)**
Range: **480 km (298 miles)**
Capacity: **2 pilots + 3 passengers**

Helicopter: **Bell Model 206L-1 LongRanger II**
Manufacturer: **Bell Helicopter Company**
Type: **light transport**
Year: **1974**
Engine: **500 shp Allison 250-C28B**
Rotor diameter: **11.28 m (37 ft)**
Fuselage length: **10.56 m (34 ft 8 in)**
Overall length: **12.46 m (40 ft 10 in)**
Height: **2.91 m (9 ft 6 in)**
Empty weight: **978 kg (2,156 lbs)**
Gross weight: **1,836 kg (4,047 lbs)**
Maximum speed: **241 km/h (150 mph)**
Hovering ceiling IGE: **—**
Service ceiling: **—**
Range: **620 km (385 miles)**
Capacity: **2 pilots + 5 passengers**

the weight savings from composite materials. The technical data given is provisional.

Bell Model 207 Sioux Scout

Predecessor of the AH-1 Cobra series, this experimental helicopter used the dynamics system and rear fuselage of a Bell OH-13 Sioux, married to a new gunship front fuselage. It had tandem seats with the operator of the twin turret (housing two 7.62 mm weapons) behind the pilot. The one model built was evaluated by the US Army. Engine: 260 shp Lycoming TVO 435. Rotor diameter: 11.28 m (37 ft).

Bell Model 209/309

Bell Helicopter undoubtedly has the most experience in the field of gunship helicopters. The first specification for this type of aircraft was produced in 1963, when Bell submitted the Model 204 Warrior (not built) and then the Model 207 Sioux Scout. In August 1964, the USAF launched the AAFSS (Advanced Aerial Fire Support System) programme, as an interim solution until the Cheyenne project being undertaken by Lockheed was completed (this in fact never went into service but would in any case have taken a number of years). Bell proposed the Model 209, the prototype of which had already been flying for some months. The HueyCobra, as the new helicopter was called, had obvious advantages over the other competitors, as 85 per cent of its parts were interchangeable with the UH-1D series, including the tail boom, dynamic components and the 1,400 shp engine, while the cockpit was a new design derived from the Sioux Scout.

In December 1965, the US Army asked for the prototype to be sent to the Edwards Air Force Base for evaluation. They were impressed by the aircraft's performance, and in the light of developments in the Vietnam War they ordered two prototypes on 4 April 1966, followed by an order for 110 production aircraft. The two prototypes had a number of differences compared with the original machine, the most notable of which was that the retractable undercarriage had been abolished and replaced by fixed skids to simplify construction. The US Army made a very happy choice with this helicopter, as can be seen from its unbroken service record from autumn 1967 to date.

The HueyCobra has a classic arrangement with a single main rotor and an anti-torque tail rotor. The main rotor is derived from that of earlier Bell military helicopters but is without the stabilizer bar. The two blades consist of an extruded light alloy section going from the leading edge to the point of widest cross-section, behind which is a thin sheet of light alloy, bonded to the honeycomb core.

In the AH-1G and 1Q versions, the HueyCobra has a Lycoming T53-L13 turbine capable of delivering up to 1,419 shp but derated to 1,115 shp to improve service life and dependability. The AH-1J version for the US Marine Corps, on the other hand, is powered by the T400-CP400 system developed by Pratt & Whitney (Canada), consisting of twin PT6 turbines with a maximum power on take-off and in emergency of 2,050 shp and 1,800 shp maximum continuous power. The light

alloy, semi-monocoque fuselage has a small frontal cross-section with a maximum width of only 0.965 m (3 ft 2 in), and a good aerodynamic profile, although the weapons installations carry a heavy drag penalty. Small stub wings are connected to the fuselage with a span of just over 3 m (9 ft 10 in). These provide appreciable lift in fast flight and can carry weapons from four attachment points up to a maximum of seventy-six 70 mm air-to-air rockets.

Exclusively designed for military use, the HueyCobra has armour protection for the crew and major components, as well as a powerful defensive armament, consisting, in the 1G and 1Q versions, of an

Helicopter: **Bell Model 209 (AH-1J SeaCobra)**
Manufacturer: **Bell Helicopter Company**
Type: **two-seat combat**
Year: **1969**
Engine: **1,800 shp Pratt & Whitney T400-CP400**
Rotor diameter: **13.41 m (44 ft)**
Fuselage length: **13.59 m (44 ft 7 in)**
Overall length: **16.14 m (52 ft 11 in)**
Height: **4.12 m (13 ft 6 in)**
Empty weight: **2,910 kg (6,415 lbs)**
Gross weight: **4,535 kg (10,000 lbs)**
Maximum speed: **330 km/h (205 mph)**
Hovering ceiling IGE: **3,800 m (12,470 ft)**
Service ceiling: **3,215 m (10,550 ft)**
Range: **550 km (342 miles)**
Armament: **One 20 mm cannon, 4 underwing attachments for rockets and machine guns**

Helicopter: **Bell Model 209 (AH-1T)**
Manufacturer: **Bell Helicopter Textron**
Type: **two-seat combat**
Year: **1980**
Engine: **1,970 shp Pratt & Whitney T400-WV-402**
Rotor diameter: **14.63 m (48 ft)**
Fuselage length: **14.68 m (48 ft 2 in)**
Overall length: **16.26 m (53 ft 4 in)**
Height: **4.15 m (13 ft 7 in)**
Empty weight: **3,635 kg (8,014 lbs)**
Gross weight: **6,350 kg (14,000 lbs)**
Hovering ceiling IGE: **3,800 m (12,470 ft)**
Service ceiling: **3,795 m (12,450 ft)**
Range: **576 km (358 miles)**
Armament: **various weapons and TOW missiles**

Bell AH-1J Sea Cobra – 1969

The US Marines received 38 Bell AH-1G HueyCobras in 1969, armed with a 20 mm cannon, whilst awaiting the twin-engine AH-1J Sea-Cobra.

One of the Bell AH-1S HueyCobras fitted with TOW missiles and ordered by the Japan Ground Self-Defense Force for trials.

Emerson Electric gun turret under the chin with two machine guns with six 7.62 mm rotating barrels, firing 8,000 rounds, or two XM-129 40 mm grenade launchers with 300 projectiles each. On the 1J version, the chin turret has an XM-97 20 mm cannon with three rotating barrels. Instead of rocket launchers, four containers for twenty-eight 70 mm rockets can be fitted to the underwing attachments, two XM-1E1 pods, each with a Minigun or eight TOW wire-guided antitank missiles in two pairs of containers.

Production of the Bell AH-1G began in 1967, followed in June of that year by delivery of the first 20 aircraft for the US Army, which were operational in Vietnam by the following autumn. Orders for the HueyCobra rose steadily from a total of 838 helicopters in October 1968 to 1,008 by January 1970. The later AH-1S version was still in production in 1984.

Thirty-eight AH-1Gs were assigned to the US Marine Corps in 1969, which later ordered 49 AH-1J SeaCobras — the twin turbine version. This was identical in size to the AH-1G and had similar armament. The Iranian armed forces ordered 202, while the AH-1G was ordered by the Royal Australian Air Force (11) and Spanish Navy (4). A few dual control TH-1G trainers were built, while other AH-1Gs were transformed into AH-1Q TowCobras with infra-red sights and eight Hughes TOW missiles, expressly designed for antitank warfare. New-build TowCobras to this standard were designated AH-1S, while the Marines have received the AH-1T (with a stretched fuselage and TOW missiles), a derivative of the Sea-Cobra using some dynamic components from the Bell 214. Other users of the Cobra family include Greece, Israel and Japan. On a typical mission, the AH-1 could reach its target

in half the time of the Iroquois and stay in the combat zone longer, with twice the fire power of a conventional helicopter.

Having always regarded the Model 209 as a temporary solution until a higher-performance machine was available, Bell decided to press ahead with a new project for the American armed forces and on 28 September 1971 announced the development of a new combat helicopter which flew on 10 September 1971. This was the Model 309 King-Cobra, clearly derived from the Model 209, with a 1.10 m (3 ft 7 in) longer, more robust fuselage supporting a larger diameter rotor measuring 14.63 m (48 ft). Both the main and tail rotors had wider chord blades and the blades of the former had double swept tips to reduce noise levels and improve performance at high speed. The nose was also modified to accept new apparatus, the available space

for ammunition was increased and the wing span was taken to 3.96 m (13 ft).

Of the two prototypes built, the first was offered to the Marines in the usual configuration with Turbo Twin Pack T400 engines, while the second prototype (which flew in January 1972) was offered to the Army with a different powerplant — the 2,890 shp Lycoming T55-L7C turbine, derated to 2,050 on take-off. On 11 April 1972, the first prototype was damaged in an accident. The second took part in comparative trials with the Lockheed Cheyenne and Sikorsky S-67 Black-hawk, but the US Army decided that none of them matched its requirements.

The KingCobra was a highly sophisticated aircraft with the latest equipment including an automatic stabilization system, autotrim system, laser day and night sight, infrared fire control system, night vision

TV and an inertial navigation system.

From the Model 309, Bell derived a new prototype attack helicopter, the Model 409 (US Army designation YAH-63), which it entered for the AAH (Advanced Attack Helicopter) competition won by the aircraft proposed by Hughes. The YAH-63 had a different profile from the KingCobra, including a conspicuous ventral fin and a tail plane at the top of the tail fin.

Bell Model 212

The American armed forces, by far the biggest users of the Huey series of helicopters, informed Bell that a twin-engine solution, even with the same power rating, would have advantages in terms of reliability and crew morale, above all on missions over the sea or enemy territory. Accordingly, Bell produced its first twin-turbine powered helicopter at the beginning of 1965, derived from a modified Model 205. The programme was financed by Bell and did not lead to any orders, but when the Texan company decided to fit the helicopter with a PT6T-3 powerplant manufactured by Pratt & Whitney of Canada, the Canadian government announced its support for development of the new helicopter. Shortly afterwards, the Canadian armed forces ordered 50 Bell 212s and the American armed forces ordered 141 (79 for the USAF, 40 for the US Navy and 22 for the US Marine Corps).

The model 212 has an identical fuselage to the Model 205, except for the very compact side-by-side twin engine installation and the nose which is 15 cm (6 in) longer. It has also been produced for the commercial market. In addition, it has been manufactured under license in Italy by Agusta, who built a demonstration prototype in 1971, initially in a civil configuration for VIP transport, but later transformed into a military configuration (corresponding to the UH-1N). The aircraft can fulfil various roles, being suited to hot climate and high altitude as well as civil operation. The Italian Air Force became interested in the Agusta AB-212 and acquired a few for air base rescue services.

Agusta's biggest undertaking was the redesigning of the original airframe to produce the shipboard AB-212 ASW version as a replacement for the old AB-204 employed by the Italian Navy. This version was well-received and has been exported to Greece, Turkey, Peru, and Spain. Distinctive features of the AB-212 antisubmarine helicopter include a special anticorrosive treatment for the powerplant, a

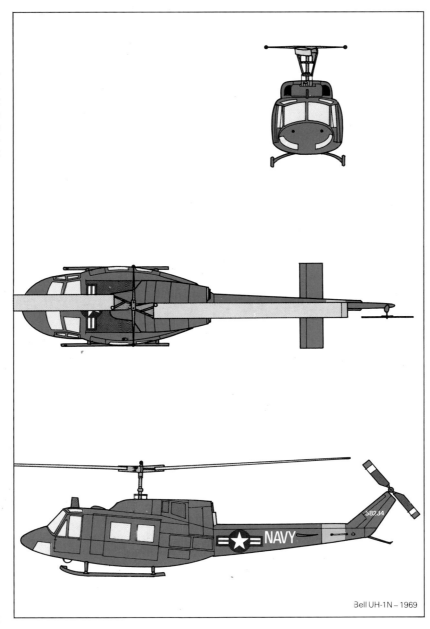

Bell UH-1N – 1969

search radar housed in a dome on the cabin roof, special electronics, sonar, antisubmarine and antiship armament, consisting either of two Mk.44 antisubmarine torpedoes, two AS-12 missiles, or two antiship missiles, depth charges and flares. The crew consists of two pilots and two operators.

More recently, the 212 has also been fitted with a new, four-blade rotor with redesigned blades. This variant, designated Model 412, has been in production in the USA and Italy since 1981. The four-blade rotor can also be fitted to the old 212s.

Bell Model 214

The programme for the Bell 214 — a much more powerful version of the UH-1H, was announced in 1970. The prototype was in fact a scaled-up,

strengthened and improved Model 205. The tail rotor drive linkage was replaced by rigid push-pull rods, the main rotor improved with wider blades and the transmission derived from that of the Cobra, but the main difference was the engine, which was the first in the Huey series to offer a substantial increase in power, making the 214 particular-

ly suitable for hot climates and high altitudes.

Following the test flying of these improvements with a single 214 Huey Plus, powered by a 1,900 shp Lycoming TS3 engine, Bell built a 214A demonstration aircraft which was shipped to Iran for evaluation trials in conjuction with the Iranian armed forces. This resulted in an order in late 1982 from Iran for 287 214As to be built by Bell, with a further 50 214As and 350 twin-engined 214STs to follow from an Iranian production line.

A total of 296 214As were delivered, plus 39 in the C rescue variant, but Iranian production was frustrated by the fall of the Shah in the 1979 revolution. A commercial variant built by Bell with a 2,930 shp T550 turbine was designated the 214B Biglifter.

Helicopter: **Bell Model 212 (UH-1N)**
Manufacturer: **Bell Helicopter Company**
Type: **tactical transport**
Year: **1969**
Engines: **2 × 1,800 shp Pratt & Whitney Canada PT6T-3**
Rotor diameter: **14.69 m (48 ft 2 in)**
Fuselage length: **12.92 m (42 ft 5 in)**
Overall length: **17.46 m (57 ft 3 in)**
Height: **4.39 m (14 ft 5 in)**
Empty weight: **2,517 kg (5,550 lbs)**
Gross weight: **5,085 kg (11,210 lbs)**
Maximum speed: **203 km/h (126 mph)**
Hovering ceiling IGE: **3,930 m (12,894 ft)**
Service ceiling: **5,305m (17,405 ft)**
Range: **440 km (273 miles)**
Capacity: **2 pilots + 13 troops**

Helicopter: **Bell Model 412**
Manufacturer: **Bell Helicopter Company**
Type: **transport**
Year: **1981**
Engines: **2 × 1,308 Pratt & Whitney (Canada) PT6T-3B Twin Pac**
Rotor diameter: **14.02 m (46 ft)**
Fuselage length: **12.92 m (42 ft 5 in)**
Overall length: **17.46 m (57 ft 3 in)**
Height: **4.39 m (14 ft 5 in)**
Empty weight: **2,753 kg (6,069 lbs)**
Gross weight: **5,216 kg (11,496 lbs)**
Maximum speed: **230 km/h (143 mph)**
Range: **420 km (260 miles)**
Capacity: **pilot + 14 passengers**

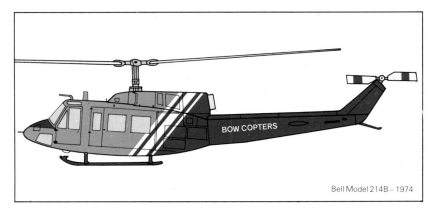

Bell Model 214B – 1974

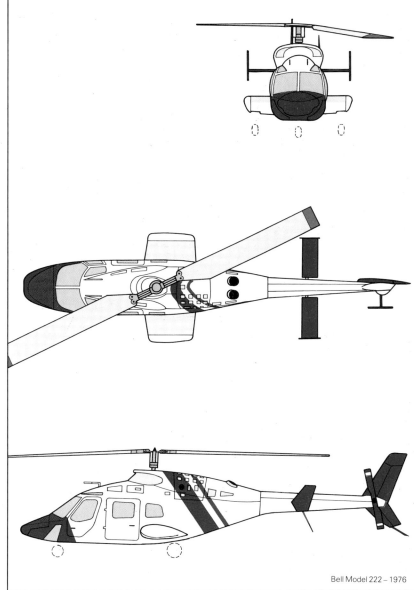

Bell Model 222 – 1976

Bell Model 214ST

The 214ST was originally designed specifically for production in Iran with development funded by the Imperial government. An interim prototype was built by Bell in 1977, introducing two 1,625 shp General Electric CT7 engines and incorporating a stretched and widened fuselage. Construction of three definitive ST prototypes began in 1978 but the fall of the Shah in 1979 forced Bell to rethink the original military transport plan, and to relaunch the aircraft with their own funding as a 7,938 kg (17,500 lb) gross weight commercial helicopter produced at Fort Worth.

Initial orders included several for offshore oil support and utility transport roles, in which configuration the aircraft seats 18 passengers plus two crew. The twin engines drive a one-hour run-dry transmission with fiberglass rotor blades and elastomeric bearings in the rotorhead. The 214ST is cleared for two-pilot IFR operation, and is the first large Bell helicopter to offer an optional wheeled undercarriage instead of skids.

Helicopter: **Bell Model 214B**
Manufacturer: **Bell Helicopter Company**
Type: **civil transport**
Year: **1974**
Engine: **2,930 shp Lycoming T550**
Rotor diameter: **15.24 m (50 ft)**
Overall length: —
Height: **4.84 m (15 ft 10 in)**
Empty weight: **3,382 kg (7,456 lbs)**
Gross weight: **6,260 kg (13,800 lbs)**
Maximum speed: **259 km/h (160 mph)**
Hovering ceiling IGE: **4,877 m (16,000 ft)**
Range: **480 km (298 miles)**
Capacity: **2 pilots + 14 passengers**

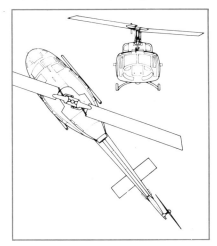

Bell Model 222

Bell began developing a twin turbine light helicopter in the late sixties, but it was not until January 1974 that a mock-up of what was to become the Bell 222 was exhibited at the annual convention of the Helicopter Association of America. Towards the end of 1975 Bell announced that the Model 222 was passing from the design to the construction stage. The first prototype flew on 13 August 1976 — considerably later than originally planned owing to the decision to investigate thoroughly the market and operators' requirements before building the new aircraft. The second prototype followed in October 1976, and by March 1977 all five prototypes were operational. The final development stages for these

aircraft also took longer and were less straightforward than the targets fixed in 1974 had suggested. The specifications of the Bell 222 were in fact considerably modified in the light of results from test flights. Necessary modifications included both structural elements such as the tail plane and endplate fins, and flight controls.

The Bell 222 is a classic design with a light alloy structure, and a fuselage built around a large cabin which can seat two pilots and five or six passengers in the executive trim. In all configurations, there is a bench seat at the back for three, which fits into the L-shape of the fuel tank behind it. The executive Bell 222 is sold with full IFR capability. One alternative is the offshore configuration for ferrying eight passengers to offshore oil platforms.

The large main rotor with two wide blades is of steel with a honeycomb core. The blades are held to the rotor hub by standard Bell elastomeric bearings. The tail rotor is also metal with two blades. The twin Lycoming LTS-101-650 engines are mounted side-by-side above the fuselage and have integral particle separators. The fuel is contained in three tanks, one in the fuselage and two in the sponsons into which the main landing gear members retract.

A few dozen Bell 222s have already been sold to operators in Europe, Latin America and the Far East. The first customers included the Metropolitan Police in London and the Japanese National Police. The Bell 222B is one of two current production versions: it too has IFR capability, but has more powerful

Helicopter: **Bell Model 222**
Manufacturer: **Bell Helicopter Textron**
Type: **transport**
Year: **1976**
Engines: **2 × 675 shp Lycoming LTS-101-650C-2**
Rotor diameter: **12.12 m (39 ft 8 in)**
Fuselage length: **10.98 m (36 ft)**
Overall length: **14.52 m (47 ft 8 in)**
Height: **3.24 m (10 ft 7 in)**
Empty weight: **2,076 kg (4,577 lbs)**
Gross weight: **3,470 kg (7,650 lbs)**
Maximum speed: **265 km/h (165 mph)**
Hovering ceiling: **3,235 m (10,615 ft)**
Range: **724 km (450 miles)**
Capacity: **2 pilots + 6 passengers**

turbines and a 135 kg (298 lb) bigger payload. The other is the 222UT utility variant, with a skid undercarriage and other weight and cost saving changes.

Bell 409

A competitor in the AAH programme (won by the Hughes AH-64), the Bell 409 (AH-63) was derived from the Model 309 KingCobra. It retained the latter's two-blade main rotor and tail rotor, but had a completely redesigned fuselage, with a large ventral fin, stub wings and a horizontal tail plane on top of the dorsal fin. Two prototypes were built. Engines: 2 × 1,536 shp General Electric T700-GE700. Rotor diameter: 15.54 m (51 ft). Overall length: 18.51 m (60 ft 9 in). Height: 3.73 m (12 ft 3 in). Gross weight: 7,237 kg (15,955 lbs). Maximum speed: 325 km/h (200 mph). Hovering ceiling: 1,980 m (6,496 ft).

Bell X-22

Unlike its predecessors, the Hiller X-18 and Curtiss-Wright X-19, the Bell X-22 was designed to study the possibility of a V/STOL tactical transport aircraft and had annular wing surfaces containing ducted propellers. It was built to a US Navy contract, and was derived from an earlier project for which only a mock-up had been produced. Two X-22A prototypes were built and made hundreds of flights with conventional, short and vertical take-offs. Although they proved to be far the most efficient aircraft of the kind yet developed, they were not considered suitable for operational service, as the maximum speed was only 370 km/h (230 mph), as compared with the 525 km/h (325 mph) envisaged.

Bell XV-15

After the partially encouraging experiments with the Bell XV-3, at the end of the sixties the Texan company built an experimental aircraft with tilt rotors designated the Model 300, which was followed shortly afterwards by a NASA contract for the design and development of the Model 301, in which the US Army subsequently became interested. The first prototype was completed in January 1977 and made its first hovering flight the following May, while the complete conversion to horizontal flight was achieved in July 1979. In the course of test flights the performance of the XV-15 proved that the designers had overcome the problems regarding stability in horizontal flight which spelled defeat for the XV-3. The

system of fitting an aircraft with tilt rotors has the advantages of reduced noise level and of increased safety because, unlike other VTOLs, this is the only one which can land by autorotation in an emergency.

Bell-Boeing JVX

Following intensive flight trials with two XV-15s the US Navy issued a contract in April 1983 to Bell and Boeing Vertol, for the joint development of a Joint Services Advanced Vertical Lift Aircraft (JVX) for assault transport and other roles, using the tilt-rotor concept. The programme anticipates a first flight in 1987 and the start of production deliveries to the US Marine Corps in 1991.

Aircraft: **Bell XV-3**
Manufacturer: **Bell Helicopter Company**
Type: **experimental convertiplane**
Year: **1955**
Engine: **450 hp Pratt & Whitney R-985**
Rotor diameter: **10.06 m (33 ft)**
Overall length: **9.23 m (30 ft 3 in)**
Height: **4.11 m (13 ft 6 in)**
Empty weight: **1,634 kg (3,602 lbs)**
Gross weight: **2,179 kg (4,804 lbs)**
Maximum speed: **291 km/h (180 mph)**
Hovering ceiling IGE: **2,256 m (7,400 ft)**
Service ceiling: **4,570 m (15,000 ft)**
Range: **410 km (255 miles)**

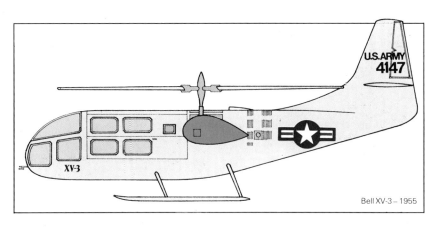
Bell XV-3 – 1955

Bell XV-3

This convertiplane was developed by Bell in collaboration with the American armed forces. It was the first aircraft in the world to make the transition from vertical to horizontal flight by rotating its wings, which had two articulated, three-blade rotors, doubling up as propellers in cruising flight. Two prototypes were built for the development programme, the first of which flew as a helicopter in August 1955. The four-seat fuselage with a large window area had a radial engine at the center to drive the rotors, while the wing movements were accomplished by electric motors. The landing gear consisted of two helicopter-type skids. The development programme for the XV-3 was suspended in 1966.

Aircraft: **Bell X-22A**
Manufacturer: **Bell Aerosystems**
Type: **experimental**
Year: **1966**
Engines: **4 × 1,250 shp General Electric YT58**
Propeller diameter: **2.13 m (7 ft)**
Wingspan: **11.96 m (39 ft 3 in)**
Length: **12.07 m (39 ft 7 in)**
Height: **6.31 m (20 ft 8 in)**
Gross weight: **8,020 kg (17,680 lbs)**
Maximum speed: **370 km/h (230 mph)**
Hovering ceiling OGE: **1,830 m (6,000 ft)**
Range: **890 km (553 miles)**
Capacity: **2 crew + 60 passengers**

Bell X-22A – 1966

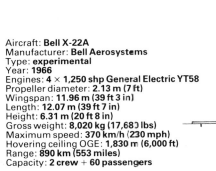

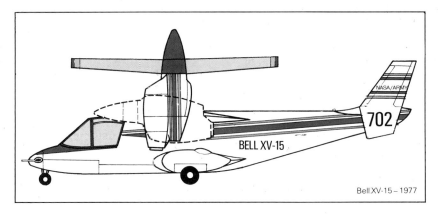
Bell XV-15 – 1977

Aircraft: **Bell XV-15**
Manufacturer: **Bell Helicopter Textron**
Type: **tilt rotor experimental**
Year: **1977**
Engines: **2 × 1,550 shp Lycoming T53**
Rotor diameter: **7.62 m (25 ft)**
Fuselage length: **12.82 m (42 ft)**
Overall length: **10.54 m (34 ft 6 in)**
Height: **3.85 m (12 ft 8 in)**
Empty weight: **4,350 kg (9,590 lbs)**
Gross weight: **5,900 kg (13,000 lbs)**
Maximum speed: **558 km/h (347 mph)**

BOEING
Boeing Vertol Company (USA)

Boeing, as the colossus of the American aviation scene, has built so many successful military and commercial jets that it holds the record for the greatest numbers of large aircraft constructed by any one company. It was founded in 1915 in Seattle, on the Pacific coast of the United States, through the entrepreneurial zeal of William Edward Boeing and Conrad Westervelt.

The first post-war civil aircraft built by Boeing was the Stratocruiser, while the company's most recent contribution to the United States Strategic Air Command is the extraordinary B-52 bomber (the Stratofortress). From 1952 Boeing concentrated its efforts on developing commercial aircraft, starting with the B-707, joined over the years by the larger B-727, the giant B-747 and more recently the B-757 and 767.

While continuing to manufacture conventional airplanes on a very large scale, Boeing entered the field of helicopter construction in 1960. In that year, the company purchased the Vertol Corporation of Morton (Pennsylvania) which became Boeing's Vertol Division. Boeing Vertol specialized in large helicopters and won several orders from the military, building the Model 107 (CH-46) for the US Navy and Marine Corps as well as the CH-47 Chinook for the Army. The latter has been extremely successful, both with the American armed forces and on the export market — it has been sold in more than 13 countries.

Boeing has also played a significant part in many space and armament programmes such as the development of the Lunar Orbiter and the Minuteman missile.

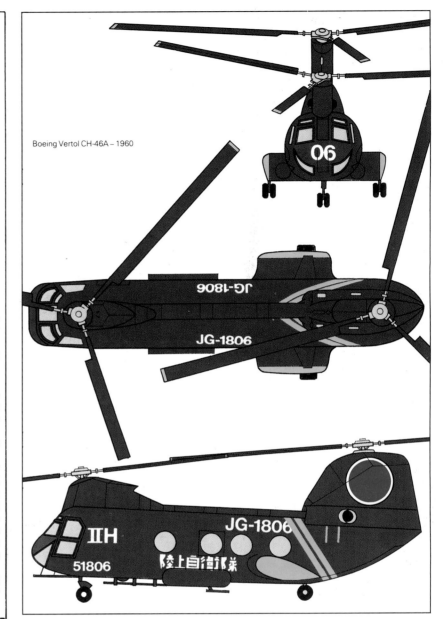

Boeing Vertol CH-46A – 1960

Boeing Vertol Model 107

In 1956, the Vertol Aircraft Corporation began developing a turbine-powered member of the "flying banana" family pioneered by Frank Piasecki. The result was a new design which was more compact than the previous angular-fuselage type, with a watertight belly to permit ditching and the powerplant installed at the base of the tail pylon.

The new Model 107 prototype with two 877 shp Lycoming T53 turbines flew on 12 August 1958. In July of that year, the US Army ordered 10 Model 107s, designated YHC-1A, with the uprated 1,065 shp General Electric YT58 turbine and a rotor diameter increased by 60 cm (2 ft). The first YHC-1A flew on 27 August 1959, but in the meantime, the US Army had ordered five YHC-1Bs (Model 114), a scaled-up variant which was better suited to meet its

need for a tactical transport helicopter, and consequently the order for the Model 107 was reduced to only three machines. The third of these was later returned to the company, which converted it into the Model 107-II, prototype of the civil version.

However, when the US Navy set up a new design competition for a medium-lift transport helicopter in 1960, this was won by the Boeing Vertol 107M, a modified version of the YHC-1A. A batch of 50 was initially ordered, the first of which was tested in October 1962. Designated CH-46A Sea Knight, the 107M was used for troop transport. During the Vietnam War the Marines also installed a 7.62 mm machine gun, which was fired through the cabin door. A total of 498 have been ordered by the Marine Corps and 24 by the US Navy. Several variants have been produced including the CH-46A for the Marines (160); the

UH-46A Sea Knight for the US Navy (24); the CH-46D with an uprated engine for the Marines (266); the UH-46D for the US Navy (10); the UH-46B for evaluation by the USAF; the RH-46E minehunters for the US Navy, and the CH-46F for the Marines (174), which is similar to the CH-46D but with improved electronics. Seven civil aircraft were used by New York Airways from 1962, while 18, designated CH-113, were ordered by the Canadian Air Force and 14, designated HPK-4, by Sweden.

The Model 107 has also been built under license in Japan by Kawasaki Heavy Industries in civil and military versions: the KV-107/II-2 commercial version for passenger transport adopted by Kawasaki, the Thai government and New York Airways; the KV-107/II-3 minehunters; the KV-107/II-4 for tactical transport, 59 of which have been

Helicopter: **Boeing Vertol Model 107M (CH-46A)**
Manufacturer: **Boeing Vertol Company**
Type: **tactical transport**
Year: **1960**
Engine: **1,050 shp General Electric T58-GE6**
Rotor diameter: **15.24 m (50 ft)**
Fuselage length: **13.66 m (44 ft 10 in)**
Overall length: **25.70 m (84 ft 4 in)**
Height: **5.09 m (16 ft 8 in)**
Empty weight: **5,627 kg (12,405 lbs)**
Gross weight: **9,700 kg (21,385 lbs)**
Maximum speed: **270 km/h (168 mph)**
Hovering ceiling IGE: **1,590 m (5,216 ft)**
Service ceiling: **4,510 m (14,796 ft)**
Range: **370 km (230 miles)**
Capacity: **2 pilots + 26 troops**

built for the Japanese Ground Self-Defense Force; the KV-107/II-5 rescue version for the Japanese Air Self-Defense Force and the Swedish Navy (38 built); the KV-107/II-7 six-eleven-seat VIP transport version, only one of which has been built for the Thai government; and the KV-107/IIA version for hot climates and high altitudes.

Boeing Vertol Model 114

In September 1958, the US Army commissioned Boeing Vertol to develop a medium transport helicopter capable of lifting a 2,000 kg (4,409 lb) load in all weathers. Boeing submitted a scaled-up version of its Model 107, and the new Model 114 project, the first in the very popular line of Chinook helicopters, was declared winner of the design competition in March 1959.

That it is a direct descendant of the Model 107 may be clearly seen in the broad, blunted, square fuselage section common to both aircraft. The Chinook's fuselage is in fact built around a large cargo bay, in front of which is the flight deck

Boeing Vertol CH-47C Chinook – 1968

Helicopter: **Boeing Vertol Model 114 (CH-47C)**
Manufacturer: **Boeing Vertol Company**
Type: **transport**
Year: **1968**
Engines: **2 × 3,802 shp Lycoming T55-L-11A**
Rotor diameter: **18.28 m (60 ft)**
Fuselage length: **15.54 m (51 ft)**
Overall length: **30.17 m (99 ft)**
Height: **5.66 m (18 ft 7 in)**
Empty weight: **9,243 kg (20,377 lbs)**
Gross weight: **20,865 kg (45,986 lbs)**
Maximum speed: **306 km/h (190 mph)**
Hovering ceiling IGE: **—**
Service ceiling: **4,570 m (15,000 ft)**
Range: **390 km (242 miles)**
Capacity: **44 troops**

and above it, at either end, the pylons holding the transmission for the two rotors. The two turbine engines are installed on either side of the aft pylon. Behind the cargo bay is a hydraulically-actuated ramp which greatly facilitates loading and unloading operations. On either side of the fuselage are two large fairings, housing the fuel tanks, landing gear shock absorbers and battery for the electrical system. The cargo bay has a volume of circa 42 cu.m (1,483 cu.ft) and can carry either 44 troops, 24 stretcher cases plus two medical attendants, or various items of equipment, representing a weight of between eight and 11 tonnes. A hoist at the front of the bay can be used for lifting loads vertically through a hatch in the middle of the floor or for lowering items to the ground. The Chinook also has a cargo hook at the center of gravity for carrying slung loads, enabling it to operate as a flying crane.

The contra-rotating tandem rotors comprise a hub and three blades 18.28 m (60 ft) in diameter. The articulated blades are composed of a steel spar and light alloy

The Italian Army's twin turbine CH-47Cs have been built under license by Elicotteri Meridionali. Others have been exported to Libya, Morocco, Egypt, Greece and Tanzania. The CH-47 Chinook transport helicopter, which is deployed in many countries, first proved its worth in Vietnam.

Boeing

honeycomb panels, with a fiber-glass reinforced plastic skin.

The two turbine engines are regulated automatically by the flight deck controls and fuel control system. A 67 shp Solar turbine at the base of the aft pylon drives the electric generators and hydraulic pumps. At the front end of each turbine is a 90° gearbox, from which a shaft leads to the combining transmission. The two turbine engine transmissions, apart from changing the direction of drive and reducing the r.p.m., each have a freewheel which enables the rotors to autorotate, overriding the engine in the event of engine failure. To minimize the vibrations transmitted to the fuselage by the rotors, the helicopter has five vibration absorbers, one in the nose, two under the cockpit floor and two inside the aft pylon. The landing gear consists of four non-retractable units. The front wheels are of the non-steerable type, while the rear wheels are steerable (but are locked during flight).

Five Boeing Model 114s, as chosen by the selection committee, were duly ordered by the US Army. These were followed by steadily increasing orders: the CH-47B soon replaced the original model, and came to be chosen by the US Army as the standard troop transport for the First Cavalry Division (Airmobile). The CH-47B — recognizable by the two thin fins at the base of the rear ramp — was followed by the CH-47C which had new 3,802 shp T55-L-11A engines, strengthened transmission and new, larger capacity fuel tanks. The first CH-47C flew on 14 October 1967 and deliveries began in spring 1968. In Vietnam, the Chinook, together with Bell helicopters, shouldered most of the burden of operations.

Over 800 Chinooks have been built in all, about half of which were still in service at the beginning of the eighties, mostly updated to the standard of the CH-47D version with 4,431 shp T55-L-712 turbines. As well as for the US Army, the Chinook has been built for the Royal Australian Air Force (12) and the Spanish Ejercito del Aire (12), and others have been sold to Argentina, Canada, Great Britain and Thailand. An important agreement was signed in 1968 with Elicotteri Meridionali (a company created by Agusta in 1967) to manufacture the Boeing helicopter under license in Italy. After a number of setbacks, an order was confirmed for 26 CH-47Cs for the Italian Army and the first wholly Italian aircraft were delivered in 1974. The Italian order was followed first by an order for the Iranian Army (initially 20 aircraft) and then for Libya, Morocco, Egypt, Tanzania and Greece.

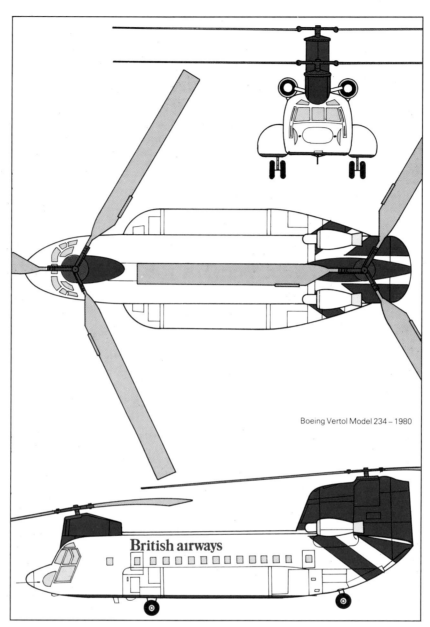

Boeing Vertol Model 234 – 1980

Helicopter: **Boeing Vertol Model 234**
Manufacturer: **Boeing Vertol Company**
Type: **commercial transport**
Year: **1980**
Engines: **2 × 4,750 shp Avco Lycoming AL-5512**
Rotor diameter: **18.29 m (60 ft)**
Fuselage length: **15.87 m (52 ft)**
Overall length: **30.18 m (99 ft)**
Height: **5.68 m (18 ft 8 in)**
Empty weight: **9,576 kg (21,111 lbs)**
Gross weight: **21,318 kg (46,998 lbs)**
Maximum speed: **269 km/h (167 mph)**
Hovering ceiling: **3,155 m (10,350 ft)**
Service ceiling **4,570 m (14,995 ft)**
Range: **1,010 km (627 miles)**
Capacity: **44 passengers**

Boeing Vertol Model 234

After having developed an updated version of the CH-47 Chinook in 1976, designated the CH-47D, which incorporated improvements to the dynamic components (e.g. rotor transmission) and avionics systems, Boeing Vertol completed a project in summer 1978 for a commercial version of the same aircraft, primarily intended for operators of oil platforms but also suitable for the prospecting of remote areas.

The airframe of the Model 234 is based on that of the military Chinooks, but has many new features such as fiberglass blades of larger chord in place of metal ones, different-sized fairings along the sides of the fuselage containing fuel, a longer nose to house the weather radar and front landing gear wheels shifted farther forward.

Two versions of the Model 234 are available: a long-range version with lateral fairings almost twice the size of the original Chinook ones, which have 6,360 kg (14,021 lb) fuel capacity, and a utility version in which the fuel tanks of 1,826 kg (4,025 lbs) are contained in four smaller fairings level with each wheel. The helicopter can be converted from one version to the other. This takes about eight hours' work by two specialists. The three rotor blades are interchangeable and maintenance has been reduced to a minimum, with considerable savings in running costs. The service life of the engines has also been increased to 1,800 hours TBO.

The passenger compartment of the long-range version has 44 seats arranged in four rows with a central corridor and there is an ample baggage compartment at the rear of the fuselage; it has a crew of three. A typical mixed combination in the utility version consists of 11 passengers and 7,250 kg (16,000 lbs) of freight. This version also has a cargo hook at the center of the fuselage capable of lifting up to 12,700 kg (27,998 lbs).

The first order for the Boeing

Boeing Vertol 237

Competitor in the UTTAS programme to choose a utility helicopter for the US Army (won by the Sikorsky UH-60). Of the three prototypes built (1974), one was modified for the LAMPS III programme. It had a four-blade rotor of composite material. Engines: 2 × 1,500 shp General Electric 700. Rotor diameter: 14.94 m (49 ft). Overall length: 18.50 m (60 ft 8 in). Height: 2.92 m (9 ft 7 in). Empty weight: 4,422 kg (9,750 lbs). Gross weight: 8,944 kg (19,718 lbs). Maximum speed: 286 km/h (178 mph). Range 595 km (370 miles). Hovering ceiling: 1,966 m (6,450 ft). Capacity: 11 troops.

Boeing Vertol 301

This big "flying crane" built for the US Army's HLH (Heavy Lift Helicopter) specification, was put into storage prior to completion when the programme was cancelled in October 1974. In 1983 plans were initiated to resume the test programme with a possible first flight in 1985. The HLH would be capable of carrying 20 tonnes over a distance of nearly 40 km (25 miles). Engines: 3 × 8,079 shp Allison T701. Rotor diameter: 28 m (91 ft 10 in). Overall length: 27.20 m (89 ft 3 in). Height: 8.70 m (28 ft 7 in). Empty weight: 26,754 kg (58,982 lbs). Gross weight: 53,572 kg (11,810 lbs).

58

BOLKOW

Bölkow Entwicklungen KG
(Federal Republic of Germany)

The Bölkow company was set up in May 1956 at Stuttgart with the object of building a series of light aircraft and helicopters. The first project, the Bo.102 was not a true helicopter but a ground-trainer for vertical flight training purposes. The Bo.103 single-seat helicopter was subsequently developed to test a new rotor design using fiberglass blades.

In 1963 Bölkow merged with Messerschmitt Werke-Flugzeug Union-Sud, and Hamburger Flugzeugbau was subsequently absorbed into the new group, which is known under the name of MBB (Messerschmitt-Bölkow-Blohm).

Helicopter: **Bölkow Bo.46**
Manufacturer: **Bölkow Entwicklungen KG**
Type: **experimental**
Year: **1964**
Engine: **800 shp Turboméca Turmo IIIB**
Rotor diameter: **10.00 m (32 ft 10 in)**
Tail rotor diameter: **1.77 m (5 ft 10 in)**
Overall length: —
Height: —
Empty weight: —
Gross weight: **2,000 kg (4,409 lbs)**
Maximum speed: **250 km/h (155 mph)**

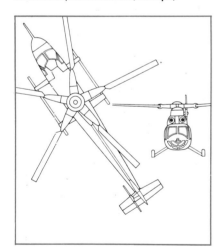

Bölkow Bo.46

The Bölkow Bo.46, three experimental prototypes of which were built for the German Ministry of Defense, served as a flying testbed for the Derschmidt semi-rigid rotor. The first model, built jointly with SIAT, began test flights in January 1964.

The Derschmidt rotor underwent a long series of wind tunnel tests, for each blade had a hinge about half-way along its radius, enabling the outer section of the blade to rotate 40° backwards or forwards in relation to the inner section connected to the hub. This enabled the movement of the advancing blade to be "delayed," thereby considerably reducing the tip speed. Conversely, by "accelerating" the movement of the outer portions, quite high rotational speeds could be achieved. However the complexity of this system prevented the Bo.46 from passing the experimental stage.

Bölkow Bo.102

The Bo-102 Helitrainer, powered by a 40 hp Hirth engine driving a simple one-bladed rotor with a counterweight, was developed in land and water based versions, both of which were semi-captive. This feature allowed the helicopter to rise to a height of 60 cm (2 ft), turn around a vertical axis and dip at up to 6° but prevented it from flying outside these limits. Rotor diameter: 6.58 m (21 ft 7 in). Length: 5.68 m (18 ft 7¼ in). Gross weight (excluding ground support system): 325 kg (717 lbs).

Vertol 234 came from British Airways Helicopters, to meet a requirement for six aircraft for offshore work in the North Sea. Since then Helicopter Service in Norway and ARCO in Alaska have also put the type in service for offshore support.

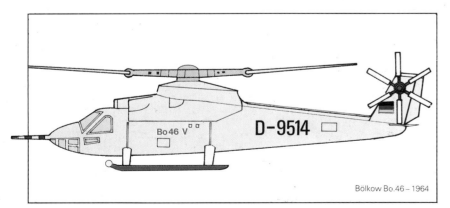

Bölkow Bo.46 – 1964

BRANTLY

Brantly Helicopter Corporation (USA)

Newby O. Branty was vice-president of the Pennsylvania Elastic Company which financed the prototype of a coaxial-rotor helicopter. Work commenced on the project in 1941 but the Second World War meant that the helicopter's maiden flight was delayed until 1946; it was aimed at the commercial market. After this project Brantly founded his own company and built both civil and military helicopters.

Bölkow Bo.103

Single-seat helicopter built in 1959 with a simple steel tube fuselage, a cockpit with transparent canopy open at the sides and a two-blade reinforced fiberglass rotor. Engine: 50 hp ILO. Rotor diameter: 6.57 m (21 ft 7 in). Gross weight: 400 kg (882 lbs). Maximum speed: 140 km/h (87 mph). Cruise speed: 114 km/h (71 mph). Range: 450 km (280 miles).

Brantly B-2/B-305

Brantly, an expert in heavy machinery, designed his first helicopter, the B-1, in 1941. It was built by the Pennsylvania Elastic Company and had coaxial, contra-rotating rotors.

The Brantly B-2 appeared in February 1953. It was highly progressive for the time, with two side-by-side seats, suitable for the executive market. Whilst other helicopters had a light steel tube fuselage, Brantly's aircraft had a carefully streamlined, skinned monocoque fuselage and a three-blade

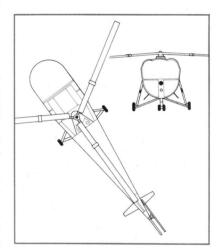

Brantly B-305 – 1964

rotor. However development of the B-2 was slow and the helicopter only went into production in 1959. Five were sold to the US Army.

The improved B-2B version had new metal blades with extruded aluminum spars and it was from this model that the B-305 was derived in 1964, with five seats, a large diameter rotor and 305 hp Lycoming opposed cylinder engine.

Helicopter: **Brantly B-305**
Manufacturer: **Brantly Helicopter Corporation**
Type: **executive**
Year: **1964**
Engine: **305 hp Lycoming IVO-540-A1A**
Rotor diameter: **8.74 m (28 ft 8 in)**
Fuselage length: **7.44 m (24 ft 5 in)**
Overall length: **10.03 m (32 ft 11 in)**
Height: **2.44 m (8 ft)**
Empty weight: **817 kg (1,800 lbs)**
Gross weight: **1,315 kg (2,900 lbs)**
Maximum speed: **193 km/h (120 mph)**
Hovering ceiling IGE: **1,245 m (4,085 ft)**
Range: **354 km (220 miles)**
Capacity: **5**

BREGUET

Société Anonyme Avions Louis Breguet (France)

Louis and Jacques Breguet were among the first aircraft constructors to become world-famous and they were also rotorcraft pioneers. In fact, Louis Breguet's Gyroplane of 1908 was one of the first helicopters to raise itself off the ground. With the outbreak of the First World War the Breguet brothers devoted their energies to airplane manufacture and only returned to the construction of helicopters when the Second World War was over. During the intervening years the company had become well known for its military and civil aircraft and Breguet played a very significant role in the recovery of the post-war French aeronautical industry.

Breguet G.IIE Gyroplane

Louis Breguet produced his third Gyroplane in 1949. This was the Model G.IIE which had a streamlined fuselage and T-tail and cabin space for a pilot and four passengers. A 450 hp Pratt & Whitney Junior engine drove two three-blade, coaxial, contra-rotating rotors fitted with Sikorsky-type controls.

Market prospects for the Gyroplane were good, thanks above all to its fast cruise speed of circa 200 km/h (125 mph), but unfortunately, the aircraft never went beyond the prototype stage, owing to lack of funds.

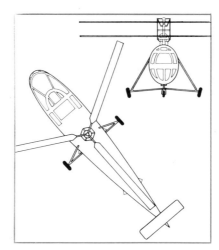

Helicopter: **Breguet G.IIE Gyroplane**
Manufacturer: **Société Anonyme Avions Louis Breguet**
Type: **four-seat experimental**
Year: **1949**
Engine: **450 hp Pratt & Whitney R-985**
Rotor diameter: **9.60 m (31 ft 6 in)**
Overall length: **9.70 m (31 ft 10 in)**
Height: **4.24 m (13 ft 11 in)**
Empty weight: **1,473 kg (3,247 lbs)**
Gross weight: **2,100 kg (4,630 lbs)**
Maximum speed: **215 km/h (134 mph)**
Hovering ceiling IGE: **1,600 m (5,250 ft)**
Service ceiling: **4,600 m (15,092 ft)**
Range: **470 km (292 miles)**
Capacity: **1 pilot + 4 passengers**

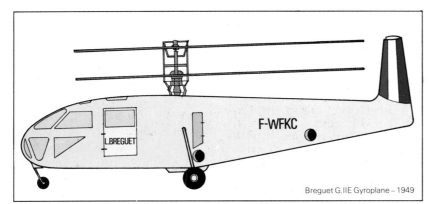

Breguet G.IIE Gyroplane – 1949

BRISTOL

Bristol Aeroplane Co. Ltd.
(Great Britain)

This company was established at Filton, near Bristol, in 1909 and was to become world-famous for its aircraft and engines. By 1914 the company had already built over 200 aircraft, many of which were highly successful in-house designs.

In the last year of the First World War about 2,000 airplanes left Bristol's assembly lines and when the Armistice was signed the company had 3,000 employees. During the 1930s work continued on military and civil aircraft; the company was also earning an impressive reputation for its design and manufacture of aero engines. In 1935, a year which was to be of crucial importance for British aviation, Bristol had a full order book and undertook a massive expansion programme. Work started that year on the twin-engine Blenheim, the first of a series of aircraft which were to be deployed in huge numbers during the Second World War.

Once the war was over, Bristol decided to diversify and while continuing with its aeronautical interests, branched out into motor car manufacture, prefabricated buildings and plastics. In 1944 Bristol set up a helicopter division with Raoul Hafner as its chief designer; in 1961 it was sold to Westland Aircraft as part of a government-encouraged rationalization policy.

The name of Bristol finally disappeared from the world of aviation in 1963, when the company became BAC's Filton division and subsequently a part of British Aerospace.

Bristol 171 Sycamore

Austrian-born Raoul Hafner, who had devoted himself to rotary wing research in the thirties, moved to England before the Second World War and took charge of the helicopter division of the Bristol Aeroplane Co. in 1944. His first aircraft, the Bristol 171 Sycamore, flew on 27 July 1947 with an American Pratt & Whitney R-985 Wasp engine, no suitable British engine being available at the time. It was of metal construction with a three-blade main rotor and was designed as an air taxi (four-five seats) and for military tasks such as air observation and casualty evacuation.

Helicopter: **Bristol 171 Mk.3 Sycamore**
Manufacturer: **Bristol Aeroplane Co. Ltd.**
Type: **general purpose**
Year: **1951**
Engine: **550 hp Alvis Leonides radial**
Rotor diameter: **14.80 m (48 ft 7 in)**
Fuselage length: **13.40 m (43 ft 11 in)**
Overall length: **13.63 m (61 ft 1 in)**
Height: **4.25 m (13 ft 11 in)**
Empty weight: **1.605 kg (3,538 lbs)**
Gross weight: **2,360 kg (5,203 lbs)**
Maximum speed: **195 km/h (121 mph)**
Hovering ceiling IGE: **1,220 m (4,002 ft)**
Service ceiling: **4,725 m (15,500 ft)**
Range: **430 km (268 miles)**
Capacity: **pilot + 4-5 passengers**

In September 1949 the Mk.2 variant flew, powered by a 550 hp Alvis Leonides 71 engine. This helicopter was put into production for the British armed forces and among the first 25 built, one (HC Mk.10) was fitted out as an air ambulance, four (HC Mk.11) were intended for Army communications, four (HC Mk.12) for the RAF (liaison, and rescue services) and three (Mk.50) for the Royal Australian Navy (search and rescue). All of these were completed to Mk.3 standard with a Leonides 173 engine.

The Bristol 171 Mk.3 civil version, whose capacity was increased to six seats, was also adopted by BEA, which began an experimental service with these helicopters between Eastleigh and Heathrow airport in 1954, which lasted for about two years. In 1950, Bristol produced another civil version, the Mk.4 with four access doors, a longer-stroke landing gear, a bigger baggage compartment and an hydraulic winch. This was primarily intended for search and rescue and air ambulance duties, and was supplied to the RAF (Mk.14), Belgian Air Force (Mk.14B), Royal Australian Navy (Mk.51) and West German Government (Mk.52).

Finally, in the mid fifties, the British company began work on development of a turbine-engined Sycamore. This was the Bristol 203 with capacity increased to 11 seats and a larger tail. But this project, using the last two airframes of the Bristol 171, was abandoned when the company was taken over by Westland, although some of its finer points were later incorporated in the Lynx.

When production of the Sycamore ended in 1959, 177 had been built. Apart from the RAF, the biggest operator of this helicopter was the German government, which used 50 for the Army and Navy. RAF Sycamores were deployed in various parts of the world where British troops were operating, and in particular played an active part in Malaysia in 1954 and during the trouble in Cyprus towards the end of 1956.

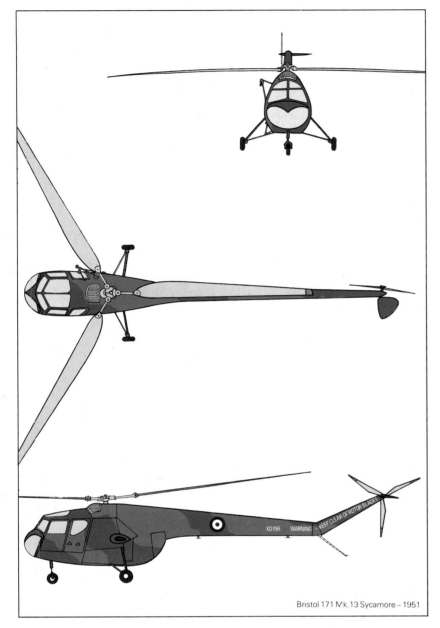

Bristol 171 Mk.13 Sycamore – 1951

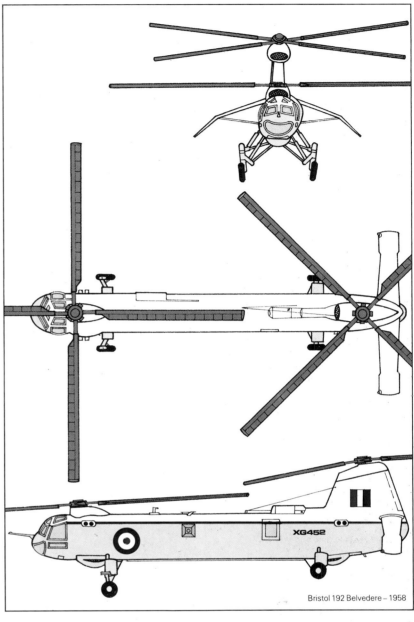

Bristol 192 Belvedere – 1958

Bristol 173/192

The Bristol 173 was the first helicopter specifically designed for commercial operation and passenger transport in particular. The first prototype, which flew on 3 January 1952, was powered by two 520 hp Alvis Leonides engines and could carry ten passengers. The tandem rotors were identical to those of the Bristol 171 Sycamore. Trials were carried out with this aircraft in 1953, from the aircraft carrier HMS Eagle. The second prototype was similar to the first but was modified to test the characteristics and effects of two stub wings and later a four-bladed rotor. The Bristol 173 Mk.3, of which three were built, with capacity increased to 16 seats and Alvis Leonides Major engines, was offered to BEA.

Unfortunately, none of these aircraft succeeded in overcoming a series of developmental problems and subsequent projects undertaken by Bristol — models 191 and 193 — in response to Royal Navy and Canadian naval specifications were no more successful. However the Type 192, the prototype of which flew on 5 July 1958, was adopted by the RAF. In the initial configuration, this aircraft had a purely manual system of control and wooden rotor blades but power controls and metal blades were standardized on the fifth prototype built in 1960. That year, three pre-production aircraft were assigned to the RAF for a series of trials for which they were based at Odiham. Twenty-six of these helicopters, called the Belvedere, were ordered and used for some years for military

transport, not only in the United Kingdom, but also in the Middle and Far East. The Belvedere was withdrawn from service in March 1969.

The production Bristol 192s had an all-metal, skinned fuselage and an anhedral tailplane, compared with the dihedral one of the Type 173. The two rotors had four metal blades and the front wheels of the fixed quadricycle landing gear were self-castoring. The helicopter's maximum capacity was 30 seats or 2,700 kg (5,952 lbs) internal payload. The instrumentation also permitted night flying.

Helicopter: **Bristol 173**
Manufacturer: **Bristol Aeroplane Co. Ltd.**
Type: **transport**
Year: **1952**
Engines: **2 × 520 hp Alvis Leonides radial**
Rotor diameter: **14.80 m (48 ft 6 in)**
Fuselage length: **16.51 m (54 ft 2 in)**
Overall length: **27.33 m (89 ft 8 in)**
Height: **4.27 m (14 ft)**
Empty weight: **3,550 kg (7,826 lbs)**
Gross weight: **4,810 kg (10,604 lbs)**
Maximum speed: **—**
Capacity: **10 passengers**

Helicopter: **Bristol 192 Belvedere**
Manufacturer: **Bristol Aeroplane Co. Ltd.**
Type: **military transport**
Year: **1958**
Engines: **2 × 1,650 hp Napier Gazelle NGa.2**
Rotor diameter: **14.80 m (48 ft 6 in)**
Fuselage length: **16.56 m (54 ft 4 in)**
Height: **5.25 m (17 ft 3 in)**
Empty weight: **5,280 kg (11,640 lbs)**
Gross weight: **9,070 kg (19,995 lbs)**
Maximum speed: **222 km/h (138 mph)**
Service ceiling: **5,270 m (17,290 ft)**
Range: **715 km (444 miles)**
Capacity: **2 pilots + 19 troops or 12 stretcher cases**

C D

CESSNA
Cessna Aircraft Company (USA)

Established in 1916 and having weathered the disastrous economic crisis of 1929, this American company became one of the foremost light aircraft manufacturers, building over 150,000 airplanes.

In 1953 Cessna made its first and, to date, only excursion into helicopter construction. A joint venture with the Siebel Company led to a new factory being opened near Prospect to develop and market the CH-1; the project was, however, abandoned in favour of Cessna's first jet aircraft.

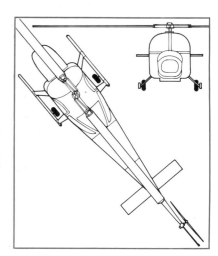

Cessna CH-1

The CH-1 was an attempt by Cessna to break into the rotary wing market. Built for commercial operation in 1953, the CH-1 was the result of Cessna acquiring the Siebel Company a year earlier.

The helicopter had a cabin very similar to that of a private aircraft. The 260 hp six-cylinder opposed Continental engine was installed in the nose, and drove a conventional two-blade rotor through a shaft passing between the two pilot seats. Only a few CH-1B commercial models were built and production ended in December 1962 when Cessna decided that the civil helicopter market was not yet ready for sound investment. However the helicopter was also evaluated by the armed forces. Ten were built for the US Army as Model YH-41 Seneca for high altitude tests, and another four were sold to Ecuador.

Helicopter: **Cessna CH-1B**
Manufacturer: **Cessna Aircraft Company**
Type: **executive transport**
Year: **1954**
Engine: **260 hp Continental FSO-52655**
Rotor diameter: **10.67 m (35 ft)**
Fuselage length: **—**
Overall length: **13.00 m (42 ft 8 in)**
Height: **2.56 m (8 ft 5 in)**
Empty weight: **943 kg (2,079 lbs)**
Gross weight: **1,406 kg (3,100 lbs)**
Maximum speed: **196 km/h (122 mph)**
Hovering ceiling IGE: **2,925 m (9,596 ft)**
Service ceiling: **3,720 m (12,205 ft)**
Range: **500 km (310 miles)**
Capacity: **1 pilot + 3 passengers**

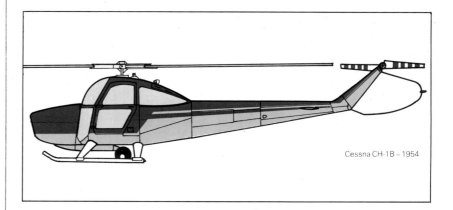

Cessna CH-1B – 1954

CIERVA
The Cierva Autogiro Company (Great Britain)

The Spanish inventor of the gyroplane, Juan de la Cierva, came to England in 1925 and formed his own company the following year. Construction licenses for Cierva autogiros were sold to companies in France, Germany, Japan and the United States. Although Cierva died in 1936, his name lived on in a new company formed at the end of the war, which subsequently merged with Saunders-Roe in 1950.

Cierva W.9/W.11/W.14

The W.9 was an experimental helicopter with a three-blade main rotor. Torque compensation was achieved by a jet of air discharged from the port side of the rear fuselage and supplied by a fan which also cooled the engine. The jet was controlled by two vanes. Engine: 205 hp Gipsy Six Series II. Rotor diameter: 10.98 m (36 ft). Gross weight: 1,200 kg (2,645 lbs).

The Cierva W.11 Air Horse, built in 1948, featured three tri-bladed rotors mounted on outriggers from the fuselage and driven from a centrally-installed engine. Two prototypes were built for the British Ministry of Supply. It could carry 24 passengers. Engine: 1,620 hp Rolls-Royce Merlin 24. Rotor diameter: 29 m (95 ft). Overall length: 27 m (88 ft 7 in). Height: 5.41 m (17 ft 9 in). Empty weight: 5,505 kg (12,136 lbs). Gross weight: 7,937 kg (17,498 lbs). Maximum speed: 225 km/h (140 mph). Service ceiling: 8,530 m (27,985 ft). Range: 530 km (330 miles).

The Cierva W.14 was a two-seat trainer and liaison helicopter also built in 1948, with a metal fuselage and three-blade rotor of mixed construction. The W.14 Skeeter project was later developed by Saro Aircraft. Engine: 145 hp D.H. Gipsy Major 10. Rotor diameter: 9.75 m

CURTISS-WRIGHT
Curtiss-Wright Corporation (USA)

The industrial empire of Glenn Curtiss produced a great variety of airplanes, some of which proved very successful, over a 50 year period. The only venture made by Curtiss into rotorcraft was M.B. Bleecker's project for a V/STOL experimental aircraft, the X-19.

(32 ft). Overall length: 11.70 m (38 ft 5 in). Height: 3.05 m (10 ft). Empty weight: 544 kg (1,200 lbs). Gross weight: 816 kg (1,800 lbs). Maximum speed: 153 km/h (95 mph). Service ceiling: 4,350 m (14,270 ft). Range: 300 km (186 miles).

Curtiss-Wright X-19

In the X-19 experimental aircraft, the four unshrouded propellers were powered by two turbines and rotated 90° at the tips of two thin wings with a 6 m (19 ft 8 in) span.

The American armed forces had expressed an interest in this formula for reconnaissance, transport and tactical support, but the X-19's performance in the airplane mode was not brilliant. Despite a maximum cruise speed of 650 km/h (404 mph), its payload capacity was less than 550 kg (1,213 lbs). The first prototype was quite badly damaged on its second flight in November 1963 and the second was never flown.

Aircraft: **Curtiss-Wright X-19**
Manufacturer: **Curtiss-Wright Corporation**
Type: **experimental**
Year: **1963**
Engines: **2 × 2,200 shp Lycoming T55-L-5**
Fuselage length: **13.23 m (43 ft 4 in)**
Total width with propellers: **10.50 m (34 ft 5 in)**
Height: **4.88 m (16 ft)**
Empty weight: **4,425 kg (9,755 lbs)**
Gross weight: **5,580 kg (12,300 lbs)**
Maximum speed: **740 km/h (460 mph)**
Range: **1,185 km (736 miles)**
Capacity: **4 troops**

DORNIER
Dornier GmbH (Federal Republic of Germany)

During the 1930s Claudius Dornier, the founder of this famous German aircraft company, made an important contribution to the clandestine re-birth of the Luftwaffe, by designing and constructing several bombers which were to prove very effective during the Second World War.

Since the 1960s, in common with many other companies, Dornier has carried out research and experiments into various vertical take-off and landing aircraft and helicopters.

Dornier Do.32

The Dornier Do.32 was one of the first helicopters designed and built by the German helicopter industry after the war. It was a small, ultra-lightweight single-seater which could be carried in a container of modest size, measuring 3.8 m (12 ft 6 in) long and less than 1 m (3 ft 3 in) wide. The container was fitted with wheels, could be towed by an ordinary motor car, and also served as a take-off and landing platform. The mini helicopter could be assembled in just five minutes.

The Do.32 was powered by a 100 shp BMW 6012 turbine which drove the rotor through a cold cycle. The prototype was tested on 29 June 1962 and completed the test programme in mid 1963, when the German company displayed a second model at the Paris Air Show. A few others were built but the two-seat derivative (with a 250 shp turbine) offered to the German government was not adopted.

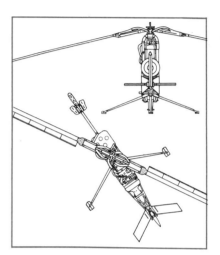

Helicopter: **Dornier Do.32**
Manufacturer: **Dornier GmbH**
Type: **experimental**
Year: **1962**
Engine: **100 shp BMW 6012**
Rotor diameter: **7.50 m (24 ft 7 in)**
Fuselage length: **3.20 m (10 ft 6 in)**
Overall length: **3.70 m (12 ft 2 in)**
Height: **1.89 m (6 ft 2 in)**
Empty weight: **151 kg (333 lbs)**
Gross weight: **270 kg (595 lbs)**
Maximum speed: **120 km/h (75 mph)**
Service ceiling: **5,000 m (16,404 ft)**
Range: **80 km (50 miles)**

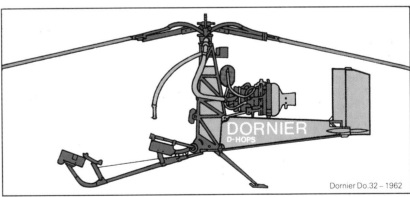

Dornier Do.32 – 1962

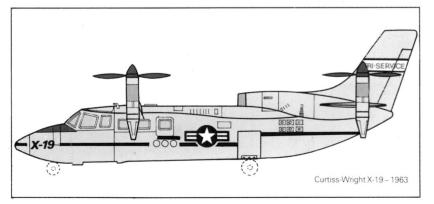

Curtiss-Wright X-19 – 1963

E F G H

ENSTROM
Enstrom Helicopter Corporation (USA)

The R.J. Enstrom Corporation was set up in 1959 to develop an experimental light helicopter designed by Rudolph J. Enstrom. The prototype made its maiden flight in November 1960 and the definitive production model has proved very successful.

In October 1968, the company was acquired by the Purex Corporation who then sold all its interest in Enstrom to F. Lee Bailey in January 1971; in January 1980 the company was bought by the Dutch concern, Brava Investments BV.

Enstrom F-280 – 1978

Helicopter: **Enstrom F-280**
Manufacturer: **Enstrom Helicopter Corp.**
Type: **light transport**
Year: **1978**
Engine: **250 shp Lycoming HIO-360**
Rotor diameter: **10.36 m (34 ft)**
Fuselage length: —
Overall length: **9.86 m (32 ft 4 in)**

Height: **2.79 m (9 ft 2 in)**
Empty weight: **708 kg (1,560 lbs)**
Gross weight: **1,179 kg (2,600 lbs)**
Maximum speed: **193 km/h (120 mph)**
Hovering ceiling IGE: **3,110 m (10,200 ft)**
Service ceiling: **3,660 m (12,000 ft)**
Range: **488 km (303 miles)**
Capacity: **1 pilot + 3 passengers**

Enstrom F-28/F-280

Production of the F-28 two-seater began in 1963 and a limited number were built before the improved Model F-28A appeared in 1968. This was followed shortly afterwards by the F-28B derivative, which had a piston engine with a turbocharger, and by the T-28 with a turbine engine.

In January 1971 production of the F-28A was resumed under the new management of F.L. Bailey; by the end of 1977 over 500 had been produced. The F-28A was certainly not an innovatory aircraft, but its good performance was due to its light structure and clean lines. The extensively-glazed forward section of the fuselage accommodated the pilot and two passengers on a single bench seat.

The powerplant — a 205 shp Lycoming HIO-360-C1B driving a three-blade, articulated metal rotor by means of a simple transmission system — was installed at the center of the fuselage. There were two fuel tanks with a total capacity of 115 liters (25.3 gallons). The semi-monocoque aft fuselage section had a small vertical fin and two-blade light alloy tail rotor.

Numerous improvements have been made to the F-28 over the years. In 1980, no fewer than five different models were in production or under development. They included the Model F-280 Shark which has a redesigned fuselage, broad dorsal fin, horizontal tail surfaces and increased fuel capacity. The F-28C is basically identical to the F-28A but has a Rajay turbocharger and, unlike the other models, the tail rotor is on the port side and turns in the opposite direction to that of previous models. The F-28F is similar to the F-28C, but has a single-piece windscreen and a new instrument panel to improve forward and downward visibility. Maintenance has also been simplified and the aircraft has a 225 shp Lycoming powerplant. A four-seat version was also developed in prototype form, the Model F-280L

EUROPEAN HELICOPTER INDUSTRIES

This company was launched as a joint venture, the two shareholders being Agusta (Italy) and Westland (Great Britain), with the aim of building and selling the helicopter which was originally known as "The Sea King Replacement" and was subsequently given the designation EH-101. The company has its headquarters in London.

Hawk, whilst a five-seater, the Model F-480 with an Allison 250C-20B turbine, has been projected.

Apart from being used as an executive helicopter or for light transport, the little Enstrom is very widely used for agricultural work. Production in 1983 focused on the Model F-28F Falcon and the F-280C.

EH-101

This triple turbine helicopter under development by European Helicopter Industries is envisaged as a multirole naval, civil and utility machine. Although it is being promoted to meet a joint British and Italian naval requirement for a new antisubmarine helicopter, the EH-101 has also been proposed for commercial use. The airframe is unusually compact to permit operation even from small vessels such as frigates. For passenger transport, the fuselage will be furnished with a maximum of 30 seats and have an internal height of 1.80 m (5 ft 11 in). Comfort apart, this will be a great advantage when carrying freight and supplies.

Nine pre-production aircraft will be built under the EH-101 programme, of which four will be used to type test the basic aircraft and the rest for evaluation and completion of the naval, civil and utility versions.

FAIRCHILD
Fairchild Industries (USA)

Fairchild's famous "Flying Boxcar," the C-119, was only one of a lengthy and varied succession of aircraft which culminated in the best close-support plane of its era, the A-10A. Sherman Mills Fairchild started building airplanes in 1925 when he founded the Fairchild Airplane Manufacturing Corporation. Today, under its present name of Fairchild Industries the corporation consists of 11, highly diversified, operating companies. The company's headquarters is at Germantown in Maryland, a few miles from Hagerstown where the first assembly lines turned out a great number of very popular and famous light aircraft.

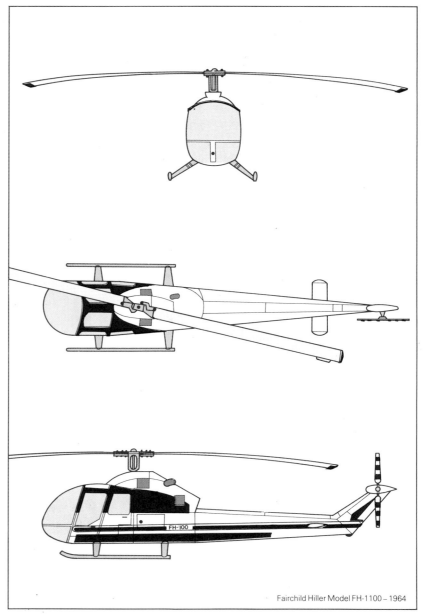

Fairchild Hiller Model FH-1100 – 1964

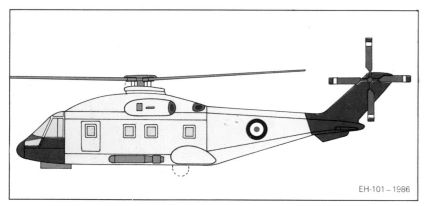

EH-101 – 1986

Helicopter: **EH-101**	Helicopter: **Fairchild Hiller Model FH-1100**
Manufacturer: **European Helicopter Industries**	Manufacturer: **Fairchild Hiller Corporation**
Type: **naval and multipurpose**	Type: **light transport**
Year: **1986 (projected)**	Year: **1964**
Engines: **3 × 1,690 shp General Electric T700-GE401**	Engine: **317 shp Allison 250-C18**
Rotor diameter: **18.59 m (61 ft)**	Rotor diameter: **10.79 m (35 ft 5 in)**
Fuselage length: **15.85 m (52 ft)**	Fuselage length: **9.08 m (29 ft 9 in)**
Overall length: **22.90 m (75 ft 2 in)**	Overall length: **12.13 m (39 ft 9 in)**
Gross weight: **14,200 kg (31,300 lbs)**	Height: **2.83 m (9 ft 3 in)**
Maximum speed: **333 km/h (207 mph)**	Empty weight: **633 kg (1,395 lbs)**
Range: **1,020 km (634 miles)**	Gross weight: **1,247 kg (2,749 lbs)**
Capacity: **2 pilots + 30 passengers**	Maximum speed: **204 km/h (127 mph)**
Armament: **naval version, 2 torpedoes**	Service ceiling: **4,325 m (14,190 ft)**
	Range: **560 km (348 miles)**
	Capacity: **1 pilot + 3 passengers**

Fairchild Hiller Model FH-1100

In May 1961, the Hiller Model 1100 was one of three projects chosen by the US Army for evaluation as a Light Observation Helicopter. Five prototypes were commissioned, designated OH-5A, the first of which flew in January 1963. The OH-5A had a 250 shp Allison T63-A5 turbine and an articulated rotor, with a stabilization system similar to that used on the L4 commercial helicopter.

The LOH production contract was awarded to the Hughes OH-6A, but in 1964 Hiller, who in the meantime had become an affiliated company of Fairchild Stratos, decided to adapt their aircraft for the civil market, as Bell had done with the Model 206. The Fairchild Hiller was less successful than the Bell helicopter, which was ordered in substantial numbers by the American government. The authorities rejected it, as there was no possibility of increasing its size, as had been done with the Bell 204/205. However the civil market was still open to the Fairchild, as one of the requirements of the LOH specification was that the designs submitted should conform to civil aviation regulations.

The fuselage of the FH-1100 was in two sections: a semi-monocoque structure at the front and tail boom at the rear. It had a two-blade, semi-rigid main rotor and two-blade, anti-torque tail rotor, both of metal, and driven by an Allison 25C-C18 turbine.

It received FAA civil type approval in July 1964 and deliveries began in June 1966. A total of 240 were built. The biggest user was the Canadian company, Okanagan, which ordered 30 FH-1100, while the Royal Thai Police Department bought 16. Others were sold to Argentina, Brazil, Chile, Cyprus, Ecuador, Panama, the Philippines and El Salvador.

Production of the Fairchild-built version ended in 1973 but recently, Hiller Aviation (which was reconstituted as a private, independent company in 1980) bought back the rights to build the aircraft from Fairchild and there were plans to build two a month in 1983, although in the event this was not achieved. The helicopter, which has been offered on the market in an executive version at a competitive price, is now fitted with an Allison 250-C20B turbine. It is slightly heavier, but performance has been improved not only by the more powerful engine, but also by the use of new blades and a new K-Flex transmission. Although not a new machine, the American manufacturers hope to win back some of the private customers from the Bell JetRanger and the Hughes 500.

FAIREY

Fairey Aviation Company (Great Britain)

Charles Richard Fairey was chief design engineer at Short Brothers until 1915 when he founded the Fairey Aviation Company, which specialized in military aircraft, mainly for the Royal Navy. Fairey began its involvement in helicopters in 1945. In 1960 the company was taken over by Westland.

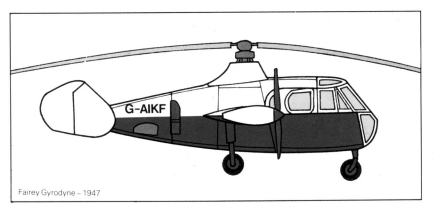

Fairey Gyrodyne – 1947

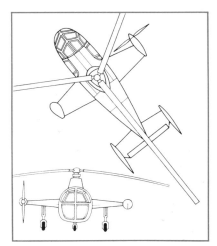

Helicopter: **Fairey Gyrodyne**
Manufacturer: **Fairey Aviation Company**
Type: **four-seat experimental**
Year: **1947**
Engine: **525 hp Alvis Leonides**
Rotor diameter: **15.60 m (51 ft 2 in)**
Fuselage length: **5.85 m (19 ft 2 in)**
Overall length: —
Height: **3.20 m (10 ft 6 in)**
Empty weight: **1,570 kg (3,460 lbs)**
Gross weight: **2,185 kg (4,817 lbs)**
Maximum speed: **200 km/h (124 mph)**
Hovering ceiling IGE: **305 m (1,000 ft)**
Service ceiling: **3,050 m (10,000 ft)**
Range: **400 km (248 miles)**

Fairey Gyrodyne

On 4 December 1947, the first of the two prototypes of the Gyrodyne — a compact and streamlined helicopter weighing just over 2,000 kg (4,410 lbs) — took off from White Waltham airport. With a 525 hp Alvis Leonides radial engine, the power from which could be transmitted in variable ratios to a three-blade rotor just over 15 m (50 ft) in diameter and to the anti-torque propeller on the starboard tip of the stub wing, the Gyrodyne behaved like a helicopter, but the same propeller also provided the necessary thrust for fast flight, when the aircraft looked almost like an autogyro. The British compound aircraft set a world speed record by flying at 200 km/h (124 mph) on 28 June 1948. An extensively modified second prototype, renamed Jet Gyrodyne, flew in January 1954; it had two blade-tip jets, fed with air from two compressors driven by the usual Alvis Leonides radial.

Helicopter: **Fairey Rotodyne**
Manufacturer: **Fairey Aviation Company**
Type: **transport**
Year: **1957**
Engines: **2 × 3,000 shp Napier Eland turbines**
Rotor diameter: **31.72 m (104 ft)**
Fuselage length: **19.67 m (64 ft 6 in)**
Overall length: —
Height: **7.06 m (23 ft 2 in)**
Empty weight: —
Gross weight: **14,968 kg (33,000 lbs)**
Maximum speed: **307 km/h (190 mph)**
Range: **720 km (450 miles)**
Capacity: **40**

Fairey Rotodyne

From the Jet Gyrodyne, Fairey developed the much more ambitious Rotodyne which flew for the first time on 6 November 1957. It was a large compound aircraft with a four-blade rotor more than 31 m (101 ft 8 in) in diameter, driven by blade-tip jets fed with compressed air bled from two 3,000 shp Napier Eland turboprops mounted in nacelles on a 14.17 m (46 ft 6 in) span wing. The same engines drove two four-blade propellers which gave a good cruise speed of approximately 300 km/h (185 mph), while the stocky fuselage had very good cubic capacity.

On 5 January 1959, the Rotodyne established a world speed record for rotary wing craft of 307 km/h (191 mph) and its appearance aroused great interest among commercial operators. The RAF also considered ordering the type, but amalgamations within the British aeronautical industry at that time and problems with noise from the tip jets prevented full-scale production, and the Rotodyne project was abandoned in 1962.

Fairey Ultra Light

Of the interesting British prototypes not adopted in the fifties, the Fairey Ultra Light is worth mentioning.

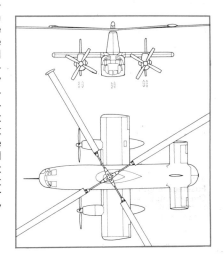

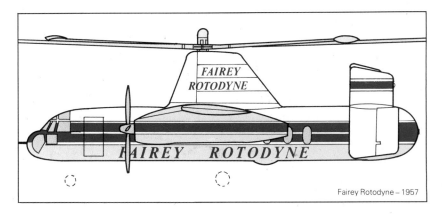

Fairey Rotodyne – 1957

This was a tiny two-seater which used most of the jet from its French Turboméca Palouste turbine engine for propulsion. Air from the centrifugal compressor was sent to the blade tips where it was mixed with the same fuel as was supplied to the turbine, to create additional thrust using tiny combustion chambers.

The project was originally developed to meet a British Army specification for an aerial observation platform and, in September 1956, was displayed at Farnborough, operating from the back of a standard truck. It demonstrated outstanding capabilities: in particular, a rate of climb of 6.75 m/sec (22 ft/sec) and a rate of descent in autorotation of 20 m/sec (65 ft/sec). Subsequent development included trials with the Royal Navy, operating from the deck of a destroyer, HMS Undaunted, but the project was eventually cancelled in 1959.

GYRODYNE
Gyrodyne Company of America (USA)

In 1946 the Gyrodyne Company of America was formed by Peter Papadokus in order to develop a design which combined the features of a fixed-wing airplane with those of a rotorcraft. Gyrodyne's products met with only limited commercial success; nearly all the designs adopted contra-rotating rotors.

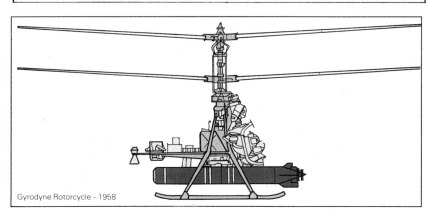
Gyrodyne Rotorcycle – 1958

Gyrodyne Rotorcycle

In response to a US Navy request for an individual helicopter, numerous "flying motorcycles" were built, with various propulsion systems, from reciprocating engines coupled in the normal way to coaxial, contra-rotating rotors, to rocket-propelled rotor blades.

The tiny Gyrodyne Rotorcycle used the first solution. The engine, tricycle landing gear and equipment were mounted on a tubular fuselage structure. A derivative of the Rotorcycle was produced in large numbers. The helicopter was in fact transformed into a remote-controlled torpedo craft for the Navy's DASH (Drone Antisubmarine Helicopter) programme. The original Porsche engine was replaced by a small Boeing turbine in the DSN-1/QH-50 and skid landing gear fitted so that it could take off and land from the deck of a medium-sized vessel such as a destroyer; it was radar-controlled.

Helicopter: **Gyrodyne Rotorcycle (QH-50)**
Manufacturer: **Gyrodyne Company**
Type: **remote-controlled torpedo craft**
Year: **1958**
Engine: **365 hp Boeing T50-B0-15**
Rotor diameter: **6.10 m (20 ft)**
Fuselage length: **2.22 m (7 ft 3 in)**
Overall length: **—**
Height: **2.96 m (9 ft 8 in)**
Empty weight: **470 kg (1,036 lbs)**
Gross weight: **1,056 kg (2,328 lbs)**
Maximum speed: **148 km/h (92 mph)**
Hovering ceiling IGE: **4,965 m (16,290 ft)**
Service ceiling: **4,875 m (16,000 ft)**
Range: **230 km (143 miles)**
Armament: **2 Mk. 44 or Mk. 46 torpedoes**

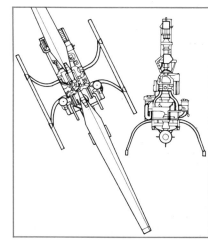

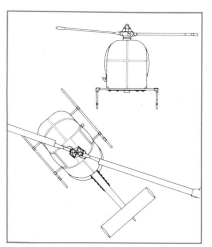

Helicopter: **Fairey Ultra Light**
Manufacturer: **Fairey Aviation Company**
Type: **multipurpose**
Year: **1955**
Engine: **250 hp Turboméca Palouste**
Rotor diameter: **8.61 m (28 ft 3 in)**
Fuselage length: **4.57 m (15 ft)**
Overall length: **—**
Height: **8.61 m (28 ft 3 in)**
Empty weight: **290 kg (640 lbs)**
Gross weight: **817 kg (1,800 lbs)**
Maximum speed: **153 km/h (95 mph)**
Hovering ceiling IGE: **3,109 m (10,200 ft)**
Range: **300 km (186 miles)**

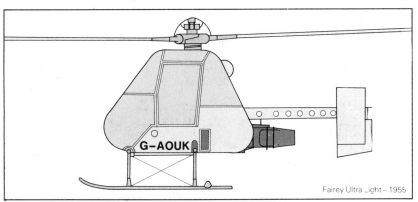
Fairey Ultra Light – 1955

HILLER
Hiller Aircraft Corporation (USA)

In 1942 Stanley Hiller founded the Hiller Aircraft Company and two years later his first aircraft took to the air. Hiller's design had coaxial rotors and was developed jointly with the Kaiser Corporation; soon afterwards, however, Hiller severed his links with Kaiser and developed more of his own original designs, under the company name of United Helicopters, which was changed again in the late 1950s to the Hiller Aircraft Corporation. In 1964 the company was bought by Fairchild and was henceforward known as the Fairchild Hiller Corporation.

Hiller 360

The Hiller UH-12, derived from the Model 360 two-seater of 1948 with a 180 hp Franklin engine, occupies an important place in the history of the American helicopter industry in the fifties. Stanley Hiller Jnr., who built the aircraft, was something of a whiz kid, in that he designed and built his first helicopter, the XH-44, in 1944 at the age of only 18. It was the first efficient American helicopter with coaxial, contra-rotating rotors. The later Hiller 360 leapt to fame in the summer of 1949 when it made the first transcontinental commercial flight. With an uprated engine and new UH-12A rotor blades, it was purchased by the US Army and Navy for battlefield evacuation and observation tasks, with the designation H-23 Raven, whilst the Navy ordered the same basic model as the HTE-1 for training.

Its successor, the H-23B, powered by a 200-210 hp Franklin engine, was the first version used by the US Army as a trainer. A considerable number were built: 216 were assigned to the Primary Flying School at Fort Walters and another 237 were used for various tasks.

The UH-12B normally had skid or flotation gear, but a wheeled undercarriage was fitted to a batch ordered by the US Navy (the HTE-2). In 1955 a new variant, the UH-12C, appeared. It retained the 200 hp Franklin engine, but had all-metal rotor blades and a "goldfish bowl" cockpit canopy. From 1956, 145 were delivered to the US Army as the H-23C. A purely military version, the OH-12D, flew on 3 April 1956 and 483 went to the US Army. The Franklin engine had been replaced by the more powerful 320 hp Lycoming VO-540, and the transmission had also been changed to

Hiller HJ-1 Hornet

The Hiller HJ-1 was developed from the earlier HJ-2 Hornet, which was the first American helicopter with blades driven by ramjets. It was evaluated by the US Army in 1952 and a small batch of 12 were built with the military designation H-32, while the US Navy commissioned a single prototype (HOE), intended as a Light Observation Helicopter, but the production programme did not go ahead.

The HJ-1, which was a two-seater with a light metal structure and fiberglass and laminated plastic skin which could be dismantled in a matter of minutes, had a two-blade metal rotor with a Hiller 8RJ2B ramjet at each blade tip as the main propulsion system, and an auxiliary piston engine which turned the rotor at up to 50 r.p.m. to start up the ramjet. The tail boom had a double anhedral stabilizer.

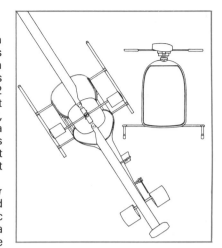

Helicopter: **Hiller HJ-1 (H-32)**
Manufacturer: **Hiller Aircraft Company**
Type: **observation**
Year: **1952**
Engines: **2 × 18 kg (40 lb) Hiller 8RJ2B ramjets**
Rotor diameter: **7.00 m (30 ft)**
Fuselage length: —
Overall length: —
Height: **2.44 m (8 ft)**
Empty weight: **246 kg (542 lbs)**
Gross weight: **489 kg (1,078 lbs)**
Maximum speed: **129 km/h (80 mph)**
Service ceiling: **2,100 m (6,890 ft)**
Range: **50 km (31 miles)**
Capacity: **2**

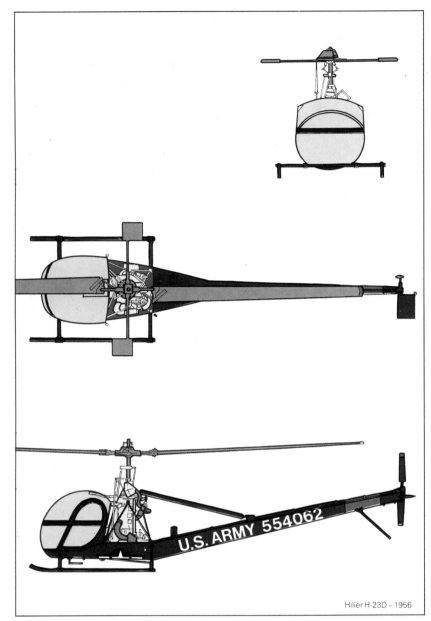

Hiller H-23D – 1956

Hiller HJ-1 Hornet – 1952

Helicopter: **Hiller H-23D**
Manufacturer: **Hiller Aircraft Company**
Type: **training/observation**
Year: **1956**
Engine: **320 hp Lycoming VO-540-1B**
Rotor diameter: **10.80 m (35 ft 5 in)**
Fuselage length: **8.53 m (28 ft)**
Overall length: **12.40 m (40 ft 8 in)**
Height: **2.98 m (9 ft 9 in)**
Empty weight: **807 kg (1,780 lbs)**
Gross weight: **1,270 kg (2,800 lbs)**
Maximum speed: **154 km/h (96 mph)**
Hovering ceiling IGE: **3,290 m (10,794 ft)**
Service ceiling: **4,940 m (16,207 ft)**
Range: **360 km (224 miles)**

increase the service life of the helicopter.

The commonest version of this sturdy little helicopter was the UH-12E which had a more powerful engine. The US Army replaced nearly all the OH-23Ds by Hiller 12Es, designated OH-23G. In 1960 the Model E4 was developed from the Hiller 12E, with a longer cabin to seat four and an anhedral stabilizer on the tail boom. Twenty-two of these were acquired by the US Army as the OH-23F, for geodetic research.

The last civil variant, which appeared in 1963, was the Hiller 12L-4 which was also used as a test-bed for a PT6 turbine, but the project was taken no further.

Total sales of the Hiller 12E family exceeded 2,000; more than 300 were exported. Operators of the Hiller included Argentina, Canada, Chile, Colombia, Great Britain, Guatemala, Japan, Morocco, Mexico, the Netherlands, Peru and Uruguay.

Hiller Model 1099

Built in 1961, this was the prototype of a turbine-powered transport helicopter using dynamic components of the earlier Hiller models, but with an entirely new, more capacious fuselage (six seats). Engine: 550 shp Pratt & Whitney PT6. Rotor diameter: 10.86 m (35 ft). Overall length: 12.57 m (41 ft 3 in). Fuselage length: 8.05 m (26 ft 5 in). Height: 3.18 m (10 ft 5 in). Empty weight: 862 kg (1,900 lbs). Gross weight: 1,588 kg (3,500 lbs).

Hiller YROE-1 Rotorcycle

Ultra-lightweight helicopter designed in 1958 and tested for the US Marine Corps who used five. It could be dismantled and carried in a small container. Engine: 43 hp Nelson H59. Rotor diameter: 5.63 m (18 ft 6 in). Fuselage length: 2.10 m (6 ft 11 in). Empty weight: 136 kg (300 lbs). Gross weight: 252 kg (555 lbs). Maximum speed: 106 km/h (66 mph). Service ceiling: 3,660 m (12,000 ft). Range: 267 km (166 miles).

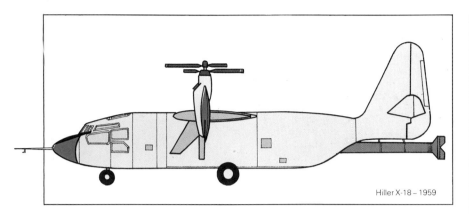

Hiller X-18 – 1959

Hiller X-18

In February 1957, the USAF ordered ten models of the Hiller X-18, a stocky tilt-wing convertiplane powered by two 6,000 shp Allison turboshafts. This aircraft, weighing nearly 15 tonnes, had the fuselage of the Chase YC-122, a twin-engine tactical transport aircraft, while the engines and propellers were taken from a discontinued programme for a vertical tail landing fighter aircraft initiated by the US Navy. Compressed air ejected from a large pipe at the tail controlled longitudinal trim during flight as a helicopter.

The X-18 was tested in November 1959 and made a total of about 20 flights, but the system proved unsatisfactory.

Aircraft: **Hiller X-18**
Manufacturer: **Hiller Aircraft Corporation**
Type: **experimental**
Year: **1959**
Engines: **2 × 5,850 shp Allison T40 turbines**
Wingspan: **14.63 m (48 ft)**
Fuselage length: **19.20 m (63 ft)**
Overall length: —
Height: **7.49 m (24 ft 7 in)**
Empty weight: —
Gross weight: **14,970 kg (33,000 lbs)**
Maximum speed: **402 km/h (250 mph)**

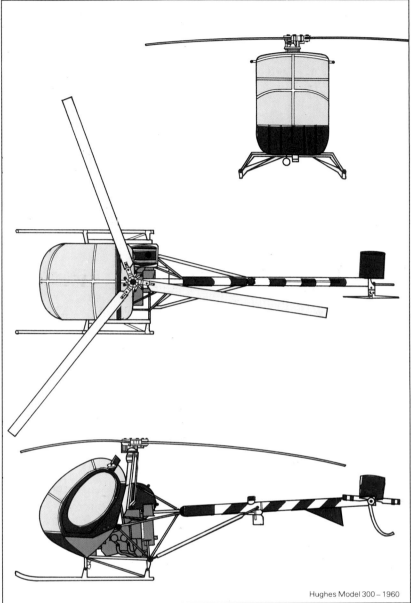

Hughes Model 300 – 1960

HUGHES.
Hughes Aircraft Company (USA)

Howard Robard Hughes, the industrialist, playboy, financier, film producer and director started to take an interest in aviation in 1925 but the company named after him was founded some years later, in 1936, when Hughes was still mainly concerned with competition flying.

In the event, the company only designed and completed a few airplanes, among them the XF-11 fighter prototype. It was developed at the request of the US Army Air Corps but went no further than the experimental stage. Hughes became world-famous as a result of his gigantic HK-4 Hercules flying-boat which had a wingspan of 97.65 m (320 ft) and was powered by eight 3,042 hp Wasp Major engines. This "monster" only managed one very short flight a few feet above the water on 2 November 1946.

Another outsize Hughes project was the XH-17 experimental helicopter designed by Kellett. In the early 1950s the Hughes business interests were re-organized: the Hughes Aircraft and the Hughes Helicopter divisions were merged with the Hughes Tool Company. The Hughes Helicopter division has built a succession of interesting civil and military helicopters over the years and continues to do so, although following the death of Hughes it was sold by his estate and now operates under the aegis of the McDonnell-Douglas Corporation.

Hughes Model 269/300

A market survey carried out in 1955 by the Hughes Tool Company, an American company active in many areas of the aeronautical industry, showed that the time was ripe for a low-cost lightweight two-seat helicopter. The Aircraft division began building the Model 269 in September 1955. This helicopter had a fully-glazed cockpit with side-by-side accommodation for two, an open-framework fuselage and a three-blade articulated rotor. The prototype flew in October 1956, but it was not until 1960 that Hughes decided to develop this machine further by producing an improved version, the Model 269A, to which many aerodynamic and structural refinements had been made. The aircraft also proved ideal for police work and other duties. About 20 a month were being produced by mid

Helicopter: **Hughes Model 269A (300)**
Manufacturer: **Hughes Tool Company**
Type: **trainer/general purpose**
Year: **1960**
Engine: **180 hp Lycoming HIO-360-A1A**
Rotor diameter: **7.71 m (25 ft 3 in)**
Fuselage length: **6.80 m (22 ft 4 in)**
Overall length: **8.80 m (28 ft 10 in)**
Height: **2.66 m (8 ft 9 in)**
Empty weight: **474 kg (1,045 lbs)**
Gross weight: **757 kg (1,669 lbs)**
Maximum speed: **144 km/h (90 mph)**
Hovering ceiling IGE: **2,895 m (9,500 ft)**
Service ceiling: **4,460 m (14,630 ft)**
Range: **480 km (298 miles)**
Capacity: **2 passengers + 136 kg (300 lbs)**

1963 and by spring 1964, 314 had been built.

The Hughes 269A was more interesting than the earlier prototype from a structural point of view. It had a redesigned, more compact cockpit and a steel tube fuselage. The landing skids were curved upwards at the front, and two small wheels could be added to facilitate ground handling. There was a small, asymmetrical butterfly tail unit. The project was submitted to the US Army who ordered five, designated YHO-2-HU, for evaluation at Fort Rucker, and a number of recommendations by Army engineers were adopted by Hughes to improve the design and establish production. In summer 1964, the Army chose it as a primary trainer and ordered 20, designated TH-55A Osage. Two subsequent orders brought the total number of the Osage in 1965 to 396. In 1967, another order was received, bringing the total to 792. Deliveries ended in March 1969.

The various two-three seat versions of the 269 (later redesignated Model 300) were very successful abroad, notably the agricultural version, but they were also sold to air forces and operators in Algeria, Brazil, Colombia, Ghana, Haiti, India, Kenya, Nicaragua, Sierra Leone, Spain and Sweden. The final variant, the 300C which had a more powerful engine and a new main rotor, could carry 45 per cent more payload than the first models.

The Hughes 300 has been built under license by Kawasaki in Japan and by Breda-Nardi in Italy. In both countries, the parts were initially imported from the United States with full-scale production following later. In 1983 the US production rights were sold to the Schweizer Aircraft Company in New York.

Hughes Model 369/500

In 1960, the US Department of Defense issued Technical Specification 153 for a Light Observation Helicopter (LOH) capable of fulfilling various roles: personnel transport, escort and attack missions, casualty evacuation and observation.

Twelve companies took part in the competition and Hughes submitted the Model 369, nicknamed the "flying egg" on account of its shape. The Hiller and Bell aircraft were selected as finalists, but the US Army later included the Hughes helicopter as well — which was offered at an exceptionally low price — under the designation OH-6, and five prototypes were ordered in spring 1961. The Bell was subsequently eliminated from the contest and the Hughes 369 was redesignated OH-6A "Cayuse." The first of the five prototypes flew on 27 February 1963 and was delivered to Fort Rucker air base the following November, to begin trials for the Army.

The Hughes aircraft was very interesting from a structural point of view. For example, the fully-articulated rotor had four blades of

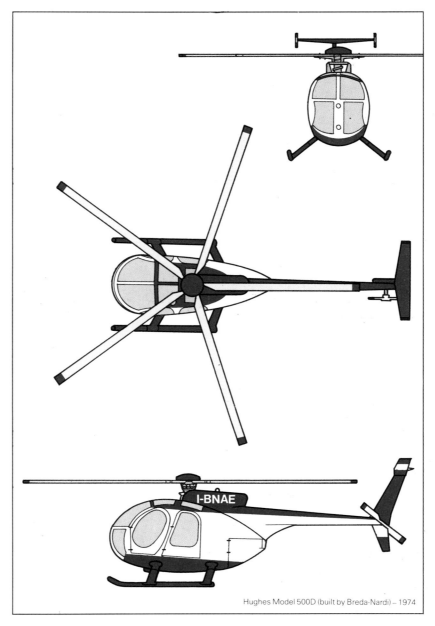

Hughes Model 500D (built by Breda-Nardi) – 1974

constant chord, consisting of an extruded light alloy spar, to which a single sheet of light alloy was bonded to form the profile of the blade. The fuselage had a light alloy, semi-monocoque structure and its remarkable robustness afforded the occupants good protection even in heavy landings. However if the compactness of the fuselage made the Hughes OH-6 light and sturdy, with low drag, it reduced the helicopter's versatility, as its small internal volume was clearly restrictive, despite being perfectly in accordance with Technical Specification 153.

The aircraft had an Allison 250 turbine engine, which was very light and compact, with a maximum power derated from 400 to 282 shp, which afforded obvious advantages in terms of service life and safety. The sophisticated avionics included a track indicator, VHF and UHF

Helicopter: **Hughes Model 500D**
Manufacturer: **Hughes Helicopters**
Type: **multipurpose**
Year: **1974**
Engine: **411 shp Allison 250-C20B**
Rotor diameter: **8.02 m (26 ft 4 in)**
Fuselage length: **7.01 m (23 ft)**
Overall length: **9.24 m (30 ft 4 in)**
Height: **2.48 m (8 ft 2 in)**
Empty weight: **512 kg (1,130 lbs)**
Gross weight: **1,157 kg (2,550 lbs)**
Maximum speed: **244 km/h (152 mph)**
Hovering ceiling IGE: **2,500 m (8,202 ft)**
Service ceiling: **4,389 m (14,400 ft)**
Range: **600 km (373 miles)**
Capacity: **1 pilot + 4 passengers**

transceivers and ADF. A wide choice of weapons fits was available.

Following trials, the choice of the OH-6A for large-scale production was announced in May 1965 with an initial order for 714, which was later increased to 1,300 with an option on another 114. Production reached a maximum of 70 helicopters in the

first month. In all 1,434 were built, the last of which were delivered in August 1970.

The Cayuse established no fewer than 23 world records in March-April 1966: 2,800 km (1,740 miles) closed circuit; 3,561 km (2,213 miles) in a straight line; 227.7 km/h (141 mph) over a 2,000 km (1,243 mile) closed circuit and 8,601 m (28,218 ft) altitude in horizontal flight. It won other records in the various classes for helicopters of a variety of weights, including a speed record of over 277 km/h (172 mph).

Apart from the five prototypes built for the US Army, Hughes built four others for its own research purposes, one of which was converted into a civil version designated Model 500, which flew at the beginning of 1967. The subsequent Model 500C variant had a 405 shp Allison 250-C20 turbine. One OH-6A was later modified under a research programme for ARPA (the advanced research office of the US Department of Defense) to reduce noise levels and has been nicknamed "The Quiet One." It introduced a five-blade main rotor, four-blade anti-torque rotor, exhaust silencer and various noise blanketing devices on the air intakes. The new rotor has 67 per cent of the r.p.m. of the original one, allowing 270 kg (595 lbs) more payload to be carried at a maximum speed of 278 km/h (173 mph). A second experimental prototype, the OH-6C, with an Allison 250-C20 turbine, reached a speed of 322 km/h (200 mph) during a test flight from Edwards Air Force Base.

The H-500MC was a military export version of the Hughes 500C, with major improvements including a more powerful main rotor of larger diameter transmission capable of withstanding higher torque values, an all-metal tail rotor and a maximum fuel capacity of 242 liters (53 gallons). The side windows are also different and high skid landing gear can be fitted. The armament is similar to that of the OH-6A.

Hughes OH-6A helicopters have been exported to the Brazilian Air Force (9) and Navy (6), and the Japanese Ground Self-Defense Force (29). The 500M version has been supplied to the Colombian Air Force (4), Italian customs (over 60), the Spanish Navy (6 in the ASW version), Denmark, Argentina, Bolivia, Mexico and the Philippines.

A later version, the 500D (500MD military) is distinguished externally from earlier models by a T-tail and five-blade rotor. The powerplant is also different — an Allison 250-C20B delivering an absolute maximum of 411 shp and 355 shp maximum continuous power. The increase in power and adoption of the new tail unit have led to a general improvement in structural robustness, particularly of the landing gear, the lower part of the cabin and tail boom, plus, of course, the transmission.

Current production includes the 500E, which introduces a lengthened and redesigned cabin among other improvements, and the 530F which introduces an uprated Allison 250-C30 engine for high altitude operations. Military variants of these new versions were introduced in 1984.

One of the most important orders for Hughes helicopters was for 29 of the Model 369HM built under license by Kawasaki and delivered to the Japanese Army in January 1972. The Japanese OH-6J is virtually identical to the American OH-6A, except for its performance and weight, which are conditioned by the 318 shp Mitsubishi-Allison 250-C18A powerplant.

In Italy, Breda-Nardi have held the license to build and market Hughes Model 300 and 500 helicopters since 1969. Apart from various commercial orders, Breda-Nardi has supplied the NH-500M to the Italian customs. Its characteristics are the same as those of the American aircraft.

Hughes 385

This was a large experimental helicopter built in 1964 to study blade-tip nozzle jet propulsion. Some of the parts were taken from existing aircraft. The version for the US Army was designated XV-9A and had a three-blade constant chord metal rotor. There was room for two pilots seated side by side in the cockpit. Engines: 2 × 2,850 shp General Electric YT-4 GE6. Rotor diameter: 16.76 m (55 ft). Fuselage length: 13.72 m (45 ft). Height: 3.66 m (12 ft). Empty weight: 3,904 kg (8,607 lbs). Gross weight: 6,946 kg (15,313 lbs). Maximum speed: 222 km/h (138 mph). Service ceiling: 5,270 m (17,290 ft).

Hughes AH-64A – 1975

Hughes AH-64A

The US Army's AAH (Advanced Attack Helicopter) programme is the biggest Western programme of its kind: it calls for an aircraft capable of operating day and night in all weathers, which can be based with front line troops if necessary. Of the two contestants, the Bell YAH-63 and the Hughes YAH-64, the latter was the first to become airborne; it flew in September 1975, and two prototypes of each helicopter were delivered to the Army for comparative trials in May 1976. When these were completed in December of that year, the Hughes aircraft was chosen and three more were built, complete with electronics and armament.

The AH-64 is an aggressive-looking helicopter seating two in tandem, with a semi-monocoque fuselage of narrow cross-section.

Helicopter: **Hughes AH-64A**
Manufacturer: **Hughes Helicopters**
Type: **two-seat attack**
Year: **1975**
Engines: **2 × 1,690 shp General Electric T700-GE-701**
Rotor diameter: **14.63 m (48 ft)**
Fuselage length: **15.06 m (49 ft 5 in)**
Overall length: **17.60 m (57 ft 9 in)**
Height: **3.83 m (12 ft 6 in)**
Empty weight: **4,662 kg (10,278 lbs)**
Gross weight: **8,013 kg (17,665 lbs)**
Maximum speed: **378 km/h (235 mph)**
Hovering ceiling IGE: **4,630 m (15,190 ft)**
Service ceiling: **6,250 m (20,500 ft)**
Range: **610 km (379 miles)**
Armament: **One 30 mm cannon + 16 Hellfire missiles**

The copilot/gunner sits in the rear seat, which is raised and has good all-round visibility. The two 1,690 shp General Electric T700-GE-701 turbines are mounted on either side of the fuselage, behind the rotor transmission, in two separate nacelles. The four-blade metal rotor is of the articulated type with the blades angled at 60°/120° in relation

to each other to reduce noise levels. The tail unit, which was modified during the aircraft's second development phase, includes an all-moving tail plane positioned slightly above the tail boom and a vertical fin to replace the earlier T-tail of the prototype. The tailwheel landing gear is fixed.

Apart from the technical/dynamic and structural characteristics of this large helicopter, what is really impressive is its armament and the complexity of the electronic equipment. The highly-sophisticated avionics include TADS (Target Acquisition and Designation Sight) associated with a night vision system using passive FLIR (Forward-Looking Infra-red), low light level TV, a laser rangefinder and target designator for use with Hellfire missiles, all associated with a computerized fire control system. The armament includes a 30 mm XM-230E1 automatic cannon firing 750 rounds, and 16 Hellfire antitank missiles or seventy-six 2.75 inch rockets beneath the stub wings. All the most vulnerable parts are protected by armour against shots of up to 23 mm caliber.

The US Army plans to acquire 536 of these Hughes helicopters. The first production AH-64A was rolled out in September 1983 and deliveries to Army units begin in 1984.

Hughes XH-17

Experimental "flying crane" heavy lift aircraft which was studied for the US Air Force in 1952 but was not mass produced. It had two General Electric J35 turbojets at the sides of the fuselage. It could carry a load of over 12,000 kg (26,455 lbs) slung from the fuselage framework. Rotor diameter: 39.60 m (130 ft). Gross weight: 23,600 kg (52,028 lbs). Cruise speed: 96 km/h (60 mph). Service ceiling: 4,570 m (15,000 ft). Range: 64 km (40 miles).

K L M

KAMAN
Kaman Aerospace Corporation (USA)

After working with Igor Sikorsky, Charles H. Kaman decided to found his own company in 1946. Kaman's first helicopter, the K-125, adopted the intermeshing side-by-side rotor configuration which eliminated the need for an anti-torque tail rotor. It first flew in 1947.

Kaman Aerospace Corporation has two factories in Connecticut, carrying out advanced research and development into helicopter structures and rotor technology.

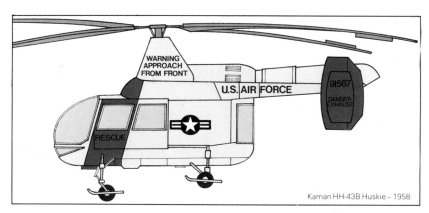

Kaman HH-43B Huskie – 1958

Kaman K-600

The K-600 appeared in 1950 in response to a US Navy design competition for a new, four-seat liaison helicopter. It was an original design with twin contra-rotating intermeshing two-blade rotors and a servoflap system for cyclic and collective pitch control.

The Kaman K-600 was intitially ordered by the Marines (HOK-1) and the US Navy (HUK-1), while the US Air Force ordered it for rescue and fire-fighting missions (HH-43A). After a first batch of 16, the USAF requested a more powerful version with a Lycoming T53-1-L-1 turbine. The prototype for 116 HH-43Bs flew on 27 September 1956, and was followed by the first production model in December 1958. All of them carried water and foam or compressed nitrogen fire-fighting equipment. They were exported to Burma, Colombia, Morocco, Pakistan, Thailand and Iran.

Helicopter: **Kaman HH-43B Huskie**
Manufacturer: **Kaman**
Type: **rescue**
Year: **1958**
Engine: **860 shp Lycoming T53-L-1B**
Rotor diameter: **14.33 m (47 ft)**
Fuselage length: **7.67 m (25 ft 2 in)**
Overall length: —
Height: **4.74 m (15 ft 6in)**
Empty weight: **2,027 kg (4,865 lbs)**
Gross weight: **2,708 kg (5,970 lbs)**
Maximum speed: **193 km/h (120 mph)**
Hovering ceiling IGE: **6,400 m (21,000 ft)**
Service ceiling: **7,620 m (25,000 ft)**
Range: **445 km (276 miles)**
Capacity: **1 pilot + 2 firefighters + 450 kg (992 lbs) of fire-fighting equipment**

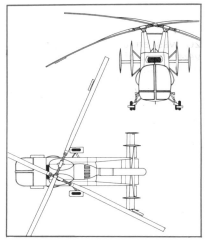

Kaman K-17

Experimental two-seater built in 1958 powered by a ''cold-jet'' rotor system: the 400 hp Blackburn Turboméca Turmo 600 turbine drove a compressor which fed compressed air to blade-tip nozzles. Rotor diameter: 11.28 m (37 ft). Empty weight: 431 kg (950 lbs). Gross weight: 907 kg (2,000 lbs). Maximum speed: 129 km/h (80 mph). Hovering ceiling: 1,525 m (5,000 ft). Range: 250 km (155 miles).

Kaman K-20

In 1956, the US Navy set up a design competition for a new, high-speed, long-range multipurpose helicopter. The contest was won by the Kaman K-20, and the American company accordingly received a contract to build 12 aircraft designated HU2K-1. Trials were lengthy, partly on account of the number of innovations made to the aircraft, and the first models, designated UH-2A Seasprite, only went into service at the end of 1962.

This was a conventional type of turbine-powered helicopter, with a four-blade main rotor and three-blade anti-torque rotor, retractable tailwheel landing gear and a streamlined fuselage. The sealed hull enabled it to float in calm water. Eighty-eight UH-2As were built, and the sea-grey aircraft with its fluorescent markings became a familiar sight on American aircraft carriers. Its successor, the UH-2B, was virtually identical except for the removal of some items of equipment, which were, however, available as optional extras.

Kaman modified one UH-2B airframe for the US Army Transportation Research Command, by installing a General Electric J85 turbojet on one side of the fuselage, thereby transforming the K-20 into a compound helicopter. In this configuration, the aircraft achieved a speed of over 360 km/h (224 mph). Several of the UH-2B were acquired and evaluated by the US Army for fire support, armed with a four-gun M6 turret and two attachment points for Miniguns and unguided rockets.

Originally single-engined, the Seasprite was redesigned in 1964 with twin GET58-GE-8 turbines and the conversion was so successful that over 100 UH-2As and UH-2Bs were subsequently converted into UH-2Cs, whilst almost as many became HH-2Cs and HH-2Ds. The HH-2C was an armed and protected version, 12 of which were supplied to the US Navy for use on large destroyers. The HH-2D models were obtained by converting 31 single-engine helicopters to the standard of the HH-2C, but without the weapons and protection. The US Navy then considered the possibility of using the Seasprite for ASW and this gave rise to the SH-2D for the LAMPS (Light Airborne Multipurpose System) programme; it was similar to the HH-2D but had a search radar in a cylindrical radome beneath the cabin, MAD gear and sonobuoys (a few aircraft were also tested with dipping sonar). The launchable weapons consisted of two Mk.46 torpedoes or antiship missiles. Twenty HH-2Ds were transformed into the SH-2D ASW variant, while 194 of the SH-2F

version, which is still in service, have been built. These differ from the SH-2D in having a new rotor and stronger landing gear. In 1983 Kaman resumed production of the SH-2F to meet further US Navy orders.

Kaman SH-2F Seasprite – 1966

Helicopter: **Kaman K-20 Seasprite (SH-2F)**
Manufacturer: **Kaman Aerospace Corp.**
Type: **multipurpose naval**
Year: **1966**
Engine: **2 × 1,350 shp General Electric T58-GE-8**
Rotor diameter: **13.41 m (44 ft)**
Fuselage length: **12.30 m (40 ft 4 in)**
Overall length: **16.03 m (52 ft 7 in)**
Height: **4.72 m (15 ft 6 in)**
Empty weight: **3,200 kg (7,055 lbs)**
Gross weight: **5,810 kg (12,808 lbs)**
Maximum speed: **265 km/h (165 mph)**
Service ceiling: **6,858 m (22,500 ft)**
Range: **680 km (422 miles)**
Armament: **2 Mk.46 torpedoes**

KAWASAKI
Kawasaki Kokuki Kogyo
(Japan)

Founded in 1878, Kawasaki is one of the great manufacturing giants which has been at the heart of Japanese industrial growth. In 1922 the company set up an aircraft construction division. During the Second World War Kawasaki produced a great many fighters and light bombers and, since the war, has built the C-1 military transport. In recent years Kawasaki's energies have mainly been directed towards the construction under license of American helicopters (Bell and Sikorsky). It has also developed the multirole BK-117 as a joint venture with the German company MBB.

Kawasaki KH-4

At the beginning of the sixties, Kawasaki decided to develop a version of the three-seat Bell Model 47G-3, with a stretched cabin to make room for two rows of seats. The first KH-4 flew in August 1962 and received Japanese type approval on 9 November of that year. By the beginning of 1972, 193 of the Kawasaki KH-4 had been built, 19 of which were assigned to the Japanese Army, 23 to the Thai armed forces, four to the South Korean armed forces and one to the Philippines.

Helicopter: **Kawasaki KH-4**
Manufacturer: **Kawasaki Industries**
Type: **light transport**
Year: **1962**
Engine: **270 hp Lycoming TVO-435**
Rotor diameter: **11.32 m (37 ft 2 in)**
Fuselage length: **9.93 m (32 ft 7 in)**
Overall length: **13.17 m (43 ft 2 in)**
Height: **2.84 m (9 ft 4 in)**
Empty weight: **857 kg (1,890 lbs)**
Gross weight: **1,290 kg (2,844 lbs)**
Maximum speed: **190 km/h (118 mph)**
Hovering ceiling IGE: **5,485 m (18,000 ft)**
Service ceiling: **5,640 m (18,500 ft)**
Range: **345 km (214 miles)**
Capacity: **1 pilot + 3 passengers**

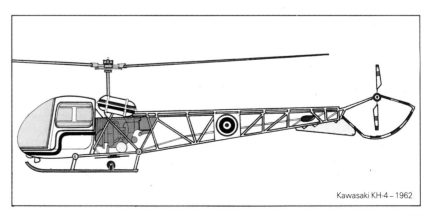

Kawasaki KH-4 – 1962

LOCKHEED
Lockheed Aircraft Corporation (USA)

Lockheed's two main aeronautical divisions, Lockheed California and Lockheed Georgia, form one of the world's oldest aeronautical concerns. Founded in 1916 by two brothers, Allen and Malcolm Loughead, the Lockheed company has produced a great number of successful civil and military aircraft. In the late 1950s the company embarked on the development of a rigid rotor helicopter which first flew under the research designation of XH-51 and from which the AH-56 Cheyenne helicopter was derived — a helicopter which met with little success.

Lockheed XH-51

The first American rigid rotor helicopter was built in 1962 and was jointly evaluated by the US Army and US Navy and subsequently by NASA. It showed excellent manoeuvrability and safety characteristics. It was fitted experimentally with a wing and auxiliary turbojet. Engine: 500 hp Pratt & Whitney PT6. Rotor diameter: 10.67 m (35 ft). Overall length: 9.69 m (31 ft 9 in). Height: 2.50 m (8 ft 2 in). Empty weight: 966 kg (2,130 lbs). Gross weight: 1,588 kg (3,500 lbs). Maximum speed: 257 km/h (160 mph). Range: 555 km (345 miles).

MBB
Messerschmitt-Bölkow-Blohm GmbH (Federal Republic of Germany)

Willy Messerschmitt founded his company in 1923. Having designed and built the famous Second World War fighter, the Bf.109, and many other outstanding aircraft, the company was re-formed after the war, initially accepting a wide range of engineering and construction contracts, but eventually it was possible to concentrate once more on aircraft production.

In 1960 the company merged with Bölkow and then in 1969 with Hamburger Flugzeugbau, forming the impressive industrial concern of MBB (Messerschmitt-Bölkow-Blohm) based in Munich, with factories at Hasbergen, Donauwörth, Hamburg, Laupheim, Manching, Munich and Ottobrunn. The shareholdings in the company were split between Willy Messerschmitt (23.3%), Blohm (27.1%), Ludwig Bölkow (14.6%), Boeing and Nord Aviation Française (9.6% each), and the Bavarian Reconstruction Institute (6.5%). By mid 1969 the MBB group employed about 20,000 people. The bulk of the company concentrated on the design and construction of light aircraft and transports, but later diversified into missile production, space programmes and helicopter construction.

The most important projects in the aeronautical sector have been the designs for a helicopter and two aircraft: the Bo.105, the Airbus and the Tornado. The Bo.105 has proved one of MBB's most successful programmes and by 1980 over 500 had been sold, both to German users and for export.

Many of MBB's present programmes involve other participants, and are often international joint ventures. The multipurpose BK-117 helicopter has been developed with Kawasaki. MBB also has a large interest in armament production and defense projects. The company is currently expanding its activities and has developed an industrial infrastructure with over 30,000 employees.

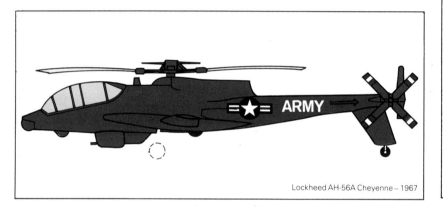

Lockheed AH-56A Cheyenne – 1967

Lockheed AH-56 Cheyenne

The ambitious AH-56 Cheyenne helicopter, with which Lockheed hoped to establish a foothold in the rotary wing sector, was in fact a resounding failure for the Californian company. It featured a rigid main and tail rotor, which Lockheed had been researching since 1959 — a rigid rotor enables helicopters to perform genuine aerobatic manoeuvres.

The AH-56A Cheyenne was driven by a General Electric T64 turbine delivering over 3,400 shp. It had a stub wing with an 8 m (26 ft 3in) span and an area of 24 sq.m (258 sq.ft), attachment points for six underwing stores weighing 900 kg (1,984 lbs) each, a streamlined fuselage with a tandem cabin seating arrangement, retractable front landing gear units, a fixed tailwheel, a rigid four-blade anti-torque tail rotor and three-blade pusher propeller at the tip of the tail boom. However the Cheyenne was technically too complicated and US Army orders were cancelled and development suspended in 1972.

Helicopter: **Lockheed AH-56A Cheyenne**
Manufacturer: **Lockheed Aircraft Corporation**
Type: **two-seat combat**
Year: **1967**
Engine: **3,435 shp General Electric T64-GE-16**
Rotor diameter: **15.36 m (50 ft 5 in)**
Fuselage length: **18.31 m (60 ft)**
Wingspan: **8.14 m (26 ft 8 in)**
Height: **4.18 m (13 ft 8 in)**
Empty weight: **5,323 kg (11,735 lbs)**
Gross weight: **9,988 kg (22,020 lbs)**
Maximum speed: **389 km/h (242 mph)**
Service ceiling: **7,925 m (26,000 ft)**
Range: **1,400 km (870 miles)**
Armament: **7.8 mm machine gun; grenade launchers; TOW missiles; rocket launchers**

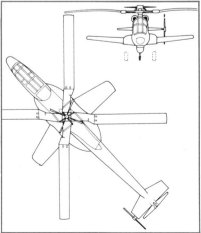

Bölkow Bo.105

The Bo.105 general purpose helicopter project begun in 1962 can be regarded as the crowning of the experience acquired by Ludwig Bölkow's company with the Bo.46 and the subsequent Bo.102 and 103. The Bo.105 started out as a lightweight five-six seater with twin turbines to improve flight safety and all-weather capabilities. The first aircraft, designated V-1, was ready for ground testing in September 1966. The helicopter had been fitted with a conventional Westland Scout articulated rotor, but in spite of this, it was destroyed by ground resonance during initial trials.

By the time the second prototype, the V-2, was ready, the rigid rotor had been thoroughly tested and was fitted to the new helicopter. The Bo.105 V-2 made its first flight at Ottobrunn (Munich) on 16 February 1967; it had a pair of Allison 250-C18 turbines and the four-blade rigid rotor, and from the outset demonstrated excellent controllability while hovering and at low flight speeds.

Further changes and modifications led to the third prototype — the V-3 fitted with two German-built MAN-Turbo 6022 turbines, and to two pre-production models, the Bo.105 V-4 and V-5, the first of which made its maiden flight on 1 May 1969. Two Allison 250-C20 turbines were later installed on the V-4, which thus became the prototype of the definitive Bo.105C. Meanwhile, from spring 1970, new "droop snoot" design blades, which had a marked downward curvature on the leading edge, were introduced. These were made by MBB, the Messerschmitt-Bölkow-Blohm und Voss group — of which Bölkow and its affiliates had become part.

In 1972, the Bo.105 went into full-scale production, and was offered with either Allison 250-C18 turbine engines or the more powerful C20. The helicopter was approved by the German Federal Authority LBA with the first powerplant in October 1970, after successfully completing autorotation trials in the autumn of 1969. Approval by the US Federal Aviation Administration followed in March 1971 and

Over 1,100 civil and military models have been sold of the Bo.105 which went into production in 1972.

was extended to the C20 engines in August 1972, while the Canadian authorities certified the Bo.105 in April 1973. The German helicopter also received a British Certificate of Airworthiness in July 1973 and was recognized by the Italian Aeronautical Register in March 1974.

There was no doubt that, with its twin-turbine engines and spacious cabin, the Bo.105 would be widely adopted for civil operations, and the German government in fact ordered 20 for its "Katastrophenschutz" programme, to ensure rapid assistance in the event of a disaster. The military version differs little from the civil one. The antitank version can carry six HOT missiles, three on either side of the cabin, with a stabilized sight on the port side.

The results of tests with the Bo.105 HGH were particularly interesting. These were completed in 1975 after two years' research aimed at improving the helicopter's performance. With special fairings, a modified tail unit and smaller skids, this helicopter reached a maximum speed of 372 km/h (231

mph), 100 km/h (62 mph) more than the conventional Bo.105. The same aircraft was also given a 6.20 m (20 ft 4 in) span wing, which enabled it to reach a speed of 404 km/h (251 mph).

The German Army has ordered the following numbers of the military version of the MBB helicopter: Bo.105M liaison and observation, 227; Bo.105 (PAH-1) antitank, 212. Other military Bo.105s have been supplied to Iraq, the Gulf States, Spain, the Philippines and Indonesia, and the Bo.105 has been built under license in these latter three countries by the CASA, NAM and Nurtanio companies, respectively.

Helicopter: **Bölkow Bo.105C**
Manufacturer: **MBB**
Type: **general purpose**
Year: **1971**
Engines: **2 × 406 shp Allison 250-C20**
Rotor diameter: **9.82 m (32 ft 3 in)**
Fuselage length: **8.55 m (28 ft)**
Overall length: **11.86 m (38 ft 11 in)**
Height: **2.98 m (9 ft 9 in)**
Empty weight: **1,110 kg (2,447 lbs)**
Gross weight: **2,300 kg (5,070 lbs)**
Maximum speed: **270 km/h (168 mph)**
Hovering ceiling IGE: **2,715 m (8,907 ft)**
Service ceiling: **5,030 m (16,500 ft)**
Range: **656 km (407 miles)**
Capacity: **4-5 passengers**

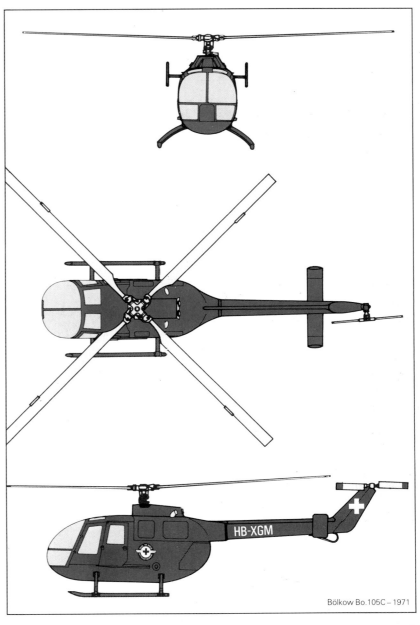

Bölkow Bo.105C – 1971

One of the German prototypes of the BK-117 which began test flights in June 1979.

The civil version has also been a major export success and was initially marketed through Boeing in the United States before MBB set up its own US facilities. By the end of 1981, total production of the Bo.105 exceeded 1,100. More than 100 Bo.105s are now in operation in the United States and these were joined in 1982 by the more recent Bo.105CBS Twin Jet II variant, with 420 shp Allison 250-C20B turbines, which, apart from having better flying capabilities, has 20 per cent more cabin room.

Further development of the Bo.105CBS led to the introduction in 1981 of the Bo.105LS (Lift Stretch) which combines the enlarged cabin with the uprated transmission of the military version and more powerful 550 shp Allison 250-C28C engines to provide a much improved hot/high performance and external lift capability.

MBB/Kawasaki BK-117

The BK-117 medium-weight multi-purpose helicopter programme was given the go-ahead on 25 February 1977 with the signing of an agreement between the German consortium Messerschmitt-Bölkow-Blohm and the Japanese company Kawasaki Heavy Industries, following more than two years' negotiation. Both partners could boast considerable experience in the rotary wing sector and the new aircraft, which was an eight-ten-seater, was intended to replace two projects studied independently by the two companies: the German Bo.107 and the Japanese KH-7. Joint development costs were to be divided equally, the financing being guaranteed by the respective governments. MBB was to be responsible for the main rotor and tail rotor, tail boom, empennage, hydraulic system and

controls, while Kawasaki was to develop the landing gear, fuselage, transmission and other minor components.

The original programme was based on four prototypes, two to be built by MBB in Munich and two by Kawasaki in Gifu, all to be completed by mid 1979. In each case, one of the prototypes was intended for flight testing and the other for static tests. However although the German company succeeded in completing its two models by the end of 1979, only one of the Japanese prototypes was ready on time.

The relationship of the BK-117 to the Bo.105 is evident in many respects. Firstly, a fair percentage of parts and systems are identical to those of the German helicopter. The hydraulic system is based on the original Bo.105 version and even the rotor is taken from the Bo.105,

suitably enlarged to match the demands of the bigger and heavier BK-117. The four-blade rotor is of the rigid type with a titanium hub and reinforced fiberglass blades. The transmission is, of course, derived from the Japanese KH-7 project: a seven-ten-seat helicopter which was to have been fitted with two 590 shp Lycoming turbine engines. The BK-117 in fact also has a pair of Avco-Lycoming LTS-101-650B-1 engines, delivering 600 shp on take-off and 550 shp maximum continuous power. The fuel tanks, with a total capacity of 605 liters (133 gallons), are housed in the lower part of the fuselage.

The executive version of the BK-117 carries a pilot and five passengers, but given the volume of 3.22 cu.m (113.7 cu.ft) there is ample room for nine passengers in the high density version or in those used for commuter and offshore

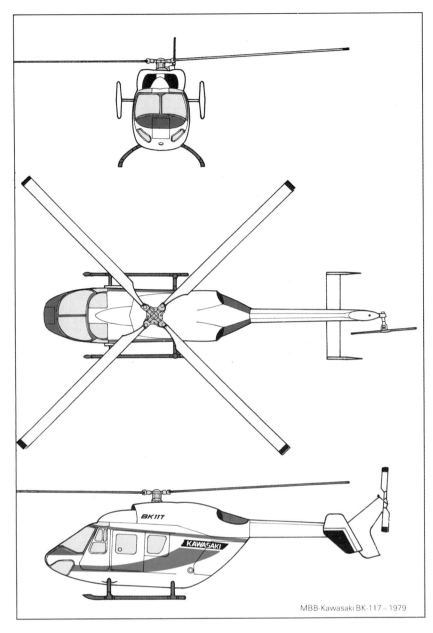

MBB-Kawasaki BK-117 – 1979

McDonnell
McDonnell Douglas Corporation (USA)

During the thirties James McDonnell worked for several design studios. On leaving that of Glenn L. Martin in 1938 McDonnell founded the McDonnell Aircraft Corporation which manufactured components for various companies before designing and building its first aircraft, the twin-engine fighter XP-67. Once the jet era arrived, McDonnell produced a useful fighter for the US Navy, the FH-1. It originally entered the field of rotorcraft by buying a controlling share in the Platt LePage Aircraft Corporation of Eddystone (Pennsylvania), but then left the scene for more than 20 years before re-entering with the purchase of Hughes Helicopters at the end of 1983.

McDonnell XH-20

This single-seater built in 1947 was powered by blade-tip ramjets delivering 30 hp each. The high fuel consumption prevented it from having a satisfactory range and the production programme for the American armed forces was never undertaken. Only one was built. Rotor diameter: 5.49 m (18 ft). Empty weight: 129 kg (284 lbs). Gross weight: 254 kg (560 lbs). Cruise speed: 80 km/h (50 mph).

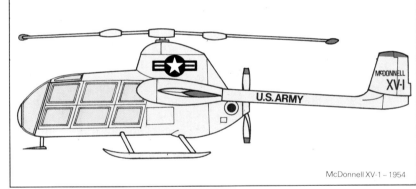

McDonnell XV-1 – 1954

services to oil platforms. In the latter roles, it can carry a substantial payload, and even bulky goods can be easily loaded through two large sliding doors, one on either side of the fuselage. Behind the passenger cabin is a large baggage hold with a capacity of 1.34 cu.m (47.32 cu.ft), which is reached through two hinged doors at the rear of the fuselage. Alternatively, the helicopter can be equipped to carry four stretchers plus two medical attendants; other roles include fire-fighting, search and rescue operations, or a cargo hook can be fitted to the cabin floor for external lift work.

The first German prototype flew on 13 June 1979 and the third (Japanese) aircraft on 10 August of that year. Production was initiated almost immediately and a year later, more than 100 BK-117s had been ordered. By the beginning of 1982, the BK-117 prototypes had

logged more than 750 flying hours and type approval by the German Federal Authorities followed shortly afterwards. Half of the 130 aircraft ordered by February 1982 were for customers in the United States, where deliveries began in early 1983.

Helicopter: **BK-117**
Manufacturer: **MBB/Kawasaki**
Type: **multipurpose**
Year: **1979**
Engines: **2 × 600 shp Avco Lycoming LTS-101**
Rotor diameter: **11.00 m (36 ft 1 in)**
Fuselage length: **9.88 m (32 ft 5 in)**
Overall length: —
Height: **3.84 m (12 ft 7 in)**
Empty weight: **1,520 kg (3,350 lbs)**
Gross weight: **2,800 kg (6,173 lbs)**
Maximum speed: **264 km/h (164 mph)**
Range: **545 km (339 miles)**
Capacity: **9 passengers**

McDonnell XV-1

This experimental aircraft was designed by a pioneer of vertical flight, the Austrian Friedrich von Doblhoff. It was built with the collaboration of the US Army and Air Force. It was one of the first examples of a compound helicopter, with a pusher propeller driven by a piston engine, and a three-blade rotor powered by air from two compressors ducted along the blades to blade-tip nozzles. The aircraft had a small wing supporting twin tail booms. The 550 hp Continental R-975 engine was housed in the rear of the fuselage. The cabin seated a pilot and three passengers. The first of two prototypes was test-flown at the beginning of 1954. In October 1956 it became the first rotorcraft to reach a speed of 320 km/h (199 mph). Development was suspended in 1957.

Aircraft: **McDonnell XV-1**
Manufacturer: **McDonnell Aircraft Corporation**
Type: **experimental compound**
Year: **1954**
Engine: **550 hp Continental R-975-16**
Rotor diameter: **9.45 m (31 ft)**
Fuselage length: —
Overall length: **15.37 m (50 ft 5 in)**
Height: **3.28 m (10 ft 9 in)**
Empty weight: **1,942 kg (4,280 lbs)**
Gross weight: **2,499 kg (5,510 lbs)**
Maximum speed: **327 km/h (203 mph)**
Hovering ceiling IGE: —
Service ceiling: **6,035 m (19,800 ft)**
Range: **955 km (593 miles)**
Capacity: **1 pilot + 3 passengers**

P S

PIASECKI

Piasecki Aircraft Company (USA)

After working as a mechanic for Kellett Autogyro, National Machine Company and Platt LePage, in 1943 Frank N. Piasecki founded the P.V. Engineering Forum (registered in 1947 under the name of the Piasecki Helicopter Corporation). In 1943 Piasecki built the second American helicopter, making use of car components and an outboard motor. He then perfected the tandem rotor system, and built the XHRP-1 for the US Navy, the first of a successful series, nick-named "flying bananas." In 1955 he resigned as president of the company and set up another, the Piasecki Aircraft Company. The original Piasecki Helicopter Corporation became the Vertol Aircraft Corporation and since 1960, the Vertol Division of the Boeing Company. The Piasecki Aircraft Company meanwhile has continued research into vertical flight up to the present day.

Piasecki 16H Pathfinder

A high-speed compound helicopter built in 1965 as a private venture for research into fast rotary wing craft. After a two-year development period, the aircraft was modified at the request of the US Army and Navy and redesignated Pathfinder II. Engine: 1,250 shp General Electric. Rotor diameter: 13.40 m (44 ft). Overall length: 11.40 m (37 ft 3 in). Height: 3.50 m (11 ft 6 in). Empty weight: 2,170 kg (4,784 lbs). Gross weight: 3,700 kg (8,157 lbs). Maximum speed: 362 km/h (225 mph). Service ceiling: 5,700 m (18,700 ft). Range: 725 km (450 miles).

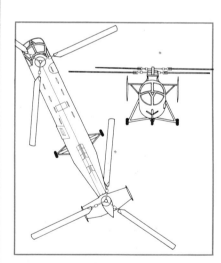

Piasecki H-21 Workhorse

From the all-metal PV-17 built in 1948, the following year Piasecki derived the HRP-2 (Rescuer) and an improved version of the Rescuer, the H-21 Workhorse. The USAF acquired 214 of the latter, and 334 of a similar model, the H-21 Swanee, were built for the US Army. The B and C variants of the H-21 were used in Vietnam, equipped with 12.7 or 7.62 mm light machine guns which were fired through the cabin doors. The H-21 used the classic single engine formula with tandem three-blade rotors. While the Navy's helicopters had a 600 hp Pratt & Whitney R-1340 engine, those for the Army had a Wright R-1820. Thirty-three of the H-21A were assigned to SAR units in the Arctic and another five were sent to Canada. Foreign operators of the H-21 included the German Army (26), French Army (98), French Navy (10), Japanese armed forces (10) and Swedish Navy (11).

Helicopter: **Piasecki H-21C Workhorse**
Manufacturer: **Piasecki Helicopter Corporation**
Type: **tactical transport**
Year: **1952**
Engine: **1,425 hp Wright R-1820-103**
Rotor diameter: **13.50 m (44 ft 3 in)**
Fuselage length: **—**
Overall length: **26.20 m (85 ft 11 in)**
Height: **4.70 m (15 ft 5 in)**
Empty weight: **3,632 kg (8,007 lbs)**
Gross weight: **6,810 kg (15,013 lbs)**
Maximum speed: **211 km/h (131 mph)**
Hovering ceiling IGE: **1,600 m (5,250 ft)**
Service ceiling: **2,880 m (9,450 ft)**
Range: **450 km (280 miles)**
Capacity: **20 troops**

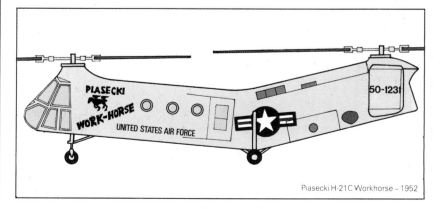

Piasecki H-21C Workhorse – 1952

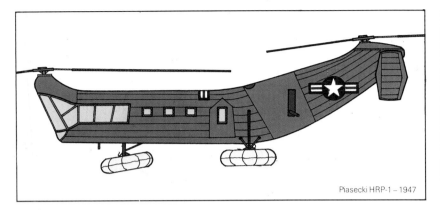

Piasecki HRP-1 – 1947

Piasecki HRP-1

The first tandem rotor helicopters built by Frank Piasecki were nick-named "flying bananas." The pro-totype, the PV-3, which was desig-nated HRP-1 by the US Navy, flew 13 months after the go-ahead was received for the project. At the time this was the world's largest helicop-ter. Tests were completed at the beginning of 1947 when P.V. En-gineering Forum, founded by Piasecki in 1943, restyled itself the Piasecki Helicopter Corporation. The first model from the initial batch of ten, which had a 600 hp Pratt & Whitney engine mounted at the rear of the fuselage, flew that summer. The tandem rotor con-figuration chosen by Piasecki allowed fairly generous center of gravity margins (important when carrying bulk loads). In addition to those used for transport and search and rescue operations by the Navy, 12 HRP-1s were assigned to the US Marines for landing exercises.

Helicopter: **Piasecki HRP-1**
Manufacturer: **Piasecki Helicopter Corpora-tion**
Type: **transport/SAR**
Year: **1947**
Engine: **600 hp Pratt & Whitney R-1340AN-1**
Rotor diameter: **12.50 m (41 ft)**
Fuselage length: **16.70 m (54 ft 9 in)**
Height: **4.55 m (14 ft 11 in)**
Empty weight: **2,358 kg (5,198 lbs)**
Gross weight: **3,133 kg (6,907 lbs)**
Maximum speed: **159 km/h (99 mph)**
Hovering ceiling IGE: **2,100 m (6,890 ft)**
Service ceiling: **2,600 m (8,530 ft)**
Range: **427 km (265 miles)**
Capacity: **8 troops or 6 stretchers**

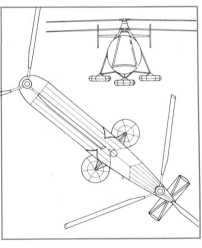

Piasecki HUP-1/HUP-2

After the first "flying banana," Piasecki immediately set to work on a specification, issued by the US Navy Bureau of Aeronautics in 1945, for a shipboard helicopter to be used on aircraft carriers and lar-ger vessels for SAR, liaison, replen-ishment and plane guard duties.

The result was the PV-14 (desig-nated XHJP-1 by the US Navy). Three pre-production aircraft, the HUP-1, were ordered in 1948; this was followed between 1950 and 1952 by a full production batch using the 525 hp Continental R-975-34 radial engine, which could carry two crew plus four-five passengers or three stretcher cases. The power-plant was installed at the center of the fuselage, which had a steel tube framework with particularly strong, fixed tricycle landing gear. The fin of the HUP-1 was subsequently eli-minated, as further improved ver-sions were fitted with an autopilot. The US Navy versions had all-

weather instrumentation and some were equipped with sonar for anti-submarine warfare.

The HUP-1 kept the classic, tan-dem rotor configuration, but had a smaller, more compact fuselage than its predecessors. This enabled the helicopter to be stowed without having to fold back the rotor blades. Once acceptance trials were over, the US Navy ordered 32 aircraft, followed by another 165 of the HUP-2, which was fitted with a more powerful engine. The Marines also used 13, while the Army acquired 70, designated H-25A, 50 of which were later transferred to the Navy as HUP-3s. Finally, 15 HUP-2s were built for the French Navy and three for the Canadian Navy. All these helicopters were withdrawn in 1956, but in the period from 1950-53, they received their "baptism of fire" in Korea, where they per-formed intensive transport, liaison and rescue missions, both on land

Piasecki H-25A – 1951

Helicopter: **Piasecki HUP-1**
Manufacturer: **Piasecki Helicopter Corpora-tion**
Type: **liaison/rescue**
Year: **1948**
Engine: **525 hp Continental R-975-34**
Rotor diameter: **10.67 m (35 ft)**
Fuselage length: **9.70 m (31 ft 10 in)**
Height: **3.80 m (12 ft 6 in)**
Empty weight: **1,913 kg (4,217 lbs)**
Gross weight: **2,724 kg (6,005 lbs)**
Maximum speed: **192 km/h (120 mph)**
Hovering ceiling IGE: **3,100 m (10,170 ft)**
Service ceiling: **3,800 m (12,467 ft)**
Range: **440 km (273 miles)**
Capacity: **2 crew + 4**

and at sea. At the height of their career, they were in fact carried aboard all the aircraft carriers of the American fleet for rescue opera-tions.

Piasecki YH-16

In 1953 the enormous XH-16 tur-boshaft tactical transport helicop-ter, the Transporter, was built. It had tandem three-blade rotors, a very

Helicopter: **Piasecki H-25A**
Manufacturer: **Piasecki Helicopter Corpora-tion**
Type: **tactical transport**
Year: **1951**
Engine: **525 hp Continental R-975-42**
Rotor diameter: **10.67 m (35 ft)**
Fuselage length: **9.70 m (31 ft 10 in)**
Height: **3.80 m (12 ft 6 in)**
Empty weight: **1,913 kg (4,217 lbs)**
Gross weight: **2,724 kg (6,005 lbs)**
Maximum speed: **185 km/h (115 mph)**
Service ceiling: **3,870 m (12,697 ft)**
Range: **574 km (357 miles)**
Capacity: **2 crew + 4**

capacious fuselage, equal in size to that of a four-engine DC-4 transport aircraft, and two engines, one at the front and the other in the rear of the fuselage. The rear engine drove the rotor at the top of a tail pylon nearly 4 m (13 ft) high. The helicopter had a horizontal stabilizer, to which ver-tical control surfaces were later added in order to overcome prob-lems of directional stability during fast flight. It weighed 14 tonnes on take-off with two pilots and 40

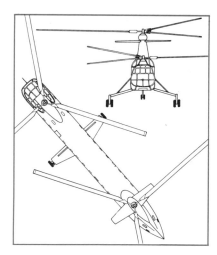

Heli-Stat began at Lakehurst, New Jersey, in 1979. The hybrid aircraft uses an airship-based envelope, attached via a skeletal structure to the front fuselage portions of four Sikorsky SH-34J helicopters, each powered by a standard Wright radial engine driving the conventional main rotor system and mounted at the four corners of the aircraft. The tail rotors are replaced by large diameter propellers to provide propulsion and full controllability.

At the beginning of 1984 it was expected that the Heli-Stat would fly in 1985, following a redesign of the structure which had failed under load tests. The following data is provisional.

Helicopter: **Piasecki YH-16**
Manufacturer: **Piasecki Helicopter Corporation**
Type: **military transport**
Year: **1954**
Engines: **2 × 1,800 shp Allison YT-38A-10**
Rotor diameter: **24.99 m (82 ft)**
Fuselage length: —
Overall length: **23.65 m (77 ft 7 in)**
Height: **7.62 m (25 ft)**
Empty weight: **10,218 kg (22,526 lbs)**
Gross weight: **15,244 kg (33,607 lbs)**
Maximum speed: **235 km/h (146 mph)**
Hovering ceiling IGE: **4,800 m (15,750 ft)**
Service ceiling: **6,980 m (22,900 ft)**
Range: **2,300 km (1,429 miles)**
Capacity: **2 pilots + 40 troops**

Aircraft: **Piasecki Heli-Stat**
Manufacturer: **Piasecki Aircraft Corporation**
Type: **experimental**
Year: **1984**
Engines: **4 × 1,525 shp Wright R-1820-84A**
Overall width: **60.05 m (197 ft)**
Overall length: **74.07 m (243 ft)**
Empty weight: **24,895 kg (54,885 lbs)**
Gross weight: **50,469 kg (111,265 lbs)**
Maximum speed: **132 km/h (82 mph)**
Service ceiling: **3,810 m (12,500 ft)**
Range: **3,307 km (2,055 miles)**
Range (with maximum payload): **80 km (50 miles)**

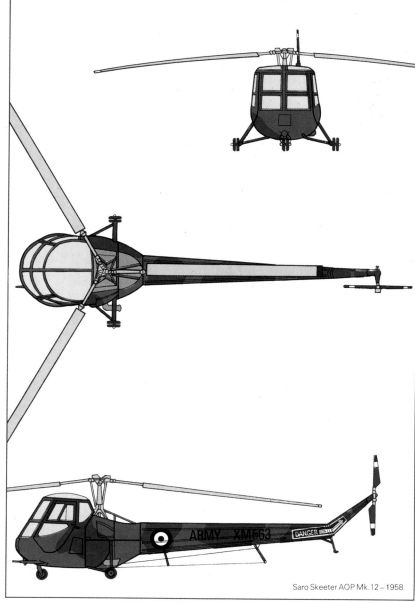

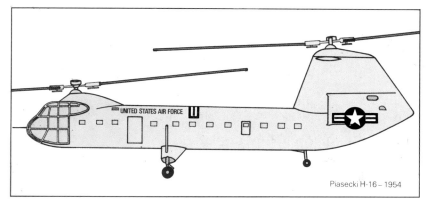

Piasecki H-16 – 1954

Saro Skeeter AOP Mk. 12 – 1958

equipped infantry on board.

The XH-16 was evaluated at length by the US Army for troop transport and the second prototype introduced two 1,800 shp turbine engines, when it first flew in 1955. Designated the YH-16A, this aircraft set an (unofficial) world record of 270 km/h (168 mph). A flying crane version was also studied, but the project was abandoned as suitable turbine engines were not available.

Piasecki Heli-Stat

The Piasecki Heli-Stat project began in the mid 1970s with a view to combining the lift capability of a lighter-than-air vehicle with the precise manoeuvrability of the helicopter, and following support from the US Forestry Service and the US Navy, construction of a prototype

SARO
Saunders Roe Ltd. (Great Britain)

Saunders Roe, the famous British aircraft manufacturer, started building motorboats in 1906 and designing and constructing aircraft in 1917. When the company's activity was at its peak, in the mid-thirties, Saunders Roe built some of its most impressive flying boats: the Cutty Sark, the Cloud and the London, as well as the giant six-engine Princess and the SR A/1 flying boat fighter.

Saunders Roe took over the Cierva company in January 1951, thus greatly increasing its potential for designing and constructing rotorcraft. In 1960 it merged with Westland.

Saro Skeeter

After a long development period, the little Saro Skeeter was first used in 1958 by the British Army Air Corps. The prototype of this attractive two-seater, which was derived from a project by the Cierva company, made its first flight on 8 October 1948, with a 106 hp Jameson FF-1 engine; this was followed a year later by a second model (Skeeter 2) which had the more powerful 145 hp Gipsy Major and a larger rotor. The two prototypes were submitted to the Ministry of Supply for evaluation after Saro (Saunders-Roe) took over Cierva in January 1951.

The Skeeter had a small, steel tube fuselage structure with a semi-monocoque tail boom section. The three-blade main rotor had metal spars with wooden ribs and a fabric

Helicopter: **Saro Skeeter AOP Mk. 12**
Manufacturer: **Saro**
Type: **general purpose/observation**
Year: **1958**
Engine: **215 hp D.H. Gipsy Major**
Rotor diameter: **9.76 m (32 ft)**
Fuselage length: **8.10 m (26 ft 7 in)**
Overall length: **8.66 m (28 ft 5 in)**
Height: **2.29 m (7 ft 6 in)**
Empty weight: **780 kg (1,720 lbs)**
Gross weight: **1,040 kg (2,293 lbs)**
Maximum speed: **167 km/h (104 mph)**
Hovering ceiling IGE: **1,680 m (5,512 ft)**
Service ceiling: **3,900 m (12,795 ft)**
Range: **340 km (211 miles)**

skin, and the two-blade tail rotor was entirely of wood. All the aircraft had tricycle landing gear, although some tests were done with skids. Refitted with a 180 hp Blackburn Bombadier engine, the helicopter was redesignated Skeeter 3, while a Royal Navy version was called Skeeter 4.

The prototype of the Skeeter 5,

built as a private venture, finally succeeded in eliminating the ground resonance problems found on the early models and was followed by the Skeeter 6 (of which three were built) with 183 hp Gipsy Major 200 engines. At this point, the British Army ordered a trial batch of four Skeeters (one of which had dual controls), followed by another 64 production models designated AOP Mk.12 (Air Observation Post). Delivery of these aircraft was com-pleted in autumn 1960 and some of them were used as trainers. The final Skeeter 8 version was offered for private use, but no orders from civil operators were forthcoming.

The Skeeter also had some success on the export market: the German Army and Navy received six and four respectively, which were transferred to the Portuguese Air Force in 1961 but never flown. One Skeeter was also used as a test-bed for the Turmo turbine.

SIKORSKY
Sikorsky Aircraft (USA)

Igor Ivan Sikorsky was a towering and intriguing figure in the history of world aviation. Born in Kiev in the Ukraine on 25 May 1889, he was a student at the St. Petersburg naval academy, but after three years he went to Paris to study engineering, which he continued on his return to Kiev in 1907. When in France again in 1909 he came into contact with some of the great pioneers of aviation and this fuelled his ideas of building a revolutionary aircraft which would take off and land vertically — the helicopter. In 1909 and 1910 in Kiev, he built two prototypes which failed to fly, mainly due to the lack of a sufficiently powerful engine. Sikorsky then devoted himself to designing and building traditional fixed-wing aircraft; among his achievements was the first large four-engine plane ever built, from which he derived an even larger bomber for the armed forces of Tsarist Russia.

The October Revolution put an abrupt end to Sikorsky's career in his own country; he was forced to flee, first to France and then to the United States, where he arrived virtually penniless. After considerable hardship, Sikorsky managed to found the Sikorsky Aero Engineering Company in 1923 and embarked on what was to be a long, fruitful career. The new company produced a succession of extremely effective transport aircraft, culminating in the four-engine S-40 Clipper in 1931.

Sikorsky's name is, however, most closely linked with the development of the helicopter, for he was the first designer to build a helicopter worthy of the name. The VS-300 made its maiden flight on 14 September 1939 (on 1 April Sikorsky's company had become the Vought Sikorsky Aircraft Company, a division of the United Aircraft Corporation). The VS-300 was so well-received that it led to a development contract from the US Army, from which Sikorsky derived the series R-5 and R-6. The civil and military S-51 helicopter was a development of the R-5.

The S-52 was the first American helicopter to have metal rotor blades, whilst the S-55 represented another step forward, in that the helicopter's capacity was greatly increased, enabling it to carry troops in addition to the two crew. The S-56 assault helicopter was the result of a US Marine Corps specification, and on 8 March 1954 the S-58 made its maiden flight.

The next achievement was the S-60 heavy lift crane, capable of lifting loads in excess of 5,000 kg (11,020 lbs). Sikorsky's S-62 amphibious helicopter was the first turbine rotorcraft to be granted certification for commercial use and the S-61, which first flew in 1959, proved so successful that it was still in production 20 years later. In August 1962, the S-65 heavy-duty multipurpose helicopter made its first appearance and was offered in several configurations for the Marines and the USAF. The S-67 Blackhawk was not a successful venture but two interesting experimental projects, the S-69 (XH-59A) research helicopter and the S-72, financed by the US Army and NASA respectively, have proved valuable assets in advancing rotorcraft technology.

The most recent helicopters to leave Sikorsky's Bridgeport and Stratford factories include the S-70, chosen by the US Army as a combat assault squad transport, and by the US Navy as a ship-based multipurpose helicopter (LAMPS II). The S-76 is designed as a fast civil transport but with potential for military use.

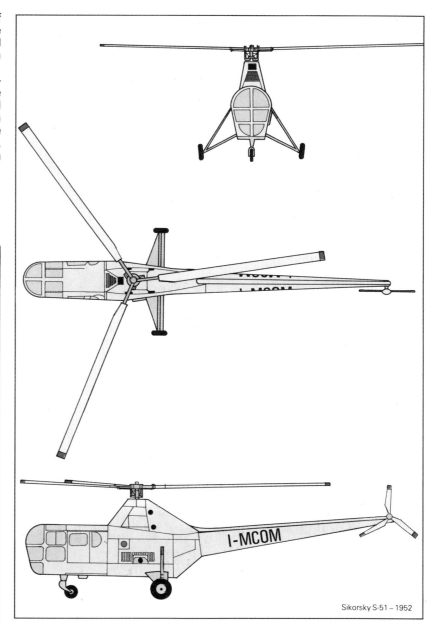

Sikorsky S-51 – 1952

Sikorsky S-51

The first helicopter to be built in large numbers was a derivative of the Sikorsky R-5, which started out as a tandem two-seater. The first of five prototypes flew on 18 August 1943 powered by a 450 hp Wasp Junior radial. This was followed by 25 YR-5A pre-production models, two of which were assigned to the Navy under the designation HO2S-1. While production of the R-5A was getting under way (34 built), five pre-series aircraft were converted into the R-5E, which had dual control, while at least 20 modified R-5As were later given new, 600 hp Wasp Junior engines and redesignated R-5D. From the latter, the S-51 was developed, with a slightly enlarged four-seat cabin and a tricycle landing gear. The first commercial helicopter designed by Sikorsky, it first flew on 16 February 1946 and was certified a month later by the

Helicopter: Sikorsky S-51
Manufacturer: **Sikorsky Aircraft**
Type: **light transport**
Year: **1947**
Engine: **450 hp Pratt & Whitney R-985AN-5 Wasp Junior**
Rotor diameter: **14.94 m (49 ft)**
Fuselage length: **12.45 m (40 ft 10 in)**
Overall length: **13.70 m (44 ft 11 in)**
Height: **3.95 m (13 ft)**
Empty weight: **1,720 kg (3,792 lbs)**
Gross weight: **2,263 kg (4,989 lbs)**
Maximum speed: **166 km/h (103 mph)**
Range: **480 km (298 miles)**
Capacity: **1 pilot + 3 passengers or 431 kg (950 lbs)**

Civil Aviation Agency and delivered to the first customer in August. It was sold to United Air Lines and Los Angeles Airways.

A total of 300 S-51s were built, some with 450 hp engines, others with 600 hp engines and larger diameter three-blade rotors. The military versions were designated R-5F (11 to the USAF), H-5G (38 fitted with a rescue hoist), H-5H (17 with amphibious wheel/pontoon landing gear), HO3S1 and S2 (90 in all, naval rescue version). The S-51 had a three-blade articulated rotor, the blades of which could be folded back to facilitate stowage. The first aircraft had manual pitch control; this was later replaced by a hydraulic system. The cabin diameter was also increased.

In 1947, Westland acquired the license to build the S-51 in Britain and produced 139 up to 1953. The British version, named the Dragonfly, had a 550 hp Alvis Leonides engine.

Sikorsky S-55

On 1 May 1949, Sikorsky's technical department was given a very important task: it was asked to create a new helicopter in just seven months, which would be capable of carrying ten passengers in addition to a crew of two.

The first of the five YH-19 prototypes ordered by the US Air Force for evaluation flew on 10 November 1949 and was characterized by a blunt-ended fuselage, which lacked the broad, triangular fillet connecting the fuselage to the tail boom which distinguished all the later series aircraft. Another characteristic of the YH-19 was the horizontal stabilizer applied to the starboard side of the tail, which was replaced in the production aircraft by two anhedral tail surfaces.

In 1951, the US Air Force ordered a batch of H-19As fitted with the same 550 hp Pratt & Whitney R-1340-57 engine as the prototypes. Production continued with the H-19B which had a 700 hp Wright R-1300-3 engine and a larger diameter main rotor; a total of 270 were built for the US Air Force, including the SH-19B version for use as a transport aircraft. From 1952, the Army also ordered the H-19, beginning with 72 H-19Cs. They were subsequently nicknamed "Chickasaw" and redesignated UH-19C and UH-19D in 1962.

Versions of the S-55 were also acquired by the US Navy, which signed its first contract on 28 April 1950. Between August 1950 and January 1958, the US Navy received

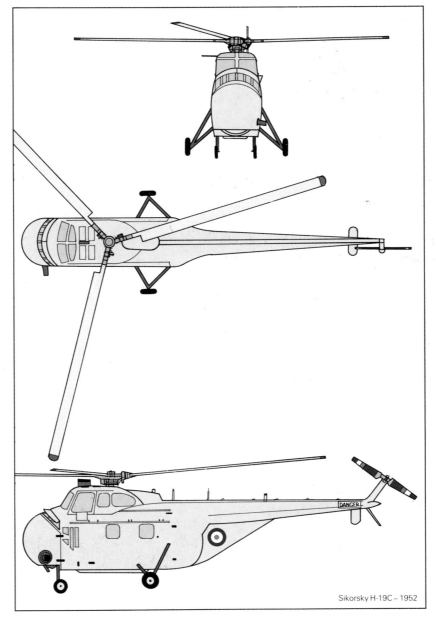

Sikorsky H-19C – 1952

119 helicopters, including ten HO4S-1 (equivalent to the H-19A) and 61 HO4S-2 (about 30 of these were built as HO4S-3G for the US Coast Guard). The Marines received 99 HRS-2 and 84 HRS-3, which corresponded to the HO4S series and were used as troop transports. The aircraft assigned to the SAR divisions of the MATS and US Army Aviation arrived in Korea when the war was nearly over, whereas the Marines were able to test their HRS-1s for rapid assault operations which anticipated full-scale landing operations.

Various techniques and roles were first tested with the S-55 in Korea which were later to form the basis of new military doctrine, such as landing operations behind enemy lines, troop support, recovery of damaged vehicles and their capacity for counterattack and engagement. Another primary task of

Helicopter: **Sikorsky S-55 (H-19C)**
Manufacturer: **Sikorsky Aircraft**
Type: **transport and general purpose**
Year: **1952**
Engine: **608 hp Pratt & Whitney R-1340-57**
Rotor diameter: **16.15 m (53 ft)**
Fuselage length: **12.85 m (42 ft 2 in)**
Overall length: **19.07 m (62 ft 7 in)**
Height: **4.066 m (13 ft 4 in)**
Empty weight: **2,245 kg (4,950 lbs)**
Gross weight: **3,266 kg (7,200 lbs)**
Maximum speed: **162 km/h (100 mph)**
Hovering ceiling IGE: **1,950 m (6,397 ft)**
Service ceiling: **3,218 m (10,558 ft)**
Range: **650 km (400 miles)**
Capacity: **10 troops or 1,296 kg (2,857 lbs)**

the helicopter was casualty evacuation or the rescuing of pilots who had come down behind the enemy lines. In the ambulance role, the S-55 could carry up to six stretchers, five of which could be hoisted on board using a mechanical winch fixed outside the cabin. The spacious cabin was designed to accommodate various seating arrangements or freight; it could

take up to ten men or a load of approximately 1,300 kg (2,866 lbs).

The most distinctive feature of the Sikorsky aircraft was the location of the engine in the nose, to enable the cabin to be placed at the center of gravity, thus allowing for considerable variations in payload without affecting stability. Special attention was also paid to the question of maintenance. The main parts were easily dismantled in an average of 12-15 hours and were all designed for ease of access (the engine, for example, could be changed in two hours, even without special equipment, and daily inspections took a maximum of 15-20 minutes). The S-55 had a monocoque metal fuselage with aluminum and magnesium light alloy bulkheads and skin. The three-blade main rotor had long-life metal blades (they demonstrated a life of over 20,000 hours in lab tests). The fuel was contained in two crash resistant tanks situated beneath the cabin in the lower part of the fuselage and had a total capacity of 700 liters (154 gallons). Each leg of the quadricycle undercarriage had its own shock absorber for maximum stability during take-off and landing and manoeuvres on the ground. Floats could also be fitted to the legs for emergency landings on water, or the undercarriage could be replaced by permanent metal amphibious landing gear.

The S-55 received American civil type approval on 25 March 1952 and the model with the Pratt & Whitney R-1340 engines became the S-55A, while the version with the Wright engine was designated S-55B. In 1952, the helicopter became the first rotary wing craft to be used for commercial links in Europe; it was then flown by the Belgian airline Sabena between the chief towns in Belgium and Lille, Rotterdam, Bonn and Cologne.

In ten years, Sikorsky produced 1,067 S-55s in military version for no fewer than 30 operators throughout the world. Another 547 were built under license (notably by Westland in England under the name Whirlwind).

One of the first production models of the Sikorsky S-51 in the civil version. This four-seat aircraft received commercial type approval in August 1946.

A Sikorsky S-55 in the colours of the Belgian company Sabena. This was the first airline to use helicopters for commercial services.

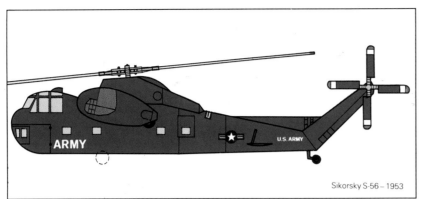

Sikorsky S-56 – 1953

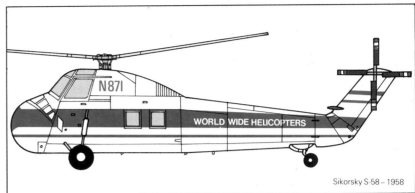

Sikorsky S-58 – 1958

Sikorsky S-56

Immediately after the S-55 had entered production, Sikorsky began working on the design of a larger helicopter, intended as an assault transport for the Marines. A twin-engine solution was chosen, and to save cabin space, it was decided to house the two large radial engines in outboard nacelles, from which two drive shafts linked up directly with the reduction gear assembly which drove the big five-blade metal rotor. The large cargo bay had a hoist capable of lifting a one tonne load. The main landing gear wheels retracted, but the tailwheel was fixed.

Some of the 60 aircraft ordered by the Marine Corps were converted into radar patrol craft (military designation HR2S-1W), with a bulbous dielectric radome under the nose, but this transformation was unsuccessful. The Army ordered 91 aircraft, designated H-37A "Mojave."

Sikorsky S-58

Another winner for Sikorsky in the fifties was the Model S-58. The prototype was developed to meet a US Navy specification for a more advanced antisubmarine helicopter than the S-55. Designated XHSS-1, it first flew on 8 March 1954 and the first production aircraft, nicknamed "Seabat," was ready by September. The Marine Corps adopted it in 1957 as "Seahorse" and the Army in 1955 as "Choctaw." As a transport helicopter capable of carrying 18 combat equipped troops or a 1,350

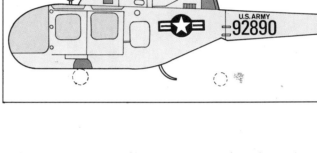

Sikorsky S-59 – 1954

kg (2,976 lb) load, the Choctaw was widely used in Vietnam. The Marines received about 500 of the S-58 in the utility version (HUS-1 and 1A).

In 1956, Westland acquired the license to build the S-58 and developed a turbine-engined version called the Wessex. Sikorsky continued producing the S-58 with the Wright radial engine; a turbine-powered conversion with a PT6T-6 Twin Pack did not become available until 1970.

Sikorsky S-59

Around 1955, the two-blade Bell rotor scored a brilliant victory over the four-blade Sikorsky. In fact, the Model XH-59 (S-59), using a 400 shp Continental XT51 turbine, was rejected by the US Army, despite its speed and the advantage of retractable landing gear, as being old-fashioned in design and unsuitable for further development. Instead, the Army chose the Bell XH-40 with a Lycoming XT53 turbine. Nevertheless, the four-seat XH-59, with retractable tailwheel landing gear and a new four-blade rotor, broke the world speed record over 3 km (1.86 mile) in 1954 by flying at 251 km/h (156 mph). The ill-fated Sikorsky aircraft had been built using a modified YH-18A airframe, itself derived from the unsuccessful postwar S-52.

Eighty-nine H-18s, using the 245 hp Franklin 0425 piston engine, three-blade rotors and fixed quadricycle landing gear, were built under the designation HOSS.1 and used by the US Marines in the Korean War.

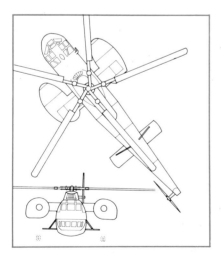

Helicopter: **Sikorsky S-56 (HR2S-1, H-37)**
Manufacturer: **Sikorsky Aircraft**
Type: **transport**
Year: **1953**
Engines: **2 × 2,100 shp Pratt & Whitney R-2800-54**
Rotor diameter: **21.95 m (72 ft)**
Fuselage length: **26.80 m (87 ft 11 in)**
Overall length: **—**
Height: **6.71 m (22 ft)**
Empty weight: **9,457 kg (20,848 lbs)**
Gross weight: **14,074 kg (31,027 lbs)**
Maximum speed: **209 km/h (130 mph)**
Service ceiling: **2,652 m (8,700 ft)**
Range: **235 km (146 miles)**
Capacity: **23 troops or 24 stretchers.**

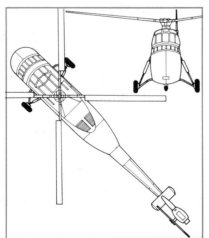

Helicopter: **Sikorsky S-58 (HSS-1, HUS-1)**
Manufacturer: **Sikorsky Aircraft**
Type: **utility transport**
Year: **1954**
Engine: **1,525 hp Wright R-1820-84**
Rotor diameter: **17.07 m (56 ft)**
Fuselage length: **14.25 m (46 ft 9 in)**
Overall length: **20.00 m (65 ft 7 in)**
Height: **4.86 m (15 ft 11 in)**
Empty weight: **3,815 kg (8,410 lbs)**
Gross weight: **6,040 kg (13,316 lbs)**
Maximum speed: **198 km/h (123 mph)**
Hovering ceiling IGE: **1,495 m (4,905 ft)**
Service ceiling: **2,896 m (9,500 ft)**
Range: **290 km (180 miles)**
Capacity: **2 pilots + 16/1,350 kg (2,976 lbs)**

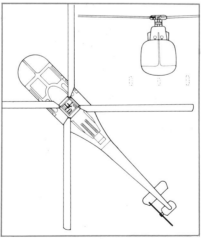

Helicopter: **Sikorsky S-59**
Manufacturer: **Sikorsky Aircraft**
Type: **observation**
Year: **1954**
Engine: **400 shp Continental Artouste XT51-T3**
Rotor diameter: **10.00 m (32 ft 10 in)**
Fuselage length: **11.95 m (39 ft 2 in)**
Overall length: **—**
Height: **2.99 m (9 ft 10 in)**
Empty weight: **749 kg (1,651 lbs)**
Gross weight: **1,226 kg (2,703 lbs)**
Maximum speed: **176 km/h (110 mph)**
Hovering ceiling IGE: **2,804 m (9,200 ft)**
Service ceiling: **4,724 m (15,500 ft)**
Range: **670 km (416 miles)**

*One of the Sikorsky S-61Bs manu-
factured under license by Mitsubishi for the Japanese Navy. These
are equivalent to the American SH-
3D.*

Sikorsky S-61

In December 1957, the US Navy
gave the go-ahead to a new programme for a very high performance
helicopter with advanced technology, to replace the out-dated S-58
(HSS-1). Sikorsky was approached
again and submitted a project for a
big twin turbine aircraft with a boat-
type hull and retractable landing
gear for amphibious operations.
The aircraft had all-weather capability, a good choice of weapons loads
and four hours' endurance. The
project was designated S-61 and
the HSS-2 prototype flew on 11
March 1959. The prototype was
followed by seven pre-production
aircraft (YHSS-2) which successfully completed service trials in 1960.
The US Navy ordered the first ten
S-61B/HSS-2 for delivery starting in
September 1961. The helicopters
were later redesignated SH-3A Sea
King. One of the first production
models set up a world speed record
of 339 km/h (210 mph) on 5 February 1962.

The main rotor of the medium-
tonnage S-61 was of the articulated
type, with five interchangeable
blades which could be folded automatically by hydraulic actuators.
The tail boom could also be folded
for stowage on board ship. The
all-metal, semi-monocoque boat-
type hull was amphibious, the twin
mainwheels retracting into two
sponsons. In the SH-3A version 255
were produced, while ten more,
ordered as HSS-2Z and subse-

quently redesignated VH-3A, were
assigned to the special American
Presidential Department for personnel transport and evacuation services in case of emergency. Nine of
the SH-3As were transformed into
RH-3As with minesweeping equipment and three were used by the
USAF for missile site support and
drone recovery. Another 12 SH-3As
were converted into the HH-3A for
battlefield rescue work, and were
fitted with two Emerson TAT-102
turrets mounted at the rear of the
two sponsons, and an in-flight refuelling probe.

In April 1962, the USAF leased
three HSS-2, transformed into 27-
seat transport aircraft for services
linking the Texas Towers radar installations. Another three S-61As

Helicopter: **Sikorsky S-61 (SH-3A)**
Manufacturer: **Sikorsky Aircraft**
Type: **twin turbine antisubmarine**
Year: **1960**
Engines: **2 × 1,250 shp General Electric T58-GE-18**
Rotor diameter: **18.90 m (62 ft)**
Fuselage length: **16.69 m (54 ft 9 in)**
Overall length: **22.14 m (72 ft 8 in)**
Height: **5.13 m (16 ft 10 in)**
Empty weight: **5,647 kg (12,450 lbs)**
Gross weight: **9,299 kg (20,500 lbs)**
Maximum speed: **267 km/h (166 mph)**
Hovering ceiling IGE: **3,200 m (10,500 ft)**
Service ceiling: **4,480 m (14,700 ft)**
Range: **1,000 km (620 miles)**
Armament: **381 kg (840 lbs) weapon load**

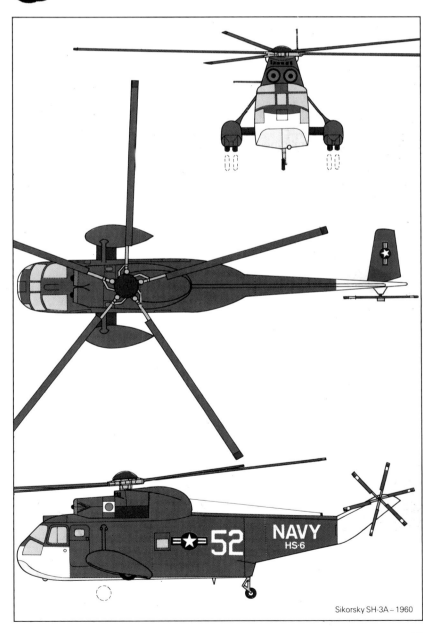

Sikorsky SH-3A – 1960

Sikorsky

were purchased for this purpose. Sixteen S-61A-4s with 31 seats were acquired by the Royal Malaysian Air Force and nine by the Danish Air Force for rescue work. In response to a Japanese naval specification, Mitsubishi obtained a license to produce the S-61; three were purchased directly from Sikorsky and by February 1972, 43 locally-produced aircraft had been delivered.

From 1966, the SH-3A was superseded by the SH-3D, which had a 1,419 shp T58-GE-10 turbine and new electronics. The first SH-3D delivered in June 1966 was one of six ordered by the Spanish Navy. This was followed by another four for the Brazilian Navy and 73 for the US Navy. The new variant was also built under license by Agusta from 1967, following an Italian naval order for an ASW helicopter to replace the old Sikorsky SH-34. An initial batch of 24 was built for the Italian Navy and 20 for the Iranian Navy (three in the VIP version); the Italian SH-3D is identical to the American model, apart from the installation of a Teledyne Doppler radar and a search radar on the left side of the nose.

In Britian, the Royal Navy also chose the S-61 to replace its old Wessex. Westland acquired the license to build the SH-3 in 1959, and the British specification called for some modifications. Thus a pair

of 1,521 shp Rolls-Royce Gnome H-1400 turbines were adopted, plus other British equipment including an Ekco all-weather radar (easily recognised by the dorsal radome), Plessey dipping sonar, Marconi Doppler navigation radar, etc.

The first British-built Sea King flew on 7 May 1969 and the first squadrons were formed the following August. Westland has built over 200 Sea Kings, including the Sea King Mk.1, 2 and 5 for the Royal Navy, 15 for the Indian Navy (Sea King Mk.42), 22 for the German Navy (Mk.41), 11 for the Norwegian Air Force (Mk.43) and 12 for the Australian Navy (Mk.50). More recently, Westland has designed and built a tactical helicopter called Commando, which is directly derived from the Sea King, and the first examples flew in 1973. Commandos have been supplied to Egypt and Qatar and, as the Sea King HC Mk.4, to the Royal Navy.

Sikorsky S-61N

The three commercial models of the S-61 — the S-61L, S-61N and the Payloader — used the same dynamic components as the military version, but had a longer fuselage.

The S-61L (land version with non-

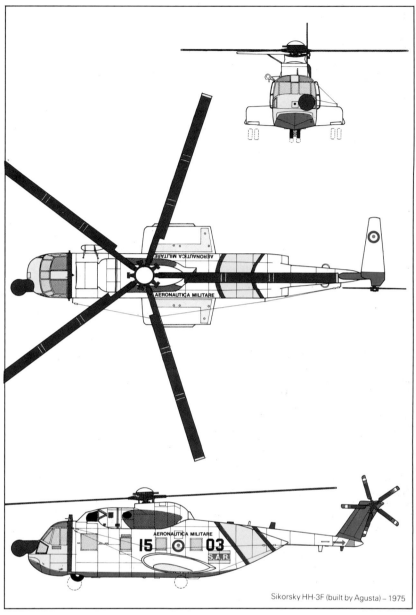

Sikorsky HH-3F (built by Agusta) – 1975

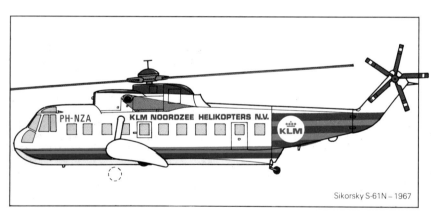

Sikorsky S-61N – 1967

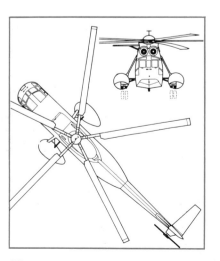

Helicopter: **Sikorsky S-61N**
Manufacturer: **Sikorsky Aircraft**
Type: **amphibious transport**
Year: **1960**
Engines: **2 × 1,500 shp General Electric TC-58-140**
Rotor diameter: **18.90 m (62 ft)**
Fuselage length: **22.20 m (72 ft 10 in)**
Overall length: **22.00 m (72 ft 2 in)**
Height: **5.63 m (18 ft 6 in)**
Empty weight: **5,675 kg (12,510 lbs)**
Gross weight: **9,980 kg (22,000 lbs)**
Maximum speed: **241 km/h (150 mph)**
Hovering ceiling IGE: **—**
Service ceiling: **—**
Range: **800 km (497 miles)**
Capacity: **2 pilots + 28 passengers**

retractable landing gear) could carry 30 passengers and a crew of three while the S-61N, which had amphibious capability, was distinguished by two sponsons into which the landing gear retracted. The former flew on 6 December 1960 and received FAA type approval in November 1961. The main operator of the S-61L was Los Angeles Airways (6), which was the first company in the world to use Sikorsky helicopters. The interior of the S-61N was quite elaborately fitted-out; the spacious cabin had a toilet, storeroom and luggage compartment, and could accommodate 26-28 passengers. Operators of the S-61N included New York Airways (4), Nippon Airways (1), British Airways Helicopters (26), Bristow Helicopters (28), Brunei Shell (2), Elivie (2), Greenlandair (5), Helikopter Service Norway (10), Japan Air Lines (1) and KLM (2).

Sikorsky S-61R

The S-61R differs significantly in a number of ways from the original S-61, in that it has a more capacious boat-type hull, modified to take a rear loading ramp, while the two sponsons have been replaced by two stub wings set farther back, into which the rear members of the tricycle landing gear retract.

The prototype was built by the company as a private venture and flown with a civil registration on 17 June 1963. However, the USAF had already placed an order with Sikorsky in February of that year for 22 aircraft, designated CH-3C, and they began to receive the first helicopters at the end of 1963. Subsequent orders brought the total number for the USAF to 133.

The CH-3C was used in the Vietnam War for rescuing pilots who had been shot down and came to be

Helicopter: **Sikorsky S-61R (HH-3F)**
Manufacturer: **Sikorsky Aircraft**
Type: **amphibious rescue**
Year: **1965**
Engines: **2 × 1,500 shp General Electric T58-GE-5**
Rotor diameter: **18.90 m (62 ft)**
Fuselage length: **19.05 m (62 ft 6 in)**
Overall length: **22.25 m (73 ft)**
Height: **5.51 m (18 ft 1 in)**
Empty weight: **5,295 kg (11,673 lbs)**
Gross weight: **9,990 kg (22,024 lbs)**
Maximum speed: **264 km/h (164 mph)**
Hovering ceiling IGE: **2,960 m (9,710 ft)**
Service ceiling: **4,145 m (13,600 ft)**
Range: **800 km (497 miles)**
Capacity: **3 crew + 25 troops or 15 stretchers**

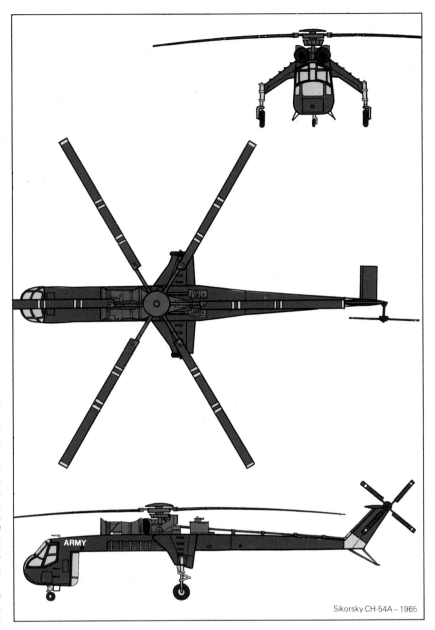

Sikorsky CH-54A – 1965

nicknamed the "Jolly Green Giant;" it was given more powerful turbines from February 1965 and redesignated CH-3E. The uprated "Green Giant" could carry 26 troops or 15 wounded, or vehicles of equivalent weight, and could also be armed with two Emerson turrets on the leading edges of the two stub wings. Forty-two CH-3Es were built, in addition to which 41 CH-3Cs were modified to this standard. The USAF also asked for specific modifications to be made to this helicopter to meet the demands of the Vietnam War: application of armour; use of supplementary fuel tanks for extended flights; self-sealing internal fuel tanks and a telescopic in-flight refuelling probe. Two of the first aircraft of the 50 to be built in the HH-3E rescue version became famous in 1967 by flying non-stop from New York to Paris (for the Air Show), covering the 6,870 km (4,269 mile) journey with nine refuellings by air tankers.

In August 1965, the US Coast Guard ordered a special version of the HH-3 which was given the designation HH-3F Pelican. This paramilitary American rescue service needed an aircraft with all-weather capability, which could safely land on water, and the HH-3F was the ideal solution. The Pelican was virtually identical to the HH-3E, apart from the lack of protection, armament and other military equipment. It had an AN/APN-195 search radar on the port side of the nose. The US Coast Guard received 40 HH-3Fs. The only foreign license-holder for this variant was Agusta, who began producing it in 1974. The 22 aircraft built by Agusta were all delivered to the Italian Air Force as replacements for the old, amphibious Grumman Albatross used for search and rescue missions at sea.

Sikorsky S-64 Skycrane

Sikorsky began designing flying cranes with the development of the S-56, which, although used in the early stages of the Vietnam War to lift and carry slung loads, was really an assault and troop transport helicopter. Using the dynamic components of this aircraft, i.e. the five-blade main rotor, four-blade anti-torque rotor and two Pratt & Whitney R-2800 engines in two outrigged pods, Sikorsky built the Model S-60 in 1959, with a fuselage reduced to the bare essentials, all the payload being carried externally. Before the S-60 was destroyed in April 1961, Sikorsky had already begun the S-64 Skycrane project. The new helicopter was similar in structure to its predecessor but had a six-blade main rotor and two 4,050 shp Pratt & Whitney JFTD-12A turbines installed side-by-side. The height of the tricycle landing

Helicopter: **Sikorsky S-64A (CH-54A)**
Manufacturer: **Sikorsky Aircraft**
Type: **flying crane**
Year: **1965**
Engines: **2 × 4,500 shp Pratt & Whitney JFTD12-4A**
Rotor diameter: **21.95 m (72 ft)**
Fuselage length: **21.41 m (70 ft 3 in)**
Overall length: **26.97 m (88 ft 6 in)**
Height: **7.75 m (25 ft 5 in)**
Empty weight: **8,732 kg (19,250 lbs)**
Gross weight: **19,068 kg (42,037 lbs)**
Maximum speed: **203 km/h (126 mph)**
Hovering ceiling IGE: **3,230 m (10,600 ft)**
Service ceiling: **2,743 m (9,000 ft)**
Range: **370 km (230 miles)**
Capacity: **9,080 kg (20,000 lbs) external load**

gear could be adjusted to adapt it to the payload. The S-64 had 2.84 m (9 ft 4 in) clearance between the ground and the bottom of the fuselage, while the main landing gear wheels on two downward-sloping strut supports were set 6.02 m (19 ft 9 in) apart. In this way, very large loads could be carried, including a special container for 23 passengers.

The German Bundeswehr was in-

terested in the flying crane and Weser Flugzeugbau lost no time in acquiring the production license. Two S-64A prototypes built in the United States were sent to Germany for evaluation by the Army Air Corps. Meanwhile, the US Army carried out its own tests on the new Sikorsky helicopter and six were ordered in June 1963 with the designation YCH-54A. Another 18 were later added to the order, followed by further contracts for a total of 90 aircraft.

The first six flying cranes were assigned to the First Cavalry Division (Airmobile) operating in Vietnam. The cranes' performance there was outstanding (one of them set a world record on 29 April 1965 by carrying a pod with 90 passengers). Other exploits by the Tarhe (as the US Army S-64 was called) during the Vietnam War included the lifting of bulldozers and tanks and retrieval of damaged aircraft.

The larger CH-54B version with twin 4,800 shp turbines and 2,300 kg (5,070 lbs) more lifting power, went into service with the US Army in 1969; 29 were built. Sikorsky also offered the Skycrane to commercial operators. The models S-64E (civil version of the CH-54A) and S-64F (derived from the CH-54B) were produced, while plans for a triple turbine version were not realized.

Sikorsky S-65

Using much of the experience gained with the S-61 and the dynamic components (rotor, transmission and anti-torque rotor) of the S-64 flying crane, Sikorsky designed a new family of helicopters designated S-65, various versions of which have been developed. On the basis of the S-61R project for the Marines, the American company proposed the S-65A with a completely redesigned, large-capacity fuselage, capable of transporting 37 equipped troops or 24 stretchers with 4 medical attendants. The US Navy, which is responsible for acquisitions for the Marines, announced the choice of the S-65A in August 1962.

The CH-53 Sea Stallion had the six-blade rotor and tail rotor of the S-64 flying crane, driven through the same transmission by new General Electric T64 engines. The fuselage no longer had the boat-type hull of the S-61, although it could land on water with two stub wings acting as stabilizers and containing the fuel tanks and, at the back, the bay for the fully retractable main landing gear units. The cargo hold, equipped with a loading ramp and an automatic loading and

Sikorsky

The Sikorsky S-65 has also been used by the Israeli Air Force since 1970.

unloading system (which can be operated even when the helicopter is in flight), can take two jeeps, antiaircraft missiles with their fire control systems or a 105 mm howitzer.

The first Sea Stallion flew on 14 October 1965, and delivery of the first 106 helicopters began in September 1966. The aircraft were assigned to Marine Squadron HMH-463 in Vietnam in January 1967. At that period, it was the largest helicopter in the Western world. On 17 February 1968, a CH-53A with modified T64 engines took off with a gross weight of 23,540 kg (51,896 lbs) and a 9,925 kg (21,880 lb) payload, establishing an unofficial record. On 23 October of the following year a Sea Stallion demonstrated surprising manoeuvrability when it performed a series of loops and rolls with Lt.-Col. Robert Guay of the Marines and Sikorsky test pilot Byron Graham at the controls, carrying a gross weight of 12,250 kg (27,006 lbs). During these manoeuvres, the helicopter supported from − 0.2 to 2.8 g.

The Sea Stallion also aroused some interest in other countries where there was a requirement for a helicopter for troop transport. Thus the S-65A was also ordered by Germany, where it was built under license by VFW-Fokker as the CH-53G. Another eight aircraft, modified for use in hot/high conditions, were exported to Israel.

In September 1966, the USAF also ordered this big helicopter for its rescue service to assist space programmes and recover pilots from war zones. The eight HH-53B ordered for the USAF were known as "Super Jolly Green Giants" and fitted with in-flight refuelling

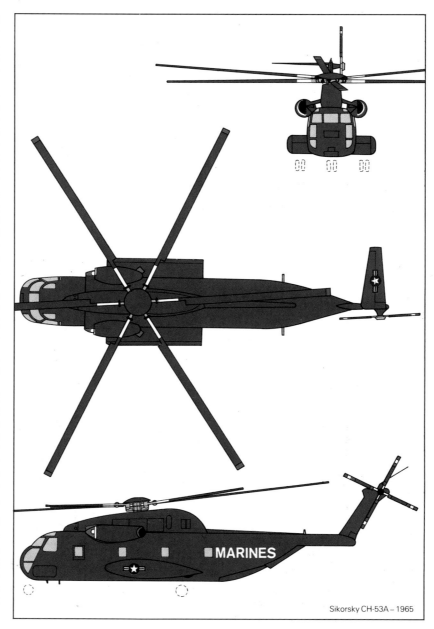

Sikorsky CH-53A – 1965

Helicopter: **Sikorsky S-65A (CH-53A)**
Manufacturer: **Sikorsky Aircraft**
Type: **tactical transport**
Year: **1965**
Engines: **2 × 2,850 shp General Electric T64-GE-6B**
Rotor diameter: **22.02 m (72 ft 3 in)**
Fuselage length: **20.47 m (67 ft 2 in)**
Overall length: **26.90 m (88 ft 3 in)**
Height: **7.60 m (24 ft 11 in)**
Empty weight: **10,662 kg (23,505 lbs)**
Gross weight: **15,875 kg (39,760 lbs)**
Maximum speed: **315 km/h (195 mph)**
Hovering ceiling IGE: **4,084 m (13,400 ft)**
Service ceiling: **5,660 m (18,570 ft)**
Range: **415 km (258 miles)**
Capacity: **2 pilots + 37 troops**

Helicopter: **Sikorsky S-65 Super Stallion (CH-53E)**
Manufacturer: **Sikorsky Aircraft**
Type: **tactical transport**
Year: **1965**
Engine: **3 × 4,380 shp General Electric T64-GE-416**
Rotor diameter: **24.08 m (79 ft)**
Fuselage length: **22.50 m (73 ft 10 in)**
Overall length: **30.02 m (98 ft 6 in)**
Height: **8.46 m (27 ft 9 in)**
Empty weight: **14,550 kg (32,077 lbs)**
Gross weight: **31,667 kg (69,813 lbs)**
Maximum speed: **315 km/h (195 mph)**
Hovering ceiling IGE: **3,267 m (10,718 ft)**
Service ceiling: **3,780 m (12,400 ft)**
Range: **500 km (310 miles)**
Capacity: **3 crew + 55 troops**

probes, jettisonable auxiliary fuel tanks, rescue hoists and all-weather avionics. Fifty-eight of the subsequent HH-53C variant with uprated turbines (3,435 shp each) were built. After having used the early production aircraft, the US Marine Corps also asked for more powerful engines to be installed, and the result was the CH-53D with 3,925 shp T64-GE-423 engines. In this version, the tail and rotor could be folded back automatically, and a high density cabin layout was available to accommodate 64 troops, equivalent to the S-65C export version. A total of 265 CH-53As and Ds were built for the Marines; the last left the factory on 31 January 1972.

To complete its experiments with the RH-3A, the US Navy borrowed nine CH-53Ds from the Marines, fitted with devices for the detection, sweeping and neutralization of all types of mines. This variant was designated RH-53D, and 30 were produced for the US Navy and six for the Iranian Navy. The RH-53 has 1,900 liter (418 gallon) supplementary fuel tanks, a 270 kg (595 lb) hoist and 11,340 kg (25,000 lb) cargo hook. At the beginning of 1973, these helicopters were used by US Navy Task Force 78 for Operation Endsweep, to free the North Vietnamese ports of mines.

The latest version of the S-65 to be built is the CH-53E Super Stallion for the US Navy. This is a much modified version with three 4,380 shp General Electric T64-GE-416 engines and strengthened transmission to withstand the increase in power. The fuselage is about 2 m (6 ft 6 in) longer than that of the CH-53D and the tail pylon is canted to port. The main rotor has also been improved and has seven composite blades (its predecessor had six light alloy ones). Thirty-three CH-53Es were initially ordered by the Marines and 16 by the US Navy. The type is still in production.

Sikorsky S-67 Blackhawk

Sikorsky, who may rightly be considered one of the giants of the helicopter industry, has taken part in all the design competitions for combat helicopters held by the American armed forces. In 1964, it submitted the S-66 project to the US Army for the AAFSS specification, calling for an aircraft with a maximum speed of approximately 418 km/h (254 mph) and ten minutes' hovering capability.

The S-66 looked very much like the Lockheed AH-56A Cheyenne (which won the contest), but had a Rotorprop tail rotor which could rotate its axis through 90° to act both as a conventional anti-torque rotor in horizontal flight and as a pusher propeller, thereby transforming the S-66 into a compound aircraft in cruising flight. When the AH-56A failed to live up to expectations, Sikorsky first offered an intermediate aircraft, consisting of an armed version of the S-61, then designed a simplified AAFSS using the maximum number of components from the S-61. The result was the S-67 Blackhawk which appeared in 1970.

Sikorsky S-67 Blackhawk – 1970

The Blackhawk looked like a helicopter with conventional rotors (those of the S-61) and had the now typical lines and features of a combat helicopter: two stub wings with a 8.33m (27 ft 4 in) span and an all-moving tail plane. The mainwheels were retractable, while the tailwheel was not. One of the most interesting features of this aircraft was the presence of speed brakes on the wing trailing edges, which could be used both as airbrakes and to improve manoeuvrability. In addition the main rotor blade tips were modified and given a sweepback of 20°, to reduce vibration, stall speed and noise.

The Blackhawk was put through a long series of tests from 1970 to 1974 but judged unsatisfactory. It nonetheless established an E-1 class world speed record on 14 December 1970 by flying at 348.971 km/h (216.84 mph) over 3 km (1.86

Helicopter: **Sikorsky S-67 Blackhawk**
Manufacturer: **Sikorsky Aircraft**
Type: **combat**
Year: **1970**
Engines: **2 × 1,500 shp General Electric T58-GE-5**
Rotor diameter: **18.90 m (62 ft)**
Fuselage length: **19.74 m (64 ft 9 in)**
Overall length: **22.60 m (74 ft 2 in)**
Height: **4.57 m (15 ft)**
Empty weight: **5,681 kg (12,525 lbs)**
Gross weight: **11,010 kg (24,272 lbs)**
Maximum speed: **311 km/h (193 mph)**
Service ceiling: **5,180 m (19,995 ft)**
Range: **354 km (220 miles)**
Capacity: **2 pilots + 15 troops**
Armament: **1.30 mm cannon; 16 TOW missiles; 70 mm rocket launchers**

miles), beating this on 19 December with a new record of 335.485 km/h (208. 470 mph) over a 15/25 km (9.32/15.53 mile) circuit. In the final stages of testing, the S-67 was fitted with night vision systems, a TAT-140 turret with a 30 mm cannon and an insulated and soundproof compartment for troop transport. The S-67 was also designed to carry an armament of 16 TOW antitank missiles, 2.75 in rockets or Sidewinder air-to-air missiles.

The Blackhawk demonstrated excellent manoeuvrability, weapon carrying capacity and versatility. At the end of the test cycle, the US Army asked for the aircraft to be modified by substituting a ducted fan for the tail unit, and in this configuration it reached a speed of 370 km/h (230 mph) in a test dive in 1974.

Sikorsky S-69

In February 1972, Sikorsky announced the development of an experimental helicopter designated S-69, which was designed to study the Advancing Blade Concept (ABC). This new system consisted of two rigid, contra-rotating rotors which made use of the aerodynamic lift of the advancing blades. At high speeds, the retreating blades were offloaded, as most of the load was supported by the advancing blades of both rotors and the penalty due to stall of the retreating blade was thus eliminated. This system did not even require a wing to be fitted for high speeds and to improve manoeuvrability, and also eliminated the need for an antitorque rotor at the tail.

The aim of the project was to evaluate the ABC with this helicopter, first using scale models for wind tunnel tests at the Ames NASA research center, and then the real aircraft, which flew on 26 July 1973. Unfortunately, however, this prototype was lost in an accident a month later. Following an enquiry, design modifications were requested, plus improvements to the control system. Tests were resumed in July 1975 with a second aircraft. When test flights as a pure helicopter were completed, a new experimental phase began with the addition of an auxiliary turbojet. In 1983 Sikorsky proposed further modifying the aircraft as the XH-59B, with a shortened fuselage and ducted fan providing forward thrust.

Sikorsky S-72

Another NASA/US Army programme involved the S-72 helicopter, used to test various integrated rotor and propulsion systems. After the first flight on 12 October 1976, the S-72 completed the first experimental phase in February 1977.

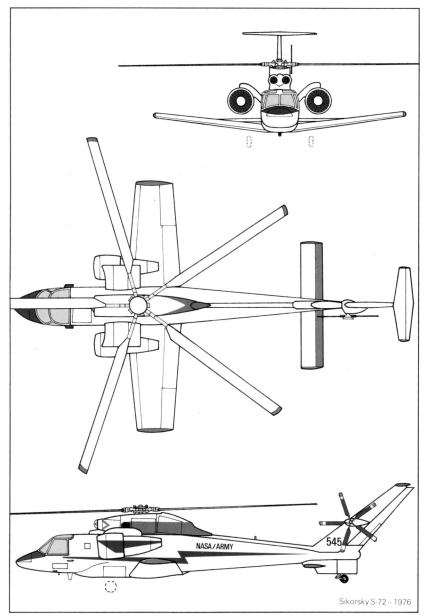

Sikorsky S-72 – 1976

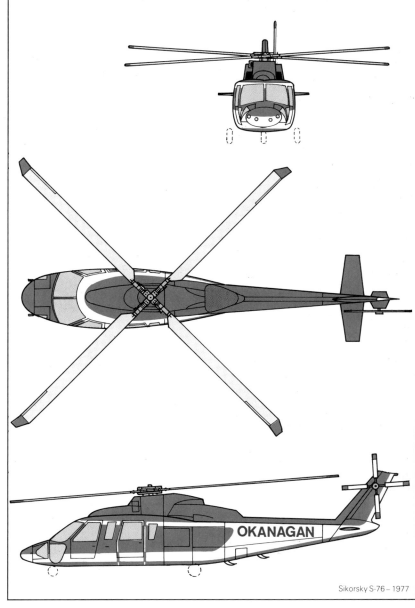

Sikorsky S-76 – 1977

The fuselage was entirely new compared with the other models by Sikorsky. It had traditional, airplane-type swept tail surfaces with a five-blade main rotor and five-blade tail rotor. Various types of blades (rigid, articulated) and transmission systems were tested.

A small, swept wing was fitted to one of the S-72 prototypes, plus two General Electric TF-34 turbofans, in two outboard nacelles. An interesting detail was the fact that the entire crew of the helicopter had ejector seats. With the supplementary turbojets, the S-72 increased its speed to about 450 km/h (280 mph). In late 1983 Sikorsky received a contract to modify one S-72 for X-wing "stopped rotor" research, a concept whereby a rigid rotor is stopped in cruise flight with the blades then acting as wings to provide lift, whilst engine power is diverted from the rotor system to give pure jet thrust.

Helicopter: **Sikorsky S-69**
Manufacturer: **Sikorsky Aircraft**
Type: **experimental**
Year: **1975**
Engine: **1,825 shp Pratt & Whitney Canada PT6T-3**
Rotor diameter: **10.97 m (36 ft)**
Fuselage length: **12.42 m (40 ft 9 in)**
Overall length: **12.62 m (41 ft 5 in)**
Height: **3.94 m (12 ft 11 in)**
Empty weight: **—**
Gross weight: **5,039 kg (11,110 lbs)**
Maximum speed: **296 km/h (184 mph)**
Hovering ceiling IGE: **2,042 m (7,000 ft)**

Helicopter: **Sikorsky S-72**
Manufacturer: **Sikorsky Aircraft**
Type: **compound helicopter**
Year: **1976**
Engines: **2 × 1,400 hp General Electric T58-GE or 2 × 4,180 kg (9,215 lb) General Electric TF-34**
Rotor diameter: **18.90 m (62 ft)**
Fuselage length: **21.51 m (70 ft 7 in)**
Overall length: **13.74 m (45 ft 1 in)**
Height: **4.42 m (14 ft 6 in)**
Empty weight: **9,544 kg (21,040 lbs)**
Gross weight: **11,895 kg (26,224 lbs)**
Maximum speed: **555 km/h (345 mph)**

Sikorsky S-76

Having concentrated almost exclusively on military aircraft thus far, Sikorsky announced plans in January 1975 for a twin-turbine helicopter for the civil market. The company had carefully evaulated the needs of potential customers and, after having examined various solutions, had already acquired a number of options. Building of the four prototypes began in May 1976 (the designation S-76 was chosen to mark the American bicentennial). The project clearly showed the experience gained with the S-70 combat helicopter. The second prototype was the first to fly, on 13 March 1977, complete with IFR avionics. From the outset, the aircraft was equipped for all-weather operation, as one of its main roles was intended to be the servicing of offshore oil rigs.

The four-blade rotor of this aircraft is exactly like that of the S-70. The blades are built around a strong titanium spar; the leading edge is also titanium, while the trailing edge has a fiberglass and nylon honeycomb structure. The entire blade is pressurized for maximum structural integrity. The rotor hub is made according to the latest techniques to minimize maintenance: the normal bearings have in fact been

Helicopter: **Sikorsky S-76**
Manufacturer: **Sikorsky Aircraft**
Type: **civil transport**
Year: **1977**
Engines: **2 × 650 shp Allison 250-C30**
Rotor diameter: **13.41 m (44 ft)**
Fuselage length: **13.44 m (44 ft 1 in)**
Height: **4.41 m (14 ft 4 in)**
Empty weight: **2,241 kg (4,940 lbs)**
Gross weight: **4,399 kg (9,698 lbs)**
Maximum speed: **269 km/h (167 mph)**
Range: **748 km (465 miles)**
Capacity: **2 pilots + 12 passengers**

replaced by elastomeric ones needing no lubrication, and special dampers virtually eliminate vibration. The powerplant is installed above the fuselage behind the drive shaft and consists of two 650 shp Allison 250-C30 turbines. There is a single 1,030 liter (227 gallon) fuel tank in the fuselage, but supplementary fuel tanks can be carried for longer journeys.

The carefully streamlined fuselage is also of composite structure. The front part is of fiberglass, the cabin section is of light alloy with honeycomb panels, while the tail, which is also of metal, has a semi-monocoque structure. The retractable tricycle landing gear is hydraulically operated. The cabin is normally furnished with seats for 14 including the crew of two, but can be modified to suit the operator. There is a large baggage compartment at the rear, with a capacity of 1.19 cu.m (42 cu.ft). The S-76 can also be fitted with an external cargo hook to carry 2,270 kg (5,004 lbs).

Over 200 Sikorsky S-76s were in operation throughout the world in 1983 and principal operators include Air Logistics, Okanagan Helicopters, VOTEC in Brazil, and Bristow in the UK. The version currently in production, the S-76 Mk.II, which won 12 world records in February 1982, has a special variant of the Allison 250 which yields five per cent more power than the previous model.

Sikorsky S-70 Black Hawk

At the end of 1978, the production models of the UH-60 — the US Army's new tactical transport helicopter for the infantry divisions — began coming off the line at the Sikorsky works. The Army had undertaken to buy about 1,100 of these helicopters over a six-seven-year period, as a first step to modernizing its airlift capability to "hot spots."

The Black Hawk is designed as a Utility Tactical Transport Aircraft System (UTTAS) to replace the ubiquitous Bell UH-1 in air support, airmobile cavalry and air ambulance units, with greatly enhanced capabilities for these three roles. For example, in the fire support role, 15 Black Hawks can do the work of 23 UH-1s. In airmobile cavalry divisions, seven UH-60s can carry the loads for eight units, and for casualty evacuation, the new helicopter can carry the same load of four stretchers as the Huey, but at a higher speed and with better chances of survival in a hostile environment.

The process which led to the acquisition of the Black Hawk began

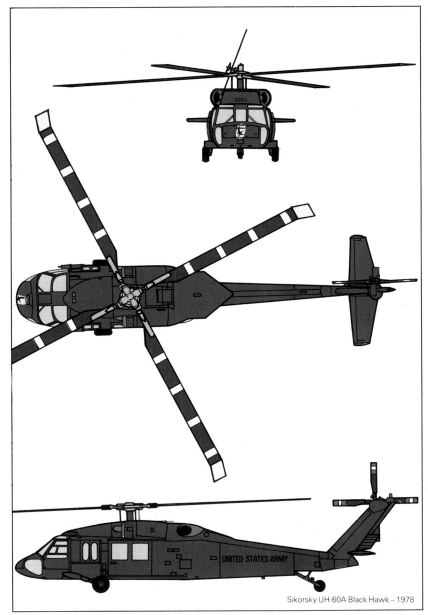

Sikorsky UH-60A Black Hawk – 1978

Helicopter: **Sikorsky S-70 (UH-60A Black Hawk)**
Manufacturer: **Sikorsky Aircraft**
Type: **tactical transport**
Year: **1978**
Engines: **2 × 1,543 shp General Electric T700**
Rotor diameter: **16.35 m (53 ft 8 in)**
Fuselage length: **15.26 m (50 ft)**
Overall length: **19.76 m (64 ft 10 in)**
Height: **5.13 m (16 ft 10 in)**
Empty weight: **4,950 kg (10,913 lbs)**
Gross weight: **7,470 kg (16,468 lbs)**
Maximum speed: **360 km/h (224 mph)**
Service ceiling: **5,790 m (19,000 ft)**
Range: **600/1,060 km (373/659 miles)**
Capacity: **11 troops or 1,200 kg (2,645 lbs)**

Helicopter: **Sikorsky S-70L (SH-60B Seahawk)**
Manufacturer: **Sikorsky Aircraft**
Type: **multipurpose naval/antisubmarine**
Engines: **2 × 1,690 shp General Electric T700**
Rotor diameter: **16.35 m (53 ft 8 in)**
Fuselage length: **15.26 m (50 ft)**
Height: **5.23 m (17 ft 2 in)**
Empty weight: **6,191 kg (13,650 lbs)**
Gross weight: **9,908 kg (21,843 lbs)**
Maximum speed: **249 km/h (155 mph)**
Service ceiling: **5,790 m (19,000 ft)**
Range: **1,100 km (683 miles)**
Armament: **2 Mk. 46 torpedoes**

in 1965 when the US Army began formulating its requirements for the UTTAS. In 1972, two competing projects by Boeing and Sikorsky were chosen for prototype development and comparative trials. For its UTTAS design, Sikorsky used the very well-proven single-rotor formula, with two new, advanced turbines to achieve the performance levels required. But the rotor was completely new in design: the blades, with titanium spars of oval cross-section, have a honeycomb core, graphite root, plastic skin and titanium leading edge abrasion strip. The monobloc rotor head has elastomeric bearings, which need no lubrication. Another innovation on the Black Hawk is the four-blade tail rotor mounted on a pylon canted 20° from the vertical. The pylon permits a controlled landing in the event of the tail rotor being knocked out during fighting.

The cockpit of the UH-60A is built for two pilots and has highly sophisticated navigational equipment. It also has protective armour capable of withstanding being hit by 23 mm shells. The fuel tanks and essential flight systems are similarly protected. The helicopter has fixed, tailwheel-type high energy attenuation landing gear. Particular care has been taken on the question of maintenance: many of the helicopter's subsystems are modular for ease of removal and replacement.

During trials for the US army, the prototypes of the UH-60 underwent various structural and aerodynamic modifications but in the end, the Sikorsky project prevailed over the Boeing competitor and, in 1977, the US Army ordered the first 15 aircraft, with an arrangement to spread a subsequent order for 353 over three years. Apart from these, the Army planned to buy another

739 Black Hawks to replace the Hueys in the utility role.

While production was getting under way in Stratford, Sikorsky continued flight testing the prototypes. Helicopter number one was lost in an accident and the enquiry ascertained that a tragic maintenance error had been committed. Delivery of the production aircraft, originally planned for the end of summer 1978, was postponed by an industrial dispute and the first UH-60A did not leave the assembly line until September, making its first flight on 17 October, and another two were delivered at the end of the year. The first aircraft were assigned to the 101st Airborne Division in 1980 and production reached a rate of 12-14 aircraft a month in 1981-82. Such high productivity proved to be very positive for Sikorsky, whose volume of business had fallen considerably after the end of the Vietnam War, to less than 25 per cent of full capacity in 1976. The Black Hawk has also been offered to various NATO countries.

Whilst development of a commercial version of the S-70 has only recently been launched, the SH-60B naval version with a ten per cent more powerful General Electric T700 turboshaft is already in production. Despite being the same size as the Black Hawk, the SH-60B has the tailwheel set farther forward to make the aircraft suitable for ships' platforms, the main rotor blades can be folded electronically, and the tailplane has been rebuilt in three sections, with the outer portions folding upwards and a hinge at the rear of the fuselage to allow the tail boom to fold.

The SH-60B is intended principally for the US Navy LAMPS Mk.III role — antisubmarine and antiship warfare and target acquisition, with the following complementary roles: SAR, casevac and fleet replenishment. Naval apparatus includes radar, MAD, IFF, data processing, an acoustic processor and two Mk.46 torpedoes. The SH-60B without equipment weighs about 1,300 kg (2,866 lbs) more than the UH-60A and the all-up weight in the ASW role is higher than that of the Army version. The US Navy expects to buy 204 for use on board 115 surface vessels and first deliveries were carried out in late 1983. Countries which have shown an interest in this version include Australia, Germany, Norway, Holland, Canada and Japan.

SILVERCRAFT
Silvercraft S.p.A (Italy)

This small company developed a light helicopter in conjunction with SIAI Marchetti (Savoia Marchetti) for agricultural and transport duties. After a few had been built, the company ceased operations in the late 1970s.

Silvercraft SH-4

Silvercraft and SIAI Marchetti were aiming to produce a highly economical aircraft. The SH-4 had some original features such as the semirigid rotor and simplified mechanics, with parts which could easily be inspected from the outside and were quick to replace. The prototype flew in March 1965 with a six-cylinder Franklin engine. A preproduction model was displayed at the 1967 Paris Air Show, and a year later the SH-4 was certified by the American FAA and the Italian Aeronautical Register.

Production of a batch of about 50 SH-4s was started at the Sesto Calende works with the aid of Fiat Aviazione (Motori), who manufactured mechanical parts for the rotor transmission, but the firm ran into difficulties over the Franklin engine, which had gone out of production. An agricultural version of the SH-4 was developed, designated SH-4A.

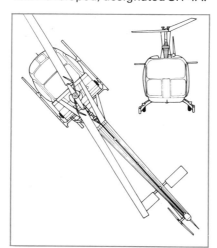

SPITFIRE
Spitfire Helicopter Company (USA)

The first project undertaken by the company was the development of a helicopter based on the Enstrom F.28A.

In 1978 the firm signed an agreement with the Polish helicopter manufacturer, WSK, for the marketing of the twin-turbine WSK-PZL Mi-2, and in 1982 it entered into collaboration with Sodian in order to produce Spitfire helicopters in Spain.

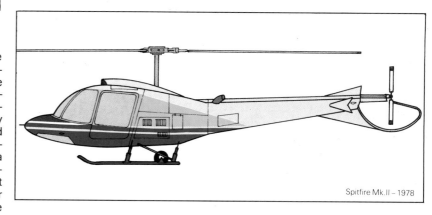

Spitfire Mk.II – 1978

Spitfire Mk.II

The Spitfire Helicopter Company began developing a light turbine-powered helicopter in the mid 1970s: the Spitfire Mk.1, based on conversions from the Enstrom F.28A. Apart from the use of a turbine, the Spitfire has a thoroughly conventional transmission system which saves a considerable amount of structural weight — about 90 kg (198 lbs) — and also economizes on cabin space.

On the subsequent Spitfire Mk. II variant, capacity has been increased from three to four seats and a more powerful 420 shp Allison 250-C20B turbine adopted. Despite the increase in weight, the overall performance of the second version is much better. Further projected developments of the formula chosen by Spitfire — who have also been responsible for marketing Polish helicopters by Pezetel in the West since August 1978 — include the turbine-engined Mk.IIIA and the twin-turbine Mk.IV four-five seat compound.

Helicopter: **Spitfire Mk.II**
Manufacturer: **Spitfire Helicopter Company**
Type: **light transport**
Year: **1978**
Engine: **420 shp Allison 250-C20B**
Rotor diameter: **9.75 m (32 ft)**
Fuselage length: **9.30 m (30 ft 6 in)**
Overall length: —
Height: **2.79 m (9 ft 2 in)**
Empty weight: **601 kg (1,325 lbs)**
Gross weight: **1,134 kg (2,500 lbs)**
Maximum speed: **217 km/h (135 mph)**
Hovering ceiling IGE: **4,085 m (13,400 ft)**
Service ceiling: **4,570 m (15,000 ft)**
Range: **495 km (307 miles)**
Capacity: **1 pilot + 3 passengers**

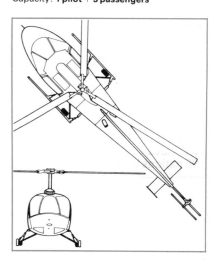

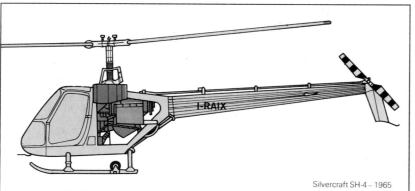

Silvercraft SH-4 – 1965

Helicopter: **Silvercraft SH-4**
Manufacture: **Silvercraft S.p.A**
Type: **light general purpose**
Year: **1965**
Engine: **235 hp Franklin 6A-350**
Rotor diameter: **9.03 m (29 ft 8 in)**
Fuselage length: **7.65 m (25 ft 1 in)**
Overall length: **10.47 m (34 ft 4 in)**
Height: **2.98 m (9 ft 9 in)**
Empty weight: **518 kg (1,142 lbs)**
Gross weight: **862 kg (1,900 lbs)**
Maximum speed: **161 km/h (100 mph)**
Hovering ceiling IGE: **3,000 m (9,840 ft)**
Service ceiling: **4,600 m (15,090 ft)**
Range: **320 km (200 miles)**

SUD-AVIATION/ AEROSPATIALE

SNCASO — SNCASE
Sud-Aviation — Aérospatiale
(France)

Sud-Aviation was created on 1 March 1957 when the two companies of Sud-Ouest Aviation and Sud-Est Aviation merged. The former had been previously known as the Société Nationale de Constructions Aéronautiques du Sud-Ouest (SNCASO) and the latter as the Société Nationale de Constructions Aéronautiques du Sud-Est (SNCASE). The two companies had both been founded before the Second World War, when France nationalized its aircraft industry, and the merged workforce totalled 22,000.

Aérospatiale and its predecessors have over 30 years' experience in helicopter design and construction, dating from the immediate post-war years when Sud-Est managed to secure the services of the famous German designer, H. Focke. After building the SE.3000, the company developed further experimental models in the Series 3000. Sud-Ouest also made its helicopter debut in the 1950s with the Ariel and the Djinn and the Fafadet "gyrodyne" experimental convertiplane.

When Sud-Est and Sud-Ouest merged the two lines of research continued under the one umbrella, the result being the Alouette and its successors. Several new types were designed, such as the Puma, the Super Frelon, the Gazelle and the Ecureuil series.

Aérospatiale's undoubted success in this sector is clearly proved by production and sales figures — over 6,000 helicopters will have been sold to a total of 95 nations by the late 1980s.

SE.3101

This single-seat experimental helicopter was designed in 1946 to study the use of auxiliary anti-torque rotors. It had two tail rotors set symmetrically at 45° on a double dihedral tail unit. Engine: 85 hp Mathis. Rotor diameter: 7.50 m (27 ft 7 in). Length: 6.90 m (22 ft 8 in). Empty weight: 400 kg (882 lbs). Gross weight: 520 kg (1,146 lbs). Maximum speed: 120 km/h (75 mph). Service ceiling: 3,000 m (9,842 ft). Range: 100 km (62 miles).

SE.3110

Another experimental helicopter derived from the SE.3101 a year later, which had a double anti-torque rotor and an enclosed cabin seating two side-by-side. Engine: 200 hp Salmson 9NH. Rotor diameter: 12 m (39 ft 4 in). Length: 11.13 m (36 ft 6 in). Empty weight: 670 kg (1,477 lbs). Gross weight: 950 kg (2,094 lbs). Maximum speed: 160 km/h (99 mph). Service ceiling: 4,500 m (14,764 ft). Range: 300 km (186 miles).

SE.3120 Alouette

General purpose civil and military three-seater, the SE.3120 was built in 1949 and had a conventional design with an articulated three-blade rotor. It was the first of the successful Alouette family of helicopters. Engine: 200 hp Salmson 9NH. Rotor diameter: 11.60 m (38 ft 1 in). Length: 10.45 m (34 ft 3 in). Empty weight: 750 kg (1,653 lbs). Gross weight: 1.150 kg (2,535 lbs). Maximum speed: 125 km/h (78 mph). Service ceiling: 4,000 m (1,312 ft). Range: 225 km (140 miles).

SE.3130 Alouette II

The French Alouette II has undoubtedly been one of the most successful civil and military light helicopters. It was derived from the SE.3120 built by Sud-Est soon after the war. The prototype had a three-blade rotor, and a 200 hp reciprocating engine. Two other prototypes followed, one of which was a three-seater. The aircraft originally had no outstanding features, but the situation changed with the introduction of the Artouste II turbine. The SE.3130 made its first flight on 12 March 1955, as did a second model immediately afterwards. Just three months after its maiden flight, the aircraft achieved world fame by setting an altitude record of 8.209 m (26,932 ft), showing its ability to operate in mountainous areas.

The structure of the Alouette II is very reminiscent of the early Bell models, in that it has a Plexiglas cockpit and open-framework fuselage. Although suited to many commercial roles, it has been used above all for military operations such as observation, liaison, search and rescue, training and casualty evacuation, and (armed with wire-guided missiles and torpedoes) in primarily offensive roles.

Mass production started in response to an order from the French Aéronavale (Fleet Air Arm), followed by others from the Armée de Terre and Armée de l'Air (Army and Air Force), amounting to a total of 363 aircraft. By the end of 1962, more than 1,000 of the Alouette II had been ordered, including 267 for the German armed forces. Other military customers for the Alouette II (redesignated SE.313B in 1967) included the Belgian Army (39), the Swiss Army (30) and the British Army Air Corps (17). Alouette IIs have also been delivered to the air forces of Austria (16), Belgian Congo (3), Cambodia (8), the Dominican Republic (2), Indonesia (3), Israel (4), Ivory Coast (2), Laos (2), Lebanon (3), Mexico (2), Morocco (7), the Netherlands (8), Peru (6), Portugal (7), South Africa (7), and Tunisia (8).

In 1964, production was switched to the SE.318C variant which differed only in the installation of an Astazou II turbine. The ALAT (Aviation Légère de l'Armée de Terre).

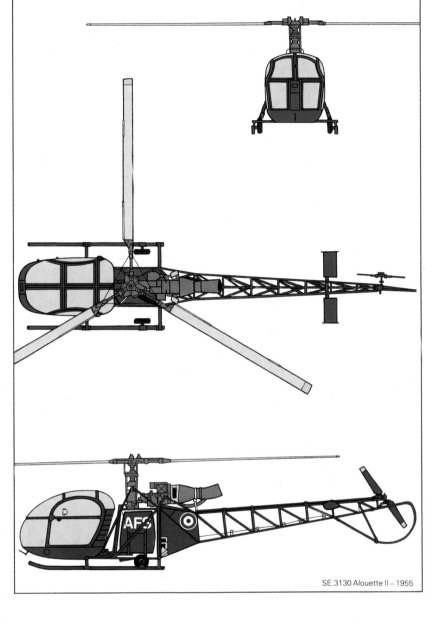

SE.3130 Alouette II – 1955

Helicopter: **SE.3130 Alouette II**
Manufacturer: **SNCASE**
Type: **general purpose**
Year: **1955**
Engine: **360 shp Turboméca Artouste IIC**
Rotor diameter: **10.20 m (33 ft 5 in)**
Fuselage length: **9.70 m (31 ft 10 in)**
Height: **2.75 m (9 ft)**
Empty weight: **890 kg (1,962 lbs)**
Gross weight: **1,500 kg (3.307 lbs)**
Maximum speed: **175 km/h (108 mph)**
Hovering ceiling IGE: **2,000 m (6,560 ft)**
Service ceiling: **3,200 m (10,498 ft)**
Range: **600 km (373 miles)**
Capacity: **4 passengers**

ordered 15 helicopters of this type and many others were sold to foreign armed forces. Production ended in 1975, by which time over 1,300 had been built.

One Alouette II Astazou was modified experimentally to test a rigid rotor with plastic blade parts, developed by the German Bölkow company. It flew in this configuration on 24 January 1966. A license to produce the Alouette II was also granted to Sweden, India and the United States, but few were built.

From the Alouette II, the SE.3131 Gouverneur executive version and the SE.3140 with a Turboméca Turmo engine were derived, as was the SE.3150, of which two were built.

SNCASO Ariel I and II

Jet-propelled experimental helicopter built by Sud-Ouest. The 1949 Ariel I had a Mathis G8 piston engine driving a compressor, which sent compressed air to the tips of the three-blade rotor. It had an oval fuselage and a conspicuous twin tail unit instead of a tail rotor. The Ariel II was also built in 1949 and used the same propulsion system but had a fully redesigned fuselage.

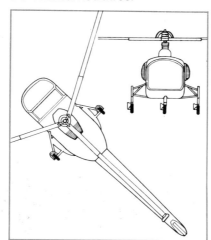

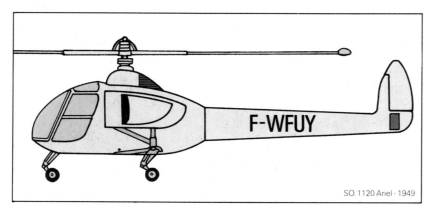

SO.1120 Ariel - 1949

Helicopter: **SO.1110 Ariel**
Manufacture: **SNCASO**
Type: **experimental**
Year: **1949**
Engine: **220 hp Turboméca Artouste**
Rotor diameter: **10.80 m (35 ft 5 in)**
Fuselage length: **7.15 m (23 ft 3 in)**
Height: —
Empty weight: **725 kg (1,598 lbs)**
Gross weight: **1.080 kg (2,381 lbs)**
Maximum speed: **170 km/h (105 mph)**
Hovering ceiling IGE: **900 m (2,952 ft)**
Range: **300 km (186 miles)**
Capacity: **2**

SO.1110/1120 Ariel

Thanks to the enterprise of a small automobile manufacturer, Turboméca, which had developed a family of small turbojets, the first French jet-propelled helicopter was also built in 1948 by Sud-Ouest.

A jet-propelled helicopter had already been developed by von Doblhoff, the reciprocating engine of which drove a compressor which sent the fuel mixture to blade-tip nozzles through the hollow rotor blades. Having ruled out direct use of the jet of a 220 hp Artouste turbine, this was used on Ariel models SO.1110 and SO.1120 for the direct drive of a compressor which fed air through the hollow rotor head and spars to burners at the tips of the three blades. The residual thrust from the turbine was used for yaw control at low velocity and in the hover, while at higher velocities, the rudder was used. The SO.1110 was a two-seater, while the SO.1120 carried three.

SO.1221 Djinn

The experience acquired by Sud-Ouest in building its two prototypes of the Ariel led to the SO.1221 Djinn. This was preceded by two SO.1220 single-seat prototypes, the first of which flew on 2 January 1953. The first definitive Model SO.1221 did not fly until the end of that year. It had an enclosed cabin, two side-by-side seats and an open-framework tail boom. The French Army promptly ordered 22 for service trials and by the end of 1960 more than 180 had been built, 100 of which were bought by the French Army and Air Force.

In the Djinn, torque reaction was offset by a turbine jet deflector mounted at the tail, which could be rotated to act as a rudder as well; two smaller fixed surfaces mounted farther out acted as stabilizers. The Djinn could take off and land quite easily on the back of an ordinary lorry. Among its many uses, it was widely adopted for agriculture.

SA.3160/319 Alouette III

The Alouette III, developed in the mid fifties, is a streamlined, rather elegant aircraft with an extensively-glazed cabin to accommodate seven. The dynamic components are derived from its predecessors and it has a 870 shp Artouste III turbine derated to 550 shp. The usual skid landing gear has been replaced by a fixed tricycle undercarriage.

The prototype made its first flight on 28 February 1959 and immediately aroused the interest of the French forces, who needed a fast, well-armed machine for the war in Algeria. Various weapons fits were examined and, apart from a number of fixed or flexible weapons, provision was made for the installation of wire-guided missiles.

Thus equipped and with a maximum speed of approximately 210 km/h (130 mph), the Alouette III suited the armed forces' require-

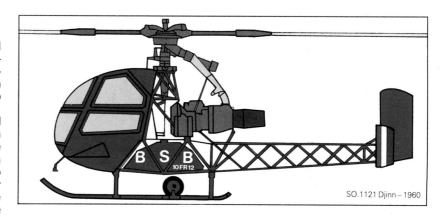

SO.1121 Djinn - 1960

Helicopter: **SO.1221 Djinn**
Manufacturer: **SNCASO**
Type: **agricultural transport**
Year: **1953**
Engine: **250 shp Turboméca Palouste IV**
Rotor diameter: **10 m (32 ft 10 in)**
Fuselage length: **5.30 m (17 ft 5 in)**
Overall lenght: —
Height: **2.36 m (7 ft 9 in)**
Empty weight: **315 kg (694 lbs)**
Gross weight: **630 kg (1,389 lbs)**
Maximum speed: **130 km/h (80 mph)**
Hovering ceiling IGE: **1,800 m (5,905 ft)**
Service ceiling: **3,000 m (9,842 ft)**
Range: **220 km (137 miles)**
Capacity: **2**

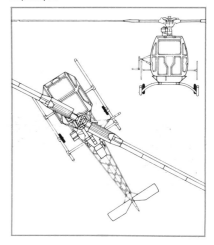

ments very well. After it had been in production for three years, Sud-Aviation built a prototype expressly designed for armed missions, with a 20 mm cannon in the redesigned nose. However, its performance was inadequate for a combat helicopter and, moreover, by that time the war in Algeria had ended.

At the end of 1970, the SA.316B version with strengthened transmission was introduced, and in 1972 the SA.316C went into production with the new 870 shp Artouste IIID turbine derated to 600 shp. Another variant which adopted an Astazou XIV turbine with the same power rating was designated the SA.319B. This last version, which was in production in the seventies, had much higher capabilities with a 25 per cent reduction in specific fuel consumption. Construction of the SA.316B and SA.319B continued for many years in France and was also

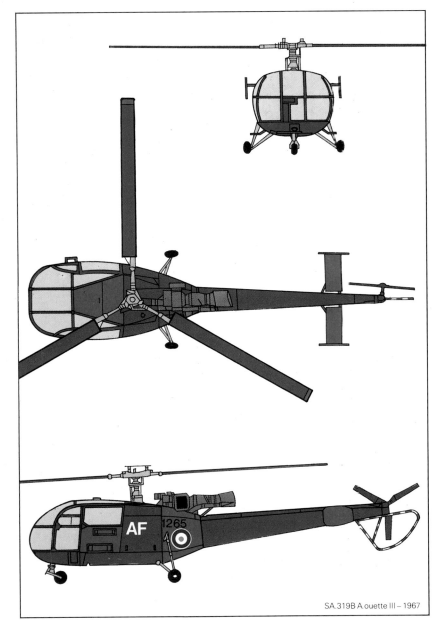

SA.319B Alouette III – 1967

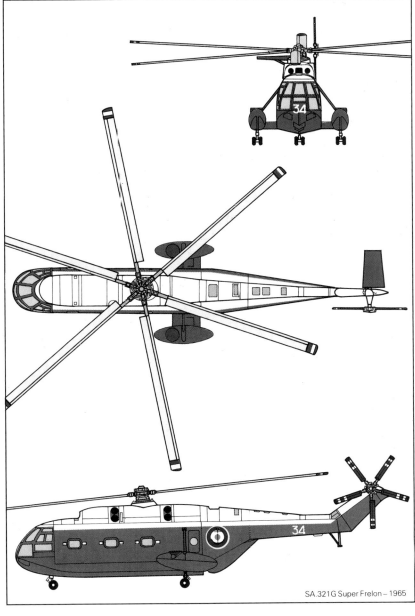

SA.321G Super Frelon – 1965

extended to India, Pakistan, Romania and Switzerland, where a number of both civil and military models have been manufactured under license. By spring 1976, over 1,350 Alouette III helicopters had been built and sold to 120 operators in 69 countries.

The helicopter was also adapted for naval use and was equipped with better navigational aids — Doppler radar, a navigation computer, autopilot and two homing torpedoes for ASW. In the antiship role, it carried two missiles.

SA.3210 Super Frelon

At the end of the fifties, the French armed forces issued a specification for a heavy helicopter for troop transport and Sud-Aviation initiated the SA.3200 Frelon project. This helicopter had three 750/800 shp

Helicopter: **SA.3160 Alouette III**
Manufacturer: **Sud-Aviation**
Type: **general purpose**
Year: **1959**
Engine: **870 shp Turboméca Artouste IIIB**
Rotor diameter: **11.00 m (36 ft 1 in)**
Fuselage length: **10.03 m (32 ft 11 in)**
Overall length: **12.84 m (42 ft 1 in)**
Height: **3.09 m (10 ft 2 in)**
Empty weight: **1,090 kg (2,403 lbs)**
Gross weight: **2,100 kg (4,630 lbs)**
Maximum speed: **210 km/h (130 mph)**
Hovering ceiling IGE: **2,000 m (6,560 ft)**
Service ceiling: **4,250 m (13,943 ft)**
Range: **500 km (310 miles)**
Capacity: **pilot + 6 passengers**

Helicopter: **SA.319B Alouette III**
Manufacturer: **Sud-Aviation/Aérospatiale**
Type: **general purpose**
Year: **1967**
Engine: **870 shp Turboméca Astazou XIV**
Rotor diameter: **11.00 m (36 ft 1 in)**
Fuselage length: **10.03 m (32 ft 11 in)**
Overall length: **12.84 m (42 ft 1 in)**
Height: **3.09 m (10 ft 2 in)**
Empty weight: **1,108 kg (2,443 lbs)**
Gross weight: **2,250 kg (4,960 lbs)**
Maximum speed: **220 km/h (485 mph)**
Hovering ceiling IGE: **3,100 m (10,170 ft)**
Service ceiling: **4,250 m (13,943 ft)**
Range: **600 km (373 miles)**
Capacity: **2 pilots + 6 passengers**

Turboméca Turmo IIIB turbines, but trials were suspended in 1963 in favour of the SA.3210 Super Frelon programme developed jointly with Sikorsky.

The influence of the American company was seen in the US-built rotor system with six blades which folded back automatically and the boat-type hull. However, the basic structure of the Super Frelon was no different from the original model: the three turbines were located side-by-side above the fuselage and the landing gear was of the fixed tricycle type. The two prototypes were followed by two pre-production models with Turmo III turbines and other variants with civil registrations.

At this point, the French government placed a firm order for 17 aircraft in the ASW version for the Aéronavale. Meanwhile, the prototype, with a modified fuselage

Helicopter: **SA.321F Super Frelon**
Manufacturer: **Sud-Aviation/Aérospatiale**
Type: **commercial transport**
Year: **1968**
Engine: **3 × 1,500 shp Turboméca Turmo IIIC**
Rotor diameter: **18.90 m (62 ft)**
Fuselage length: **19.40 m (63 ft 8 in)**
Overall length: **23.03 m (75 ft 7 in)**
Height: **4.94 m (16 ft 2 in)**
Empty weight: **7,345 kg (16,193 lbs)**
Gross weight: **13,000 kg (28,660 lbs)**
Maximum cruise speed: **230 km/h (143 mph)**
Service ceiling: **3,150 m (10,335 ft)**
Range: **625 km (388 miles)**
Capacity: **37 passengers or 5,000 kg (11,023 lbs)**

Helicopter: **SA.321G Super Frelon**
Manufacturer: **Sud-Aviation/Aérospatiale**
Type: **multipurpose**
Year: **1965**
Engines: **3 × 1,550 shp Turboméca Turmo IIIC**
Rotor diameter: **18.90 m (62 ft)**
Fuselage length: **19.40 m (63 ft 8 in)**
Overall length: **23.03 m (75 ft 7 in)**
Height: **6.66 m (21 ft 10 in)**
Empty weight: **6,863 kg (15,130 lbs)**
Gross weight: **13,000 kg (28,660 lbs)**
Maximum speed: **275 km/h (170 mph)**
Hovering ceiling IGE: **2,170 m (7,120 ft)**
Service ceiling: **3,150 m (10,335 ft)**
Range: **820 km (509 miles)**
Armament: **4 torpedoes + 2 Exocet antiship missiles**

The SA.321F public transport version of the Super Frelon in a Norwegian operator's colours.

and retractable landing gear, set the following world speed records in July 1963: 341.23 km/h (212 mph) over 3 km (1.8 miles); 350.47 km/h (217.78 mph) over 15/25 km (9.32/15.53 miles); 334.28 km/h (207.72 mph) over 100 km (62 miles) — truly outstanding results.

The second prototype was fitted out with the equipment needed by the French Navy (flotation gear, search radar, sonar and other ASW equipment), and trials with the first four pre-production Super Frelons were followed by the first production helicopter, which flew on 30 November 1965. Delivery of the SA.321G maritime patrol and ASW versions began at the same time. These were equipped with two Sylphe radars, all-weather navigation systems, an automatic stabilization system, and mine-laying and mine-sweeping equipment. The Aéronavale assigned them to Flotille 32F for both shore-based and shipboard use.

Of the 99 Super Frelons completed, 12 have been supplied to the Israeli Air Force, 16 to the South African Air Force, and nine to Libya. Others have been supplied to Iraq and China. The cabin of the Super Frelon in the military transport version is 7 m (23 ft) long and can take two jeeps or two DCA 20 mm cannon. For casualty evacuation it can take 15 stretcher cases with two medical attendants. The rear loading ramp is hydraulically operated and can remain open even in flight.

Of the three Turmo IIIC turbines, two are installed in front of the rotor drive shaft while the third, at the center rear, has an air intake on the port side and exhausts on the same side. Crash resistant tanks under the fuselage floor contain 3,900 liters (858 gallons) of fuel. A utility version has also been developed from the military version. Designated the SA.321J, it went into production in 1968 and can carry 27 passengers or 4,000 kg (8,818 lbs) internally, with a slung load of up to 5,000 kg (11,023 lbs).

The one-off SA.321F commercial transport version, test-flown in 1968, had an air-conditioned, soundproofed cabin, a sliding door on the starboard side and a rotor head fairing. The two stub wings at the sides of the fuselage were used as baggage holds, and airline-style seating provided for 34-37 passengers.

SA.315B Lama

The Lama owes its name to the fact that it was designed for operation at high altitude. The project for this variant of the Alouette originated in late 1968 in response to an Indian Air Force requirement for an aircraft capable of operating in the Himalayas, and a similar need on the part of South American air forces operating in the Andes. The first Lama, the exterior of which was almost indistinguishable from its predecessors flew on 17 March 1969 and was certified on 30 September 1970.

Structurally, the Lama is the same as the Alouette II, with high skid landing gear without wheels. The only detail which makes it immediately recognizable is a small housing for electronic equipment at the front of the cockpit. The dyna-

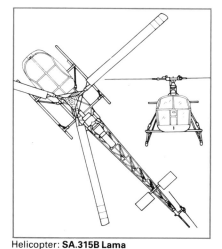

Helicopter: SA.315B Lama
Manufacturer: **Sud-Aviation/Aérospatiale**
Type: **general purpose.**
Year: **1972**
Engine: **870 shp Turboméca Artouste IIIB**
Rotor diameter: **11.02 m (36 ft 2 in)**
Fuselage length: **10.26 m (33 ft 8 in)**
Overall length: **12.92 m (42 ft 5 in)**
Height: **3.09 m (10 ft 2 in)**
Empty weight: **995 kg (2,193 lbs)**
Gross weight: **1,950 kg (4,298 lbs)**
Maximum speed: **210 km/h (130 mph)**
Hovering ceiling IGE: **3,750 m (12,303 ft)**
Service ceiling: **4,000 m (13,123 ft)**
Range: **510 km (317 miles)**
Capacity: **3 passengers**

mic components are identical to those of the Alouette III. The Lama can be used as a flying crane and is capable of lifting 1,000 kg (2,204.6 lbs) to an altitude of 2,500 m (8,202 ft). During demonstrations, the Lama took off and landed at 7,500 m (24,606 ft) above sea level. As the Chetak the SA.315B has been built under license by Hindustan Aeronautics in India.

SA.330 Puma

This aircraft was the result of a French Army specification drawn up in 1962 for a medium/light tactical and logistic transport helicopter capable of all-weather operation, defined as an "hélicoptère de manoeuvre." At the time, Sud-Aviation, who had the license to build the Sikorsky S-58, was working on a version of its own, with a 1,900 shp Turboméca Bi-Bastan turbine, which flew on 5 October 1962. However this helicopter would only have been a compromise solution and with the time and opportunity to develop something that repre-

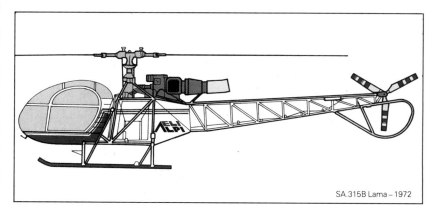

SA.315B Lama – 1972

sented a technological advance, the French company began work on the SA.330 which was to be powered by two 1,300 shp Bastan VII turbines.

In June 1963, the War Ministry allocated 20 million francs for development of the SA.330 (then called Alouette IV). A full-size mock-up, seen at the Paris Air Show that year, was similar to the final version apart from the shape of the nose. In the meantime, the Bastan engines were replaced by 1,300 shp Turmo IIIC4s which had already been tested on the Super Frelon. The first of two prototypes was ready by 15 April 1965.

The SA.330 was more closely related to the Super Frelon than the Alouette III in appearance, particularly in terms of the shape of the fuselage, which had two turbines mounted on the top, and the five-blade anti-torque rotor. The fully-articulated main rotor had four extruded aluminum blades. The payload exceeded that of the specification, the aircraft being capable of carrying 18 troops with full individual armament plus two crew. The first five pre-production aircraft with these characteristics appeared in 1967, all with civil registrations, while the sixth had a different nose, which was standardized on the production aircraft. As a result of the trials programme this compact, efficient aircraft won the approval of the French Army, which ordered 130 (designated SA.330H). Development of this helicopter received a considerable boost in 1967 when

the RAF chose the Puma for its Tactical Transport Programme, and 40 Pumas were ordered from Westland, as part of an agreement with Sud-Aviation.

The Puma remained in production in France for more than ten years in various commerical and military versions, although its specific role is for troop transport. The SA.330 can also carry a considerable weapon load, in the form of a GIAT M693 20 mm side-firing cannon, or two fixed 7.62 mm machine gun installations at the side, or wire-guided missiles such as the Nord SS11 or SS12 or HOT Euromissiles. Thirty of the SA.330B, which is the version for the French ALAT (Army Air Corps), were built from spring 1969.

The SA.330C export version also went into production in 1969, while the RAF's SA.330E Puma HC Mk.1s built by Westland in 1970-71 were assigned to No.33 and 230 Squadrons. The SA.330F civil version flew in September 1969 powered by

Helicopter: **SA.330H Puma**
Manufacturer: **Sud-Aviation/Aérospatiale**
Type: **medium transport**
Year: **1968**
Engines: **2 × 1,580 shp Turboméca Turmo IVC**
Rotor diameter: **15.08 m (16 ft 8 in)**
Fuselage length: **14.06 m (46 ft 2 in)**
Overall length: **18.15 m (55 ft 6 in)**
Height: **4.38 m (14 ft 4 in)**
Empty weight: **3,536 kg (7,795 lbs)**
Gross weight: **7,000 kg (15,432 lbs)**
Maximum speed: **273 km/h (170 mph)**
Hovering ceiling IGE: **2,230 m (7,316 ft)**
Service ceiling: **6,000 m (19,684 ft)**
Range: **570 km (354 miles)**
Capacity: **16 troops**

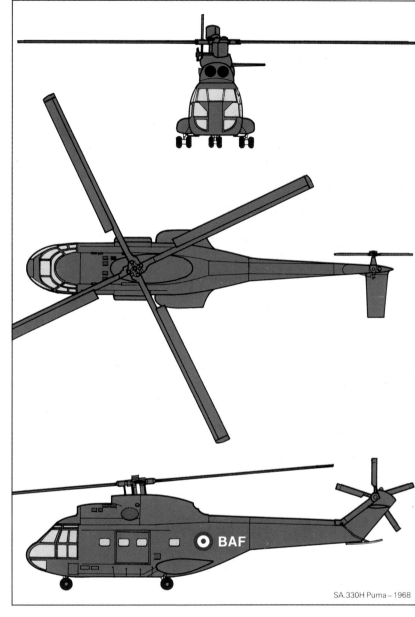

SA.330H Puma – 1968

One of the ten SA.330 Pumas in service with the British company Bristow Helicopters.

Sud-Aviation – Aérospatiale

1,290 shp Turmo IVA engines. It was later superseded by the SA.330J, introduced in 1976, and the SA.330L for military use. Both have 1,580 shp Turmo IVC engines and composite material main rotor blades. The SA.330J has also been certified for all-weather operation and has an efficient anti-icing system on both the rotor blades and air intakes.

AS.332 Super Puma

The design of this derivative of the SA.330 Puma commenced in 1974 and the definitive prototype was preceded by a modified Puma, the AS.331, which flew in September 1977 with an uprated transmission driven by two Turboméca Makila turboshafts. The first AS.332 flew on 13 September 1978 and introduced a number of further changes to improve payload, performance and survivability, and to reduce maintenance.

These changes included a new energy-absorbing landing gear with increased wheel base and track, a lengthened nose section, more efficient fiberglass main and tail rotors, greater fuel capacity, and revised fin and tail plane contours to improve handling. Subsequently in 1980 a fourth prototype introduced a cabin stretch of 0.76 m (2 ft 6 in) with two additional windows and accommodation for up to three more passengers.

There are currently five main versions of the Super Puma, based on short and long fuselage variants. The AS.332B is the standard military version, which to date has been supplied to Abu Dhabi, Argentina, Chile and Spain, whilst the AS.332F is a naval variant armed with two Exocet missiles for antishipping duties. The civil equivalent of these two short fuselage variants is the AS.332C. The two stretched variants are the AS.332M military transport and the AS.332L civil version. The latter has become popular with offshore support operators, particularly in the North Sea where six major operators had the type in service at the beginning of 1984. This included 34 aircraft with Bristow Helicopters, redesignated Tigers to signify equipment differences from the standard AS.332L.

Orders for 150 Super Pumas had been received by late 1983, including license-built aircraft being assembled by Nurtanio of Indonesia.

SA.341 Gazelle

Sud-Aviation began working on a modern replacement for its Alouette II as long ago as 1966. The aim

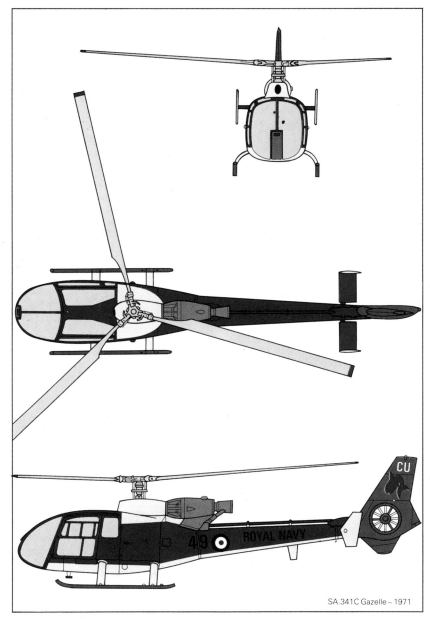

SA.341C Gazelle – 1971

Helicopter: **AS.332L Super Puma**
Manufacturer: **Aérospatiale**
Type: **medium transport**
Year: **1978**
Engines: **2 × 1,780 shp Turboméca Makila 1A**
Rotor diameter: **15.60 m (51 ft 2¼ in)**
Fuselage length: **16.25 m (53 ft 3¾ in)**
Overall length: **18.70 m (61 ft 4¼ in)**
Height: **4.92 m (16 ft 1¾ in)**
Empty weight: **4,265 kg (9,402 lbs)**
Gross weight: **8,350 kg (18,410 lbs)**
Maximum speed: **296 km/h (184 mph)**
Hovering ceiling IGE: **2,700 m (8,850 ft)**
Service ceiling: **—**
Range: **635 km (394 miles)**
Capacity: **2 pilots + 22 passengers**

Helicopter: **SA.341C Gazelle**
Manufacturer: **Sud-Aviation/Aérospatiale**
Type: **multipurpose**
Year: **1971**
Engine: **590 shp Turboméca Astazou IIIA**
Rotor diameter: **10.50 m (34 ft 5 in)**
Fuselage length: **9.53 m (31 ft 3 in)**
Overall length: **11.97 m (39 ft 3 in)**
Height: **3.15 m (10 ft 4 in)**
Empty weight: **917 kg (2,022 lbs)**
Gross weight: **1,800 kg (3,968 lbs)**
Maximum speed: **264 km/h (164 mph)**
Hovering ceiling IGE: **2,850 m (9,350 ft)**
Service ceiling: **5,000 m (16,404 ft)**
Range: **670 km (416 miles)**
Capacity: **pilot + 5**

was to develop a light observation helicopter with accommodation for five, which would use some of the main components of the Alouette II but be technically less complex. Sud-Aviation produced the SA.340 prototype at the beginning of 1967, with an Astazou IIN turbine and the same transmission, landing skids, anti-torque rotor and tail plane as the Alouette. The rotor was of the rigid type with three blades of reinforced plastic designed by Bölkow, but in the original project it was planned to replace the two-blade tail rotor by a 13-blade fan shrouded in a type of vertical fin known as a *fenestron*. This was applied to the second prototype which closely resembled the production SA.341 and flew a year later, on 17 April 1968.

The SA.341, named Gazelle, was also included in the joint production agreement with Westland in the UK.

The three British armed forces were interested in the Gazelle as a lightweight utility helicopter and the Army purchased one of the four pre-production models to equip it according to British specifications. The first production Gazelle, fitted with a 590 shp Astazou III turbine, flew on 6 August 1971.

The modern, lightweight Gazelle was designed for a series of roles such as liaison, training and air observation. Its streamlined fuselage could accommodate five and carry a 600 kg (1,322 lb) slung load, while a rescue hoist could lift 120 kg (265 lbs). With a maximum cruise speed of 264 km/h (164 mph) fully loaded, it was well suited to escort and light combat duties. For this, it could carry two small-caliber Matra rocket launchers and four wire-guided missiles with gyrostabilized sights. The armament also included two fixed 7.62 mm machine guns, a flexible machine gun in the cabin or in an Emerson Minitat turret (or one of similar design) located at the front with a periscope sight.

The Gazelles ordered by the British armed forces were given the designations SA.341B AH Mk.1 for the Army, SA.341C Gazelle HT Mk.2 for the Royal Navy and SA.341D HT Mk.3 (trainer) for the Royal Air Force, while the liaison version also used by the RAF was designated SA.341E HCC Mk.4. The 166 initially ordered by the ALAT were designated SA.341F.

The SA.341G civil version, also certified for instrument flight conditions, was distributed in the United States by Vought Helicopters, who sold about 40 before Aérospatiale set up their own US subsidiary.

AS.350/355 Ecureuil

If the Alouette II represented the first family of French helicopters, the Puma the second generation and the Dauphin the third, the Ecureuil (Squirrel) is essentially a fourth generation, not just in terms of technology and performance, but above all, in the efforts made to simplify the production process, bringing assembly line techniques for helicopters increasingly close to those for ordinary motor cars.

The AS.350 in fact uses many automobile parts such as a cooling fan from a normal Citröen car and an oil radiator by another automobile manufacturer, while the Starflex rotor has very few parts, thereby eliminating the need for lubrication. Metal blades have also been abandoned in favour of fiberglass reinforced plastic ones which have a virtually unlimited life. The use of composite materials and

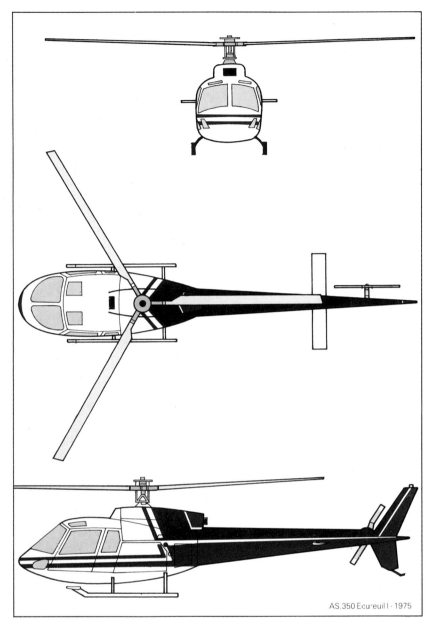

AS.350 Ecureuil I - 1975

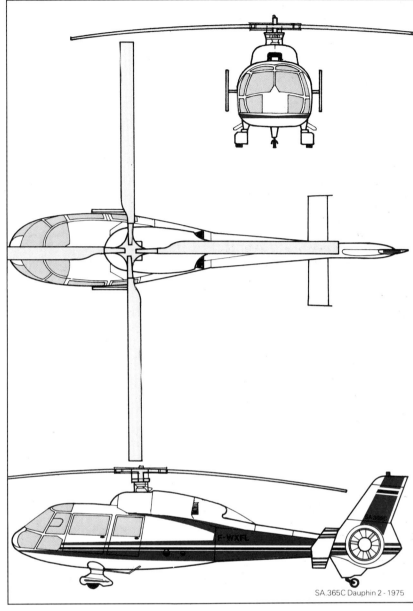

SA.365C Dauphin 2 - 1975

pressed parts has contributed a great deal to simplifying the production process. The spacious cabin, for instance, is made of thermoformed polycarbonate semimonocoque sections with ultrasonic welding. The bearings usually found in rotor hubs have been replaced by elastomeric ball joints which need no lubrication.

The first prototype of the AS.350 with a Lycoming LTS engine flew in January 1974 and the second (with a French Turboméca Arriel engine) in February 1975. Deliveries began in July 1978 after eight preproduction models had been built. By the end of December of that year, the company had 459 orders for machines of this type, only six of which were for the military version. Essentially a civil helicopter, therefore, it has been a big success in the United States, where it was called Astar and customers could opt for an American or French engine.

Helicopter: **AS.350 Ecureuil I**
Manufacturer: **Aérospatiale**
Type: **light transport**
Year: **1975**
Engine: **600 shp Turboméca Arriel**
Rotor diameter: **10.69 m (35 ft 1 in)**
Fuselage length: **10.91 m (35 ft 9 in)**
Overall length: **12.99 m (42 ft 7 in)**
Height: **3.08 m (10 ft 1 in)**
Empty weight: **1,027 kg (2,264 lbs)**
Gross weight: **1,900 kg (4,188 lbs)**
Maximum speed: **272 km/h (169 mph)**
Hovering ceiling IGE: **4,050 m (13,287 ft)**
Service ceiling: **5,800 m (19,028 ft)**
Range: **750 km (466 miles)**
Capacity: **1 pilot + 5 passengers**

The need for a light twin-turbine helicopter, particularly in America, led Aérospatiale to develop a bigger version — Ecureuil II (or Twinstar) — powered by two 420 shp Allison 250-C20F. It made its first flight on 27 September 1979 followed by the second prototype on 13 November. After 122 hours' flight testing, production went ahead at a rate of between five and seven helicopters a month, rising to 20-24 in 1981.

SA.360/SA.365 Dauphin

The SA.360 Dauphin, which was designed to replace the Alouette III, was first seen in public at the 1973 Paris Air Show, but one of the two prototypes had already flown a year before, on 2 June 1972, with a 980 shp Astazou XVI turbine, a four-blade main rotor (using the same blades as the Alouette III), a characteristic *fenestron* tail unit and fully-glazed front fuselage section. After 180 flights, the prototype was refitted with a 1,050 shp Astazou XVIII engine and new plastic rotor blades, and was modified to reduce vibrations and eliminate ground resonance.

Thus modified, flights were resumed in May 1973 and it was officially introduced at Le Bourget Air Show, where it distinguished itself by winning a series of three world records in the E1D class for helicopters from 1,750 to 3,000 kg

Helicopter: **SA.365C Dauphin 2**
Manufacturer: **Aérospatiale**
Type: **general purpose/transport**
Year: **1975**
Engine: **2 × 650 shp Turboméca Arriel 1C**
Rotor diameter: **13.29 m (43 ft 7 in)**
Fuselage length: **11.41 m (37 ft 5 in)**
Overall length: **13.20 m (43 ft 4 in)**
Height: **4.00 m (13 ft 1 in)**
Empty weight: **1,823 kg (4,019 lbs)**
Gross weight: **3,400 kg (7,496 lbs)**
Maximum speed: **280 km/h (174 mph)**
Hovering ceiling IGE: **4,900 m (16,076 ft)**
Service ceiling: **4,575 m (15,010 ft)**
Range: **580 km (360 miles)**
Capacity: **8 passengers**

(3,858 to 6,614 lbs), piloted by Roland Coffignot. With a payload equivalent to eight passengers, it flew at 299 km/h (186 mph) over a 100 km (62 mile) closed circuit; at 312 km/h (194 mph) over a 3 km (1.86 mile) straight course and at 303 km/h (188 mph) over 15 km (9.32 miles). The second prototype, which flew on 29 January 1973, was given new blades, and the first production aircraft subsequently

The SA.361 Dauphin in the un-armed military version.

introduced a stepped nose, which was standardized.

Production of the Dauphin began in 1974 with the SA.360C, but the market for this big single-engine aircraft seemed somewhat limited and it appeared to be under-powered. As a result, at the end of 1976 Aérospatiale found itself with no fewer than 15 completed Dauphin civil airframes waiting for customers. In the meantime, a military prototype had been developed, the SA.361, with a 1,400 shp Asta-zou XX turbine and Starflex rotor. This was accompanied by a second model with the same powerplant but the original rotor hub.

Production of the single-engine civil Dauphin stopped after 34 had been made, although development

of the military version continued on an experimental basis. In the SA.361H/HCL (Hélicoptère de Combat Léger) configuration, the Dauphin can carry eight HOT anti-tank missiles. With an SFIM turret, it can attack tanks even at night. Other weapons fits typical of Aérospatiale helicopters can be used (e.g. light, flexible machine guns, rocket launchers, Minitat).

The twin-engine version of the Dauphin designated SA.365 was flown on 24 January 1975. Based on the SA.360, it introduced two Turboméca Arriel turbines delivering 650 shp each. The first flight of the SA.366 took place two days after that of the prototype. It was identical except for the fact that the powerplant consisted of two 680 shp Avco

Lycoming LTS-101 turbines. The Starflex rotor was also fitted on the Dauphin 2 and production began in 1977, with demand for the aircraft steadily increasing.

Over 70 of the SA.365C were sold to civil operators and oil companies. From this model, the AS.365N variant was developed; it looked similar to its predecessor but in fact had 90 per cent new or improved parts. Modifications included extensive use of composite materials for the structure, rotor blades with a different profile, a modified fuselage and a retractable tricycle landing gear. The AS.365N is currently in production for civil or military use and just over 100 of these aircraft were in operation at the end of 1983.

The SA.366G version was developed at the same time as the AS.365N. Designed in response to an order from the US Coast Guard, it differed primarily in using American Avco Lycoming LTS-101 engines. For the search and rescue missions for which it is intended, the aircraft has sophisticated avionics equipment by Collins. It has two sliding doors, a rescue hoist and can take three stretchers and four assistants. One of the first civil models set a world speed record on 9 February 1980 by flying non-stop from Paris (heliport) to London at an average of over 294 km/h (183 mph), beating this two days later by a direct flight from Paris (Issy-les-Moulineaux) to London at 321.9 km/h (200 mph).

U W

UMBAUGH
Umbaugh Company (USA)

This company became involved in helicopter construction in the late 1950s and built the Umbaugh 18 autogyro in collaboration with the Fairchild Engine and Airplane Company.

WALLIS
Wallis Autogyros Ltd.
(Great Britain)

This small company was founded in 1961 by Wing-Commander K.H. Wallis and has produced an extremely wide range of special-purpose autogyros.

Umbaugh Model 18

The Umbaugh two-seat autogyro, developed in 1960 in conjunction with the Fairchild Airplane Company was expected by its designers to be an unprecedented success, but after the first two prototypes, few were in fact built, as very high costs restricted sales. The semi-monocoque metal fuselage had tandem seating and the tail boom supported a triple fin tail unit. The 180 hp Lycoming engine with a pusher propeller was installed at the rear of the fuselage.

Wallis WA-116/122

Wing-Commander K. Wallis flew his first autogyro in August 1961. After building nine single-seaters, construction of a two-seat variant — the WA-116T — was begun in 1969; he then tested a four-blade rotor and finally produced the WA-116F with which he won the closed circuit world record in 1974 in the 670.26 km (416.48 miles) category.

Wallis autogyros have been powered by various types of engines, within the range 72 to 160 hp (the latter is used in the two-seat Wallis WA-122) and have been employed for research programmes, including one promoted by Sperry Radar.

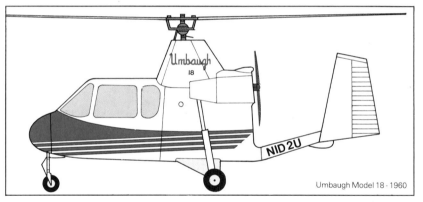
Umbaugh Model 18 - 1960

Aircraft: **Umbaugh Model 18**
Manufacturer: **Umbaugh Aircraft Corporation**
Type: **two-seat autogyro**
Year: **1960**
Engine: **180 hp Lycoming 0360**
Rotor diameter: **10.67 m (35 ft)**
Fuselage length: **6.50 m (21 ft 4 in)**
Overall length: —
Height: **3.05 m (10 ft)**
Empty weight: —
Gross weight: —
Maximum speed: **202 km/h (125 mph)**
Hovering ceiling IGE: —
Service ceiling: **4,570 m (15,000 ft)**
Range: **560 km (350 miles)**

Aircraft: **Wallis WA-116F**
Manufacturer: **Wallis Autogyros Ltd.**
Type: **light autogyro**
Year: **1969**
Engine: **72 hp McCulloch**
Rotor diameter: **6.20 m (20 ft 4 in)**
Fuselage length: **3.38 m (11 ft)**
Overall length: —
Height: —
Empty weight: **143 kg (315 lbs)**
Gross weight: **317 kg (700 lbs)**
Maximum speed: **161 km/h (100 mph)**
Hovering ceiling IGE: —
Service ceiling: —

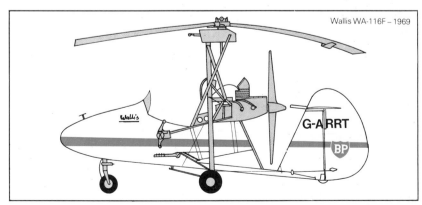
Wallis WA-116F – 1969

VFW-Fokker H3 Sprinter, see p.125

Wagner Sky-Trac, see p.125
WSK-PZL Kitty Hawk, see p.120

Yakovlev Yak 24, see p.119
Yakovlev Yak 100, see p.119

In 1983 development of a production version, powered by a Weslake engine, was under way in association with Vinten Ltd. Intended primarily for para-military use, including policing and survey work, the definitive aircraft is due to be certificated in 1984.

WESTLAND

Westland Aircraft Ltd.
Westland Helicopters Ltd. (Great Britain)

Westland was formed for the purpose of constructing aircraft under license; its first original project was a fighter seaplane built in 1915, followed by a commercial aircraft in 1919. However the company had to wait until the late 1920s for recognition, when its Wapiti general-purpose aircraft proved extremely popular.

Only after the war did Westland decide to enter the helicopter sector, the first step being an agreement concluded with Sikorsky to produce the four-seat S-51. Westland then carried out modifications on several American rotorcraft.

Following subtle government pressure aimed at amalgamating sectors of the British aircraft industry, in 1959 Westland took over Saunders-Roe, which had previously absorbed Cierva Autogiro. In 1960 this was followed by the purchase of the helicopter divisions of Bristol and Fairey. Thus the British helicopter industry came to be concentrated in the hands of Westland, with the exception of some companies building light rotorcraft which never went into production. Today the headquarters of Westland Helicopters are at Yeovil, with divisions sited at Cowes and Weston-super-Mare.

The Wessex helicopter was developed and built on a large scale for the British armed forces and for foreign military users. Helicopter designs which Westland had inherited when it acquired Bristol (such as the Belvedere) and Saro (the Scout and Wasp) were also developed and manufactured. In June 1966 Westland started the production under license of the Sikorsky SH-3 and later signed an agreement with Sud-Aviation (now Aérospatiale) for a joint venture to build the Lynx, Puma and the Gazelle. An important recent development is a co-operation agreement with Agusta for the construction of the three-turbine EH-101 helicopter.

Westland Westminster

A private venture by Westland using the main transmission, rotors and hydraulic controls of the Sikorsky S-56 with a steel tube fuselage. The prototype flew on 15 June 1958. It was proposed for civil or military operation but the project came to nothing. Engines: 2 × 2,800 shp Napier Eland E.229A. Rotor diameter: 21.95 m (72 ft). Overall length: 27.4 m (90 ft). Height: 5.04 m (16 ft 6 in). Empty weight: 10,125 kg (22,320 lbs). Gross weight: 16,345 kg (36,034 lbs). Cruise speed: 184 km/h (116 mph). Hovering ceiling IGE: 2,750 m (9,020 ft). Range: 330 km (205 mph).

Westland Whirlwind

The first S-55s received by the Royal Navy in 1950 were built by Sikorsky, but Westland acquired a license in 1950 and the first British-made S.55 flew at Yeovil in November 1952. Like the American models, the first Whirlwinds had Pratt & Whitney engines and were delivered to No.705 Squadron based at Gosport.

The RAF also ordered this helicopter for transport and rescue missions: the Whirlwind HAR Mk.2 (the same as the naval version except for some differences in equipment) joined the Transport and Coastal Command Units from 1955. With Wright R.1300 engines, the Whirlwind Mk.3 went into production for the Royal Navy in 1953 and operated for many years from both ship and shore bases. The subsequent RAF HAR Mk.4 version was modified for use in the tropics and fitted with a new variant of the Pratt & Whitney R-1340. It was used in Malaysia.

When Westland began producing the S-55, it specified that the American engine would be used until a more suitable British powerplant was available. To meet this requirement, Alvis developed a double radial called the Leonides Major, which delivered 882 hp derated to 750 hp. The re-engined Whirlwind flew in 1955. It was followed in 1956 by the Mk.7 version intended to replace the old Fairey Gannet anti-submarine aircraft.

Meanwhile, Westland had thought of adapting a turbine engine for the Whirlwind. The aircraft was first given a General Electric T.58 and then the more powerful D.H. Gnome turbine. The turbine-powered Whirlwind Series 3 flew in February 1959 and introduced a new nose profile which offered better visibility from the cockpit than the piston engine version. The

Whirlwind could carry ten men or six stretchers, or a comparable load.

The RAF adopted the Whirlwind Mk.10 version in April 1960. More than 400 Whirlwinds were built, of which nearly 100 were exported to the following countries: Austria, Brazil, Canada, Cuba, France, Ghana, Jordan, Iran, Kuwait, Spain, Saudi Arabia and Yugoslavia.

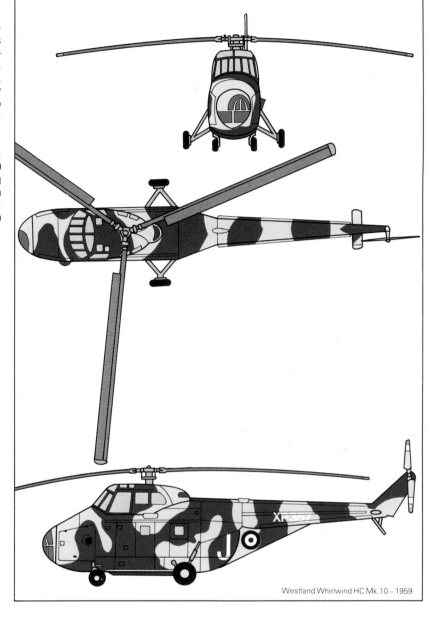

Westland Whirlwind HC Mk.10 – 1959

Helicopter: **Westland Whirlwind HAR Mk.5**
Manufacturer: **Westland Aircraft Ltd.**
Type: **general purpose**
Year: **1955**
Engine: **882 hp Alvis Leonides Mk.155**
Rotor diameter: **16.10 m (52 ft 10 in)**
Fuselage length: **12.71 m (41 ft 8 in)**
Overall length: **18.95 m (62 ft 2 in)**
Height: **4.04 m (13 ft 3 in)**
Empty weight: **2,531 kg (5,580 lbs)**
Gross weight: **3,538 kg (7,800 lbs)**
Maximum speed: **176 km/h (110 mph)**
Hovering ceiling IGE: **1,680 m (5,518 ft)**
Range: **539 km (335 miles)**
Capacity: **10 troops**

Helicopter: **Westland Whirlwind Series 3**
Manufacturer: **Westland Aircraft Ltd.**
Type: **general purpose**
Year: **1959**
Engine: **1,050 shp Rolls-Royce (B.S.) Gnome H-1000**
Rotor diameter: **16.15 m (53 ft)**
Fuselage length: **13.46 m (44 ft 2 in)**
Height: **4.76 m (15 ft 7 in)**
Empty weight: **2,130 kg (4,696 lbs)**
Gross weight: **3,630 kg (8,003 lbs)**
Maximum speed: **175 km/h (109 mph)**
Range: **480 km (298 miles)**
Capacity: **2 pilots + 10 passengers**

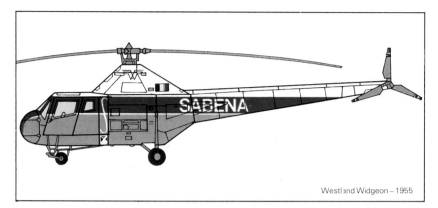

Westland Widgeon – 1955

Westland Widgeon

The long history of co-operation between Sikorsky and Westland began in 1947 with the Model S-51 which was built in Britian until the end of 1955, when the Westland Widgeon appeared. This had a re-designed cabin for four passengers plus the pilot, and a three-blade rotor driven by a 500 hp Alvis Leonides engine. About 15 were built alongside production of the larger Whirlwind, the British version of the Sikorsky S-55.

A few passenger transport versions of the Widgeon were produced, some ambulance versions with room for two stretchers and a medical attendant inside the cabin, and at least one model equipped for rescue operations with an external hoist capable of lifting up to 455 kg (1,003 lbs). A few Widgeons were also exported to Brazil and Jordan, but one of the chief operators of this helicopter was the Hong Kong police force, which used it for port surveillance.

Helicopter: **Westland Widgeon**
Manufacturer: **Westland Aircraft Ltd.**
Type: **general purpose**
Year: **1955**
Engine: **500 hp Alvis Leonides**
Rotor diameter: **14.99 m (49 ft 2 in)**
Fuselage length: **12.44 m (40 ft 10 in)**
Overall length: —
Height: **4.04 m (13 ft 3 in)**
Empty weight: **2,007 kg (4,425 lbs)**
Gross weight: **2,676 kg (5,900 lbs)**
Maximum speed: **167 km/h (104 mph)**
Hovering ceiling IGE: **1,525 m (5,000 ft)**
Service ceiling: **3,100 m (10,170 ft)**
Range: **500 km (310 miles)**
Capacity: **pilot + 4 passengers**

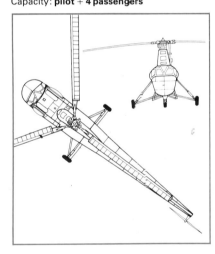

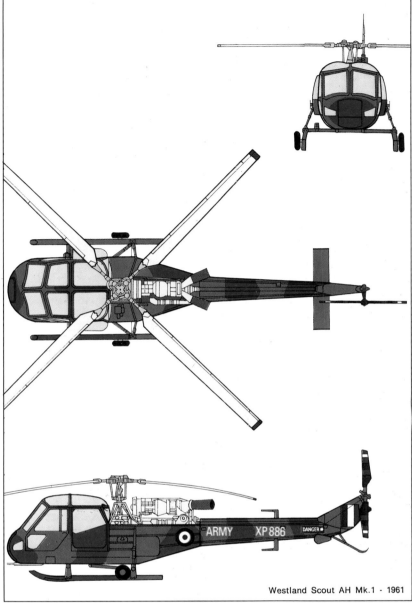

Westland Scout AH Mk.1 - 1961

Westland Wasp/Scout

Development of the Wasp/Scout family was initiated by Saro in 1957, with the aim of developing an aircraft based on the earlier Skeeter helicopter, but of more modern design, above all in terms of the powerplant. The result was the P.531 project, which aimed to use various components of the Skeeter; the first of two prototypes, both powered by a 400 shp Turboméca Turmo 603, flew on 20 July 1958. In 1959, Westland acquired Saro and decided to continue development of this interesting light helicopter. Another two prototypes were built, the first with a 1,050 shp Bristol Siddeley Nimbus engine derated to 635 shp, and the other with a de Havilland Gnome H.1000 turbine derated to 685 shp.

The British Army ordered a pre-production model and this was fol-lowed in September 1960 by an order for 66 of the P.531-2 Scout AH Mk.1 with 968 shp Rolls-Royce Nimbus turbine engines (derated to 685 shp). Another order was placed for 40 helicopters in September 1964.

The Scout was suited to all the tasks of a lightweight helicopter: observation, liaison, training, SAR. Several orders were also received from abroad: Royal Australian Navy (2), Royal Jordanian Air Force (3), Uganda (2) and Bahrain (2). The last two countries used them for police work. A total of 150 Scouts were built. Although its characteristics were not outstanding, the Scout fulfilled a role in the British Army which was played by the Bell 206 in many other armies, and has only recently been superseded by the Westland Lynx.

Development of the naval version of the Wasp proceeded more-or-less in parallel, but took longer. The Royal Navy used one of the prototypes, suitably modified with higher skids suitable for deck landings, and also ordered two P.531s powered by Nimbus turbine engines for deck landing and operational trials. The three aircraft performed exhaustive take-off and landing trials from the escort vessel HMS Undaunted in November 1959. The definitive Wasp was mainly intended for ASW from frigates of the Tribal and Leander classes and similar vessels; for this purpose it could carry one or two 122 kg (270 lb) torpedoes or 250 kg (550 lbs) of depth charges. In September 1961, the type was ordered for the Royal Navy under the name Wasp HAS Mk.1 (the first flew on 28 October 1962 with a 968 shp Nimbus engine derated to 710 shp) and went into service in October 1963, performing 200 day and night landings on HMS Nubian.

Helicopter: **Westland Scout AH Mk.1**
Manufacturer: **Westland Aircraft Ltd.**
Type: **5-seat general purpose**
Year: **1961**
Engine: **968 shp Rolls-Royce Bristol Nimbus Mk.503 turbine**
Rotor diameter: **9.83 m (32 ft 3 in)**
Fuselage length: **9.24 m (30 ft 4 in)**
Overall length: **12.29 m (40 ft 4 in)**
Height: **3.56 m (11 ft 8 in)**
Empty weight: **1,465 kg (3,230 lbs)**
Gross weight: **2,405 kg (5,300 lbs)**
Maximum speed: **211 km/h (130 mph)**
Service ceiling: **4,075 m (13,370 ft)**
Range: **510 km (317 miles)**

Helicopter: **Westland Wasp HAS Mk.1**
Manufacturer: **Westland Aircraft Ltd.**
Type: **antisubmarine**
Year: **1962**
Engine: **968 shp Rolls-Royce Nimbus Mk.503 turbine**
Rotor diameter: **9.83 m (32 ft 3 in)**
Fuselage length: **9.24 m (30 ft 4 in)**
Overall length: **12.29 m (40 ft 4 in)**
Height: **3.56 m (11 ft 8 in)**
Empty weight: **1,566 kg (3,452 lbs)**
Gross weight: **2,500 kg (5,511 lbs)**
Maximum speed : **193 km/h (120 mph)**
Hovering ceiling IGE: **3,810 m (12,500 ft)**
Service ceiling: **3,750 m (12,300 ft)**
Range: **488 km (303 miles)**
Armament: **2 Mk.44 torpedoes or 250 kg (550 lbs) weapon load**

The Saro P.531 was the predecessor of the Westland Wasp ASW helicopter, which entered service with the Royal Navy in 1964 and was later exported to South Africa, New Zealand, Brazil, the Netherlands and Indonesia.

The Wasp differed from the Scout mainly in the long-stroke landing gear with fully castoring wheels and the small tailplane on the starboard side of the tail rotor pylon. The main rotor and tail boom could be folded for stowage on board ship.

The Wasp, of which 63 were built, was primarily an antisubmarine helicopter in the ''killer'' role. It has been replaced by the Lynx in the Royal Navy but the following navies are still operating the Wasp: South Africa, Brazil, New Zealand, and Indonesia (which purchased ten second-hand aircraft from Holland when the latter's navy replaced its Wasp fleet with the Westland Lynx).

Westland Wessex

In 1956, Westland, who held the license to build the Sikorsky S-55, acquired the license for the more modern S-58. The powerplant of the latter was considered unsatisfactory and the British firm began a partial redesigning of the American aircraft to enable a 1,100 shp Napier Gazelle NGa. 11 turbine to be installed instead of the original 1,525 hp Wright R-1820-84 radial. Thus transformed, one might have assumed that the helicopter was underpowered, but the nature of turbine engines is such that it was in fact ideal. The slight loss of power was

The Westland Wessex in the tactical transport version for the Royal Air Force.

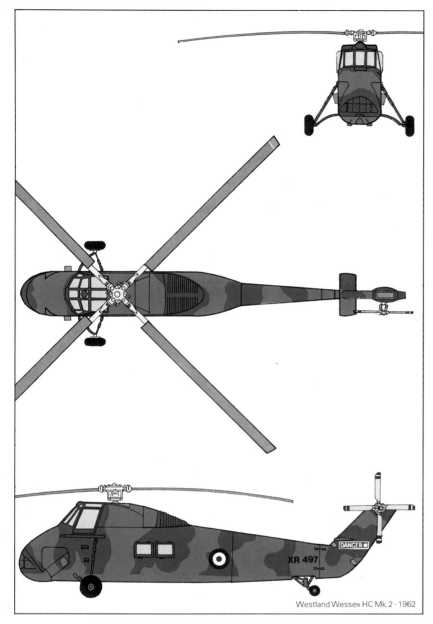

Westland Wessex HC Mk.2 - 1962

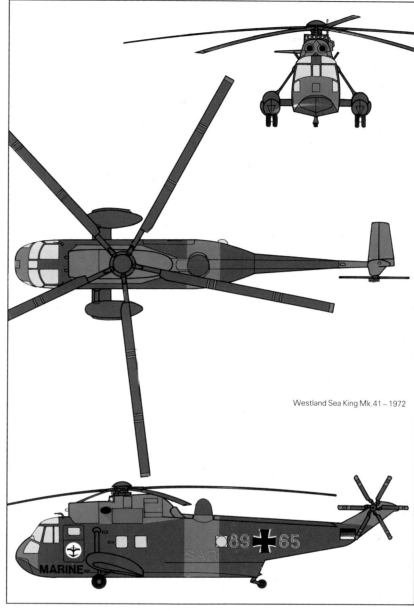

Westland Sea King Mk.41 – 1972

offset by greater reliability, a reduction in vibration and weight, easier maintenance and a lowering of specific fuel consumption.

The Royal Navy immediately ordered the new helicopter as the Wessex HAS Mk.1, to replace the older Whirlwind HAS Mk.7. The aircraft was basically similar to the Sikorsky S-58, but the nose profile was altered as a result of the installation of the turbine which, in the first production version, was a 1,450 shp Gazelle NGa.13. Later Wessex (Mk.2 and 5) were powered by twin Rolls-Royce Gnome engines and employed as troop transports. Westland built 356 Wessex in all (including those for the civil market): the HAS Mk.1 version for the Royal Navy; the HC Mk.2 tactical transport version for the RAF; the HAS Mk.3 antisubmarine version with 1,550 shp Gazelle NGa.18 turbine; the HU. Mk.5 for various roles

on the Navy's commando carriers; the HAS Mk.31 for the Royal Australian Navy; the Wessex Mk.52 for the Iraqui Navy (12); the Wessex Mk.53 for Ghana (3); the Wessex Mk.54 for Borneo and the Wessex Mk.60 commercial version.

Helicopter: **Westland Wessex HC Mk.2**
Manufacturer: **Westland Aircraft Ltd.**
Type: **tactical transport**
Year: **1962**
Engines: **2 × 1,250 shp Bristol Siddeley Gnome H.1200**
Rotor diameter: **17.07m (56 ft)**
Fuselage length: **14.74 m (48 ft 4 in)**
Overall length: **20.03 m (65 ft 8 in)**
Height: **4.93 m (16 ft 2 in)**
Empty weight: **3,842 kg (8,470 lbs)**
Gross weight: **6,124 kg (13,670 lbs)**
Maximum speed: **195 km/h (120 mph)**
Hovering ceiling IGE: **1,800 m (5,900 ft)**
Range: **770 km (478 miles)**
Capacity: **pilot + 16**

Westland Sea King

In 1959 Westland acquired the license to build the Sikorsky S-61B, to replace the Wessex in the antisubmarine role. The Royal Navy specification called for a British powerplant with different characteristics from the original one, different electronics and a wide range of mission capabilities. Westland adopted a pair of Rolls-Royce Bristol Gnome turbines for their version of the Sea King, with fully computerized controls and largely British-made ASW equipment. The resultant helicopter is readily identifiable by the dorsal radome of the all-weather search radar. Other avionics systems include Plessey dipping sonar, Marconi Doppler navigation radar and Sperry & Newmark instrumentation. With the two Gnome turbines and these avionics, the first HAS Mk.1 production Sea

Helicopter: **Westland Sea King Mk.41**
Manufacturer: **Westland Helicopters Ltd.**
Type: **search and rescue**
Year: **1972**
Engines: **2 × 1,250 shp Rolls-Royce Bristol Gnome H.1400 turbines**
Rotor diameter: **18.90 m (62 ft)**
Fuselage length: **17.02 m (55 ft 10 in)**
Overall length: **22.15 m (72 ft 8 in)**
Height: **4.85 m (15 ft 11 in)**
Empty weight: **5,613 kg (12,374 lbs)**
Gross weight: **9,300 kg (20,503 lbs)**
Maximum speed: **211 km/h (130 mph)**
Hovering ceiling IGE: **1,525 m (5,000 ft)**
Service ceiling: **3,050 m (10,000 ft)**
Range: **963 km (598 miles)**

King flew on 7 May 1969 and the first Royal Naval Squadron was formed the following August.

The Sea King is an antisubmarine helicopter with genuine all-weather capability and a fully-proven navigational and attack system. But it is not a truly amphibious vehicle, in that any length of time spent in water would irrevocably damage some items of equipment on the hull. It is therefore only designed to land on water in an emergency, the boat-type hull being guaranteed watertight for 15 minutes. The two lateral sponsons contain flotation bags to improve buoyancy. Standard ASW equipment includes two marker buoys, four smoke floats, four Mk.44 homing torpedoes or four depth charges. The Sea King can also carry out missions against surface vessels with one or two antiship missiles.

The following versions of the Sea King have been produced: Sea King HAS Mk.1, Mk.2 and Mk.5 for the Royal Navy; HAR Mk.3 (16 of the SAR version for the RAF); Sea King Mk.42 (24 for the Indian Navy), which was based on the RN version except for the communications equipment; Mk.41 for the German Navy (22); Mk.43 for the Norwegian Navy (11); Mk.45 for the Pakistani Navy (6); Mk.48 for the Belgian Air Force (5 of the SAR version); Mk.50 for the Australian Navy (12). A commando version has also been produced, of which 17 were initially delivered to the Royal Navy and at least another 30 to Egypt and Qater.

Westland Lynx

For a number of years, Westland manufactured anglicized Sikorsky-designed helicopters under license, usually with substantial modifications, but it was not until after the amalgamation of the British helicopter industry in 1959-61 that any original projects reached the hardware stage. In 1964, the Yeovil division began designing a family of military helicopters using the WG prefix, and the 13th model was based on the need to replace the Scout and Wasp used by the British forces, and to offer an alternative to the American Bell Huey, with more advanced technology.

Many components were clearly inspired by the success of the Scout and Wasp but the rotor, for example, was completely new, being of the semi-rigid type with blades of constant chord and cambered section. With these characteristics, it was possible to achieve very high tip speeds, as well as enhancing lift and reducing drag. The construction of the rotor blades was also technologically advanced, in that they had a honeycomb core and made extensive use of modern materials. The result was an aircraft which was up-to-date in terms of design and easier to maintain than comparable American aircraft. Thus it was Westland's strongest proposal for an agreement signed with

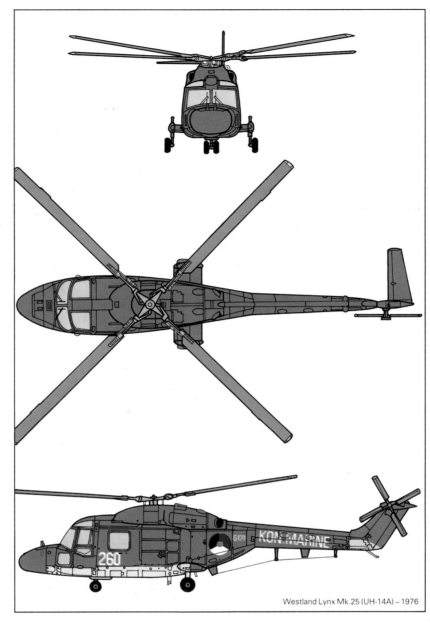

Westland Lynx Mk.25 (UH-14A) – 1976

Sud-Aviation in 1968.

The first Westland WG.13 was ready for flight testing on 21 March 1971 — rather later than foreseen. It was followed by four more aircraft in two basic configurations: the AH Mk.1 for the Army and the HAS Mk.2 for the Navy.

The Lynx demonstrated its capabilities by the records achieved in the summer of 1972. Piloted by Westland's chief test pilot Roy Moxam, it broke the world record over 15/25 km (9/15.5 miles) by flying at 321.74 km/h (200 mph), also setting a new 100 km (62 mile) closed circuit record shortly afterwards by flying at 318.504 km/h (198 mph).

The British Army ordered over 100 Lynx AH.1 for a variety of roles, from tactical transport to armed escort, antitank warfare (with eight TOW missiles), reconnaissance and casualty evacuation. A Marconi Elliott AFCS system is fitted to the Army's version of the Lynx, which

Helicopter: **Westland Lynx Mk.2**
Manufacturer: **Westland Helicopters Ltd.**
Type: **multipurpose**
Year: **1976**
Engines: **2 × 890 shp Rolls-Royce BS 360 Gem**
Rotor diameter: **12.80 m (42 ft)**
Fuselage length: **11.66 m (38 ft 3 in)**
Overall length: **15.16 m (49 ft 8 in)**
Height: **3.66 m (12 ft)**
Empty weight: **2,600 kg (5,732 lbs)**
Gross weight: **3,676 kg (8,104 lbs)**
Maximum speed: **270 km/h (168 mph)**
Hovering ceiling OGE: **2,950 m (9,678 ft)**
Range: **630 km (390 miles)**
Capacity: **10 troops or 2 torpedoes or 2 depth charges**

gives automatic stabilization on three axes and can also be used as an autopilot during extended flights. The naval version, unlike the ground-based version with skid landing gear, has a non-retractable quadricycle landing gear with oleopneumatic shock absorbers. The initial HAS Mk.2 version was ordered by both the Royal Navy and

the French Aéronavale, although they differed in their avionics, ASW equipment, and their armament (the former has four Sea Skua anti-ship missiles and the latter AS12 missiles). Uprating and other changes subsequently resulted in two distinct new variants, the HAS Mk.3 for the Royal Navy and the Mk.4 for the Aéronavale. Similar uprating for the British Army version has resulted in the AH Mk.5.

The Lynx has also met with considerable export success. After careful evaluation, it was chosen by the German Navy (12 ordered in 1981) for use on their new frigates, and six SAR and 18 ASW models have been ordered by the Royal Netherlands Navy. Other operators of the Lynx include Argentina, Brazil, Denmark, Norway, Nigeria and Qatar.

Westland Lynx 3

Derived from the latest Army and Navy variant of the standard Lynx, the Westland Lynx 3 is a stretched version, using the proven dynamic system and uprated Rolls-Royce Gem engines but with sufficient changes as to be virtually a new helicopter. The rotor system incorporates new composite main blades with paddle tips to increase efficiency by up to 40 per cent, whilst the tail rotor is similar to that of the Westland 30, rotating in the opposite direction to that on the original Lynx. The fuselage has been lengthened by 30 cm (11.8 in) to improve cabin volume and the tail boom is strengthened and similar to the boom of the Westland 30.

Two variants of the Lynx 3 are under development. The first is the Army Lynx 3 with an energy-absorbing wheeled undercarriage, mast-mounted sight, full day/night target and vision sensors, and the ability to carry a wide range of armament and other equipment. The prototype of this variant was under construction early in 1984. The second variant is the Navy Lynx 3 which dispenses with the mast-mounted sight and fits a navalized undercarriage.

Westland 30

The origins of the Westland 30, originally known as the WG-30 Super Lynx, go back to the sixties, when Westland was studying the possibility of a replacement for the Wessex and Whirlwind which were then in service with various civil and military operators.

After considering a civil version of the Lynx, the British company favoured a larger machine using many of the components of the

The Westland 30 which has been a commercial success on the civil market. The spacious cabin can seat 22 people.

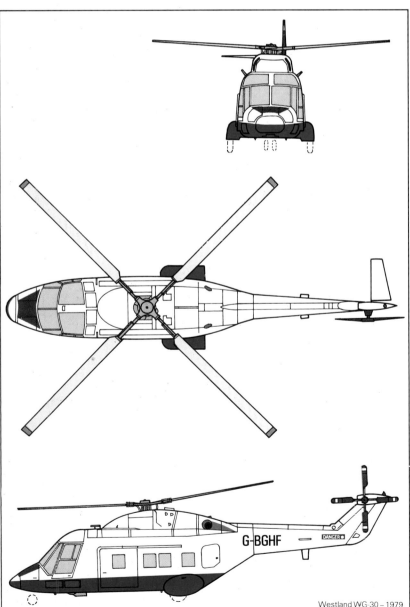

Westland WG-30 – 1979

Helicopter: Westland Lynx 3
Manufacturer: **Westland Helicopters Ltd.**
Type: **multipurpose**
Year: **1984**
Engines: **2 × 1,115 shp Rolls-Royce Gem 60**
Rotor diameter: **12.80 m (42 ft)**
Overall length: **15.47 m (50 ft 9 in)**
Height: **3.33 m (10 ft 11 in)**
Gross weight: **5,443 kg (12,000 lbs)**
Maximum speed: **259 km/h (161 mph)**
Range: **703 km (437 miles)**

Helicopter: Westland 30
Manufacturer: **Westland Helicopters Ltd.**
Type: **transport**
Year: **1979**
Engines: **2 × 1,060 shp Rolls-Royce Gem 41-1**
Rotor diameter: **13.31 m (43 ft 8 in)**
Fuselage length: **14.33 m (47 ft)**
Overall length: **15.90 m (52 ft 2 in)**
Height: **4.30 m (14 ft 1 in)**
Empty weight: **2,914 kg (6,424 lbs)**
Gross weight: **5,330 kg (11,750 lbs)**
Maximum speed: **250 km/h (155 mph)**
Hovering ceiling IGE: **2,195 m (7,200 ft)**
Range: **685 km (425 miles)**
Capacity: **2 pilots + 17/22 passengers**

military helicopter. Accordingly, the Westland 30 has the transmission, rotor blade structure, some systems and many instruments and accessories of the Lynx, but the fuselage is entirely new and is bigger, even if it resembles the Lynx aerodynamically. It is made wholly of aluminum with a traditional type of structure and skin, while composite materials are used in the tail boom. The landing gear is fixed and the main units are housed in two fairings at the sides of the aft fuselage. The fuel system comprises two 500 kg/630 liter tanks (1,102 lb/139 gallon) in the fuselage. The hydraulic system is similar to that of the Lynx as is the instrument panel with a few additions. The larger rotor should have a much longer service life than that of the Lynx on account of its slower rotational speed. Care has been taken to reduce vibrations in the fuselage.

The Westland 30 was originally intended for military use in the tactical transport and air ambulance roles, but the design has proved equally suitable for the civil market. In this role, the helicopter is approved for instrument flight, has optional airstair or sliding doors, and can take up to 22 passengers in the high density version in a comfortable, soundproofed cabin. Behind the cabin, which can be furnished to customers' requirements to carry VIPs, executives or freight, there is an ample baggage compartment reached from the rear of the fuselage. The capabilities of the Westland 30 for offshore work are particularly interesting: with a 250 km (155 mile) radius of action and 227 kg (500 lbs) fuel, the initial W30-100 variant can carry nine passengers on the outward journey and 13 on the homeward one. This type has been ordered by British Airways. In the military version, the same aircraft can carry 14 equipped troops or 17 without equipment, or six stretchers plus medical attendants.

The prototype of the Westland 30 made its first flight on 10 April 1979 in time for a successful appearance at the Paris Air Show that year. Production and delivery of W30-100 aircraft began in 1981. This version has now been superseded by the W30-160 with uprated Gem 60 engines. Westland is also now test-flying the W30-200 prototype, powered by 1,700 shp General Electric CT-7 engines, which are expected to much improve gross weight performance and payload in hot/high countries, and is also developing a new five-blade rotor system which is expected to appear on yet another new variant, the W30-300.

USSR STATE INDUSTRIES AND DESIGN BUREAUS

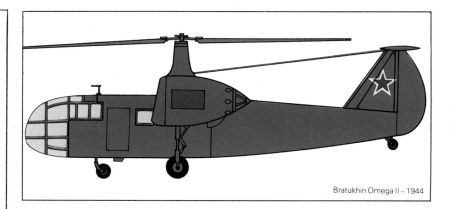
Bratukhin Omega II – 1944

The Soviet Central Institute for Aero-Hydrodynamics (TsAGI) was constituted in 1918 to develop Russian aviation expertise. B.N. Yuryev, a pioneer of vertical flight, was its director and in 1925 he began to develop helicopter designs. Although Yuryev was later transferred to other duties, by the end of 1930 his bureau had built the first TsAGI helicopter, designated 1-A. At the same time another team of designers, headed by Bratukhin, was developing an autogyro, the Model 2-A, based on La Cierva's ideas. Progress on these programmes was speeded up in the early 1930s when two famous designers, N.I. Kamov and M.C. Mil, joined the team.

Ivan Pavlovich Bratukhin was in charge of the helicopter design team of the TsAGI throughout the thirties and in 1941 he took over Yuryev's position in charge of the special OKB-3 department of the Moscow Aeronautical Institute. This unit built the Omega helicopter but when the project was reviewed in the late forties, Bratukhin's designs were abandoned and the OKB-3 was instructed to develop a helicopter which could rival the Yakovlev Yak-100 and the Mil Mi-1. From 1947 onwards Bratukhin worked on the B-11 and also on a large twin-engined transport, but neither of these went into series production.

Nikolai Ilich Kamov started work on an autogyro for the TsAGI in 1919, collaborating with N.K. Skrzhinsky in designing and constructing rotorcraft. After several programmes had been completed, a special projects division (OKB) was established in 1945, whose main brief was to carry out research into contra-rotating rotor systems, and an interesting series of military helicopters was developed. Kamov died in 1973 but his design studio continued to function under the direction of S. Mikhéev.

Mikhail Leontyevich Mil joined the TsAGI in 1931 after having completed his studies at the Novocheakassy Aeronautical Institute. During the Second World War he headed the experimental helicopter laboratory and lectured at the Kazan Aeronautical Technical Institute. Mil's OKB design studio was founded in December 1947 and has produced a very wide range of successful aircraft. After Mil's death in 1970, the design studio continued to operate with Mirat N. Tsischenko in charge.

Alexandir Sergeievich Yakovlev, one of Russia's most versatile designers and engineers, began his career in the engine division of the Zhukowsky Aeronautical Academy, graduating in 1931. He then joined the Soviet state aeronautical industry in factory number 39. His first project was the UT-2 competition two-seat sporting plane and his first military aircraft, the I-26 or Yak-1, flew in 1942. Yakovlev was an extremely prolific designer and towards the end of 1944 he decided to extend his interests to helicopter design and construction, building the Yak-24 Horse and the Yak-100. Most of the commissions received by his design bureau tended to concentrate on projects commissioned by the Soviet armed forces.

Bratukhin Omega

Ivan Bratukhin was one of the pioneers of helicopters in the Soviet Union, but he achieved no great success until 1940, when his team developed the 2MG Omega, a helicopter with contra-rotating, side-mounted rotors, similar in design to the German Focke-Achgelis Fa.61. The prototype flew in 1941 and proved stable, with a simple and reliable system of controls. In 1943, the institute decided to build a new version, known as the Omega II, with more powerful engines and a few minor modifications. The Omega II flew in 1944 and a few of them were seen at the Tushino air display in August 1946.

The subsequent G-3, developed as an artillery observation helicopter for the Army, flew in 1945. It was followed a few months later by the G-4, five of which were built between 1947 and 1948. The Bratukhin bureau developed other projects over the next two years, which retained the system of side-mounted rotors, driven directly by the engines.

Helicopter: **Bratukhin Omega II**
Manufacturer: **State Industry**
Type: **experimental**
Year: **1944**
Engines: **2 × 350 hp MG-31F**
Rotor diameter: **7.00 m (23 ft)**
Fuselage length: **8.20 m (26 ft 11 in)**
Overall length: **—**
Height: **3.24 m (10 ft 7 in)**
Empty weight: **1,760 kg (3,880 lbs)**
Gross weight: **2,050 kg (4,520 lbs)**
Maximum speed: **150 km/h (93 mph)**
Service ceiling: **3,000 m (9,842 ft)**

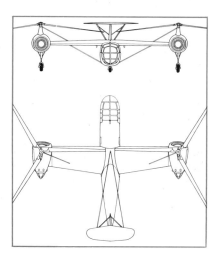

Kamov Ka-8

In attempting to produce a "flying motorcycle," or a light single-seat helicopter of the simplest possible structure, the Kamov bureau built the Ka-8 in 1947. It was derived from the Ka-17 designed two years earlier, making use of the system of twin coaxial, contra-rotating rotors which dispensed with the need for a tail rotor. The low output of the two-cylinder motorcycle engine and its unsuitability for aeronautical use handicapped the aircraft, and in fact only three were built. Engine: 44.8 hp M-76. Rotor diameter: 5.6 m (18 ft 4 in). Empty weight: 183 kg (403 lbs). Gross weight: 275 kg (606 lbs). Maximum speed: 80 km/h (50 mph). Service ceiling: 250 m (820 ft).

Kamov Ka-10 (Hat)

When the Ivchenko helicopter engine became available, it was possible to develop the Ka-8 into the Ka-10, with better flight characteristics and reliability. The first Ka-10 flew in September 1949. It was followed by three more prototypes and eight Ka-10M pre-production models; the latter were distinguished by the fact that they had a different rotor assembly and an endplate fin tail unit instead of the single fin of the Ka-10. These helicopters were tested at length, but did not enter production or service. Engine: 55 hp Ivchenko AI-4V. Rotor diameter: 6.12 m (20 ft). Fuselage length: 3.90 m (12 ft 10 in). Empty weight: 234 kg (516 lbs). Gross weight: 375 kg (827 lbs). Maximum speed: 90 km/h (56 mph). Service ceiling: 2,000 m (6,560 ft).

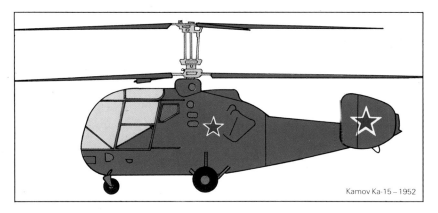

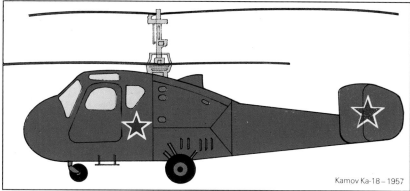

Kamov Ka-15 – 1952

Kamov Ka-18 – 1957

Kamov Ka-15 (Hen)

On the basis of past experience, whilst developing the Ka-10 "flying motorcycle," the design team also built a two-seat helicopter with an enclosed cabin and the same arrangements of coaxial, contra-rotating rotors and endplate fin tail unit, to meet a Soviet Naval Air Force specification. The new helicopter, designated Ka-15, flew towards the end of 1952 and went into production for the Soviet Navy and for civil operation as the Ka-15M. For military use, it could carry two depth charges on rails at the sides of the fuselage, which in the civil version were replaced by two stretchers or hoppers for agricultural chemicals. The powerplant was a 225 hp AI-14V air-cooled radial engine installed at the center of the fuselage, but towards the end of 1960, most Ka-15Ms were given uprated 275 hp AI-14VF engines. The NATO reporting name for the Ka-15 is Hen.

Helicopter: **Kamov Ka-15**
Manufacturer: **State Industry**
Type: **general purpose**
Year: **1952**
Engine: **225 hp AI-14V**
Rotor diameter: **9.96 m (32 ft 8 in)**
Fuselage length: **—**
Overall length: **—**
Height: **—**
Empty weight: **968 kg (2,134 lbs)**
Gross weight: **1,370 kg (3,020 lbs)**
Maximum speed: **150 km/h (93 mph)**
Hovering ceiling IGE: **680 m (2,230 ft)**
Service ceiling: **3,000 m (9,840 ft)**
Range: **300 km (186 miles)**
Capacity: **pilot + observer (2 stretchers)**
Armament: **depth charges**

Helicopter: **Kamov Ka-18**
Manufacturer: **State Industry**
Type: **general purpose**
Year: **1957**
Engine: **275 hp AI-14VF**
Rotor diameter: **9.96 m (32 ft 8 in)**
Fuselage length: **7.03 m (23 ft)**
Overall length: **—**
Height: **3.34 m (10 ft 11 in)**
Empty weight: **1,040 kg (2,293 lbs)**
Gross weight: **1,460 kg (3,218 lbs)**
Maximum speed: **150 km/h (93 mph)**
Hovering ceiling IGE: **680 m (2,230 ft)**
Service ceiling: **3,500 m (11,483 ft)**
Range: **400 km (248 miles)**

Kamov Ka-18 (Hog)

The Kamov Ka-18 (NATO reporting name Hog) was a four-seat development of the Ka-15M; it retained the same engine, rotor, transmission and control systems and landing gear. The main changes were to the fuselage, which was stretched to make room for two passengers and a baggage compartment. The prototype was completed in 1956 and flight testing began early in 1957. A limited number of the Ka-18 were built for use as air ambulances and for forestry patrol, geological survey and agricultural work. Towards the end of 1960, the production aircraft were given a 275 hp AI-14VF engine (VF stands for Vertolet Forsirovannie meaning helicopter with turbocharger) instead of the AI-14V, thus enabling the payload to be increased by about 100 kg (220 lbs) and the ceiling by 300-500 m (1,000-1,650 ft). The chord of the endplate fins was also enlarged.

The Ka-18 was evaluated but not adopted by the Soviet Air Force.

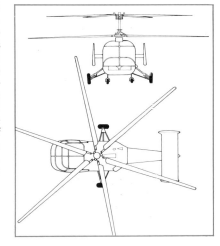

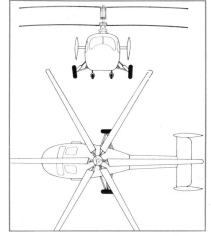

Kamov Ka-22 (Hoop)

The Ka-22 combined a square fuselage with a 20 m (65 ft 7 in) wing span. At the tips of the wings were two nacelles containing Ivchenko TB-2 engines delivering over 5,600 shp, each of which could power a 20 m (65 ft 7 in) four-blade rotor or four-blade tractor propeller. The fuselage was similar in size to the Antonov An-12 transport and could carry 100 passengers or a 16,000 kg (35,273 lb) load. The rotors apparently autorotated during horizontal flight. The Ka-22 (NATO reporting name Hoop) won the world speed record for rotary wing craft in October 1961 when it exceeded 365 km/h (227 mph). It was not mass produced.

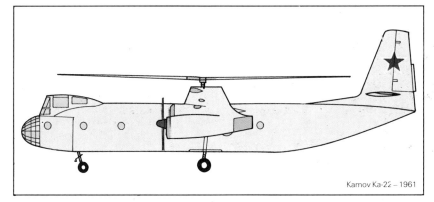

Kamov Ka-22 – 1961

Aircraft: **Kamov Ka-22**
Manufacturer: **State Industry**
Type: **experimental transport**
Year: **1961**
Engines: **2 × 5,620 shp Ivchenko TB-2**
Rotor diameter: **20.00 m (65 ft 7 in)**

Overall length: **23.00 m (75 ft 5 in)**
Height: **8.25 m (27 ft)**
Empty weight: **13,500 kg (29,762 lbs)**
Gross weight: **30,000 kg (66,138 lbs)**
Maximum speed: **365 km/h (227 mph)**
Capacity: **16,485 (36,343 lbs)**

Kamov Ka-25 (Hormone)

To meet a Soviet Naval Air Force specification in the late fifties for an antisubmarine helicopter for ship or shore-based use, the Kamov bureau developed a helicopter powered by twin turbines installed side-by-side above the cabin, which drove two three-bladed coaxial, contra-rotating rotors as on their other aircraft. It was first seen at the Tushino air display in July 1961 and was assigned the NATO reporting name Harp. The prototype may have been designated Ka-20.

The Harp was characterized by a large radome under the nose and a fairing beneath the tail boom. The armament consisted of two fixed machine guns in the nose and two small air-to-surface missiles (prob-

The Kamov Ka-25 is the Soviet Union's main shipboard antisubmarine helicopter. Unlike Western helicopters, the Hormone, which has a search radar under the nose, has all its droppable armament (depth charges and torpedoes) in a bay in the fuselage.

ably dummies) at the sides of the fuselage. The production version, designated Ka-25, differed from the prototype only in minor details, and was assigned the code name Hormone. About 460 were built between 1966 and 1975. They have replaced the piston-engined Mi-4s in the Soviet Navy and Naval Air Force and a few have been exported to Syria, India and Yugoslavia.

NATO now recognises two distinct variants of the Ka-25. The first, designated Hormone-A, is basically a ship-based and antisubmarine version operating from cruisers of the Kresta and Kara classes, Moskva and Leningrad carrier/cruisers and Kiev and Minsk ASW cruisers. The Moskva and Leningrad carrier/cruisers can carry about 18 Ka-25s; the larger Kiev and Minsk, about 30. Those of the Kara class carry three and the Kresta four (Kresta I) or five (Kresta II). Hormone-A has a search radar in a large fairing under the nose, and a towed magnetic anomaly detector (MAD), while a dipping sonar is housed in a compartment at the rear of the cabin. The helicopter also has electro-optical sensors. Some models have been seen with different types of fairings, probably containing submarine detection apparatus. Some have big hatches beneath the fusel-

age, enclosing a bay for antisubmarine torpedoes, nuclear depth charges or other types of weapons (probably air-to-surface guided missiles).

The second variant of the Ka-25, designated Hormone-B, has special electronic equipment for target spotting and guidance of surface-to-surface missiles. It has a larger more spherical radome under the nose and a cylindrical radome under the rear of the cabin. This variant has no ventral loading doors.

The Ka-25 normally has a crew of two pilots and two or three ASW equipment operators, but it also has

Helicopter: **Kamov Ka-25K**
Manufacturer: **State Industry**
Type: **flying crane**
Year: **1967**
Engines: **2 × 900 shp Glushnekov GTD-3**
Rotor diameter: **15.74 m (51 ft 8 in)**
Fuselage length: **9.83 m (32 ft 3 in)**
Overall length: **—**
Height: **5.37 m (17 ft 7 in)**
Empty weight: **4,400 kg (9,700 lbs)**
Gross weight: **7,300 kg (16,093 lbs)**
Maximum speed: **220 km/h (137 mph)**
Service ceiling: **3,500 m (11,485 ft)**
Range: **400 km (248 miles)**
Capacity: **12 passengers**

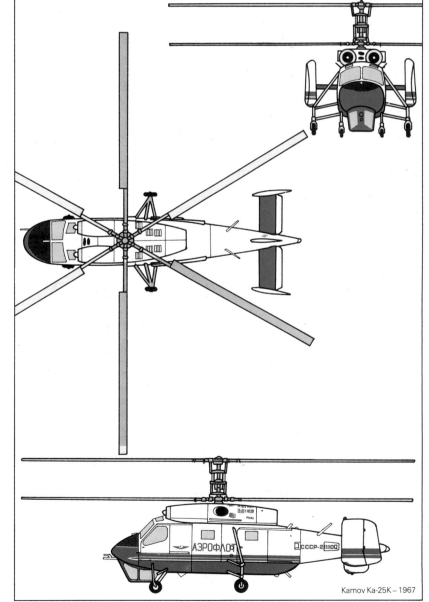

Kamov Ka-25K – 1967

secondary capability for troop transport, as the cabin is large enough to accommodate 12. Each of the four landing gear wheels can be enclosed by an inflatable pontoon surmounted by flotation bottles. This guarantees buoyancy if the aircraft is forced to ditch.

A civil variant of the Ka-25, designated Ka-25K, was displayed at the Paris Air Show in 1967. Designed for use as a flying crane, it had a gondola under the nose (in place of the fairing for the search radar of the military version), with a rearward-facing pilot seat for controlling loading and unloading operations in the hover. A hatch was provided in the cabin floor for a cable to be lowered by winch. The cabin could take either a maximum load of 2,000 kg (4,409 lbs), 12 passengers or four stretchers and an attendant. This variant was not put into production or service.

Kamov Ka-26 (Hoodlum)

The Ka-26, designed at the beginning of the sixties, is built for maximum simplicity and versatility as a "lifting system" consisting of the powerplant, contra-rotating rotor assembly, cabin, landing gear and twin endplate fin tail unit. Loads and containers of various kinds can be installed immediately behind the cabin, beneath the rotors: a pod for six passengers, an open platform, tanks for liquid or solid insecticides or other products, and spray bars for agricultural use. A variant for geophysical survey is equipped with an electromagnetic pulse generator in the cabin and a big hoop antenna outside. Thanks to its compactness and stability, the Ka-26 can operate from small platforms and has been fitted with floats and used for fish-spotting.

The Ka-26 went into service on a large scale in 1970 and has been exported for both civil and military use.

Mil Mi-1 (Hare) and Mi-2 (Hoplite)

The Mi-1, initially designated GM-1 (Gelikopter Mil, or Mil helicopter) was the first production Russian helicopter to enter service with the Soviet armed forces. Development of this aircraft started shortly after the end of the war and the first of three prototypes flew in September 1948; delivery of the production models began in 1951.

The Mi-1 was a four-seat general purpose helicopter. It was replaced in the final production runs by the Mi-1T, a three-seater with different operational equipment. A dual control trainer version was designated Mi-1U.

Once military requirements had been met by a production run of several hundred, the Mi-1 was also widely adopted for a great variety of civil tasks, such as air ambulance duties, fish-spotting or whaling, ice patrol in polar regions, highway patrol and for carrying mail.

An agricultural variant, designated Mi-1NKh, could carry 400 kg (882 lbs) or 500 liters (110 gallons) of chemicals in two hoppers at the sides of the fuselage. In 1961, the Mi-1 Moskvich passenger version was developed for Aeroflot, with an all-metal rotor, hydraulic controls, better cabin soundproofing and night flying or all-weather instrumentation. In 1956, a prototype (erroneously indentified in the West as Mi-3) was also evaluated. This had a four-blade rotor and various other external modifications, such as two lateral stretcher panniers, but it did not enter production.

Numerous Mi-1s were exported to allies of the Soviet Union, for both civil and military use, and many are still in service. From 1955, they were also produced in Poland by WSK-Swidnik, with the designation SM-1, and were built in various different versions. Most of the Polish helicopters were for export. The SM-1 provided a model for development of the SM-2, which had a stretched fuselage to accommodate five, and was produced from 1961. Production of the Mi-1 ended in 1961 in the Soviet Union and in 1965 in Poland.

Helicopter: **Mil Mi-1**
Manufacture: **State Industry**
Type: **general purpose**
Year: **1948**
Engine: **575 hp AI-26V**
Rotor diameter: **14.35 m (47 ft 1 in)**
Fuselage length: **12.10 m (39 ft 8 in)**
Overall length: —
Height: **3.30 m (10 ft 10 in)**
Empty weight: **1,880 kg (4,145 lbs)**
Gross weight: **2,404 kg (5,300 lbs)**
Maximum speed: **170 km/h (105 mph)**
Hovering ceiling IGE: —
Service ceiling: **3,000 m (9,842 ft)**
Range: **580 km (360 miles)**
Capacity: **pilot + 3 passengers**

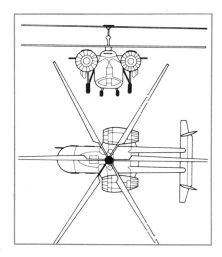

Helicopter: **Kamov Ka-26**
Manufacturer: **State Industry**
Type: **light general purpose**
Year: **1965**
Engines: **2 × 325 hp Vedeneev M-14V-26**
Rotor diameter: **13.00 m (42 ft 8 in)**
Fuselage length: **7.75 m (25 ft 5 in)**
Overall length: —
Height: **4.05 m (13 ft 3 in)**
Empty weight: **1,950 kg (4,300 lbs)**
Gross weight: **3,000 kg (6,614 lbs)**
Maximum speed: **170 km/h (105 mph)**
Service ceiling: **3,000 m (9,842 ft)**
Range: **400 km (248 miles)**
Capacity: **6 passengers or 900/1,000 kg (1,984/2,204 lbs).**

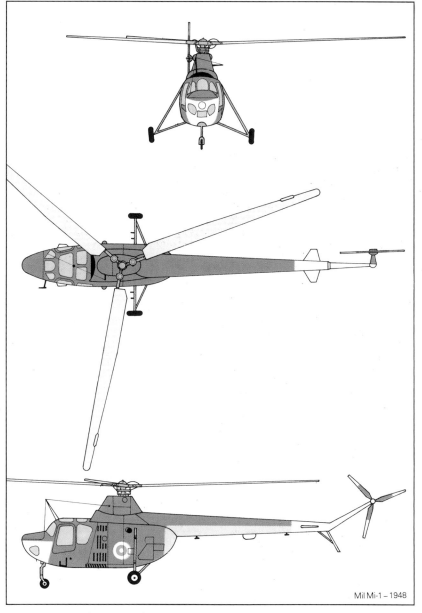

Mil Mi-1 – 1948

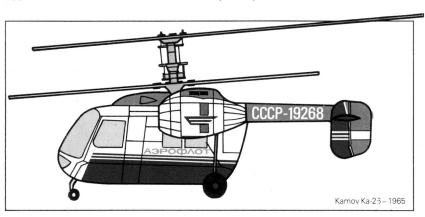

Kamov Ka-26 – 1965

In the mid fifties, the Mil bureau decided to improve the performance of the Mi-1 by developing a turbine-powered version. Two of the new Isotov GTD-350 free-turbine engines were chosen. A free-turbine engine enables the r.p.m. of the rotor to be varied, whilst those of the engine are kept constant. For half the weight of the earlier piston engine, the two GTD-350 developed 40 per cent more power. They were installed side-by-side above the fuselage, considerably increasing the available cabin space. The first prototype, designated V-2 and then Mi-2, flew in September 1961; it had the same rotor, transmission and tail unit as the Mi-1. After preliminary trials, a metal tail rotor was adopted (the Mi-1 had a wooden one) and later, from 1965, a new main rotor hub derived from that of the Mi-6.

As the Russian plants were fully occupied with production of the Mi-8 and other heavy helicopters in the Mil series, an agreement was reached with WSK-Swidnik to manufacture the Mi-2 in Poland, and they took over production and development rights in 1964. The first Polish Mi-2 had flown before this in November 1963, and once trials were completed, large-scale production began in 1965. The first production aircraft had 400 shp engines, but from 1974 these were uprated to 450 shp. Another modification was the use of fiberglass materials for the main rotor, tail rotor and stabilizer, to simplify production and improve performance.

Various versions of the Mi-2 have been built for civil and military use. One in service with the Polish Air Force is equipped with rocket launchers and air-to-ground missiles, slung from rails at the sides of the fuselage. The Mi-2 is still in production. Most of the aircraft built have been exported to the Soviet Union and other Warsaw Pact countries.

Helicopter: **Mil Mi-2**
Manufacturer: **State Industry**
Type: **light general purpose**
Year: **1961**
Engines: **2 × 400 shp Isotov GTD-350P**
Rotor diameter: **14.56 m (47 ft 9 in)**
Fuselage length: **11.94 m (39 ft 2 in)**
Overall length: **17.42 m (57 ft 2 in)**
Height: **3.75 m (12 ft 4 in)**
Empty weight: **2,370 kg (5,225 lbs)**
Gross weight: **3,700 kg (8,157 lbs)**
Maximum speed: **210 km/h (130 mph)**
Hovering ceiling IGE: **2,000 m (6,560 ft)**
Service ceiling: **4,000 m (13,125 ft)**
Range: **170 km/h (105 miles)**
Capacity: **pilot + 8 passengers or 700 kg (1,543 lbs)**
Armament: **missiles or rockets**

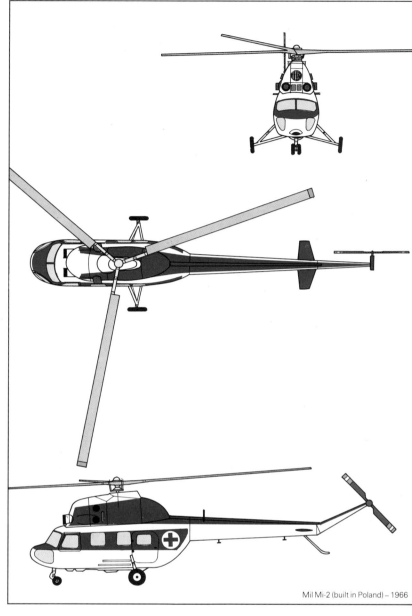

Mil Mi-2 (built in Poland) – 1966

Civil Mi-2 helicopters have been used by Aeroflot.

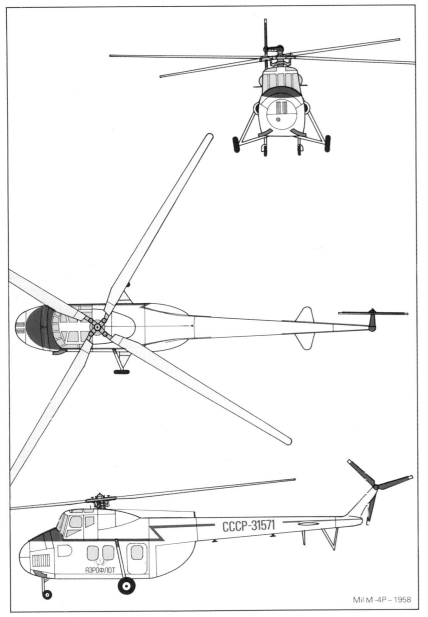

Mil M-4P – 1958

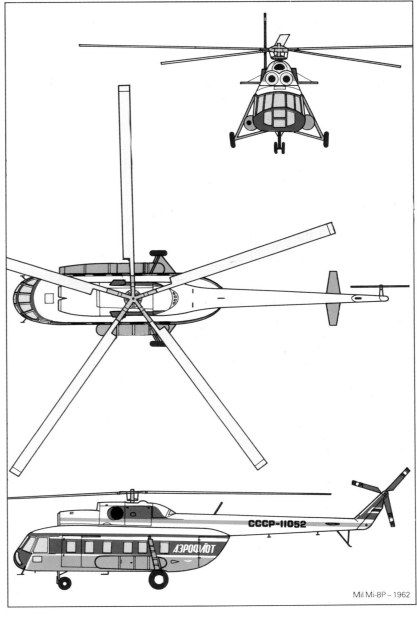

Mil Mi-8P – 1962

Mil Mi-4 (Hound) and Mi-8 (Hip)

The Mi-4 was the second Mil project to enter large-scale production. Several thousand have been built in both military and civil configurations, operating in the Soviet Union and various other countries. It has now been replaced in its original transport and antisubmarine roles by more modern, turbine-powered machines but many are still in service with support units.

The Mi-4 was first seen in public in August 1953, but it had made its first flight and entered production the year before. The first few years' output was exclusively for military use. In the basic version, NATO reporting name Hound-A, the Mi-4 is a transport helicopter, with a crew of two and provision for observer in a gondola beneath the forward fuselage. The engine is installed in the nose, leaving ample room in the

Helicopter: **Mil Mi-4P**
Manufacturer: **State Industry**
Type: **transport and general purpose**
Year: **1958**
Engine: **1,700 hp Shvetsov Ash-82V**
Rotor diameter: **21.00 m (68 ft 11 in)**
Fuselage length: **16.80 m (55 ft 1 in)**
Overall length: —
Height: **5.18 m (17 ft)**
Empty weight: **5,268 kg (11,614 lbs)**
Gross weight: **7,800 kg (17,195 lbs)**
Maximum speed: **210 km/h at 1,500 m (155 mph at 4,920 ft)**
Service ceiling: **5,500m (18,045 ft)**
Range: **250 km (155 miles)**
Capacity: **8-11 passengers or 1,600 kg (3,527 lbs)**

cabin to accommodate up to 14 combat equipped troops, small vehicles or 1,600 kg (3,527 lbs) of supplies. Access to the cabin is facilitated by rear loading doors. A lot of these aircraft have been delivered to the VVS and a close support version was also produced, with a machine gun at the front of the gondola and rails for air-to-

surface rockets on either side of the fuselage. The Mi-4 has also been used by the Soviet Naval Air Force for antisubmarine duties. In this version (Hound B), it has an under-nose search radar in front of the gondola, and a dipping sonar, which is stowed at the rear of the fuselage beneath the root of the tail boom when not in use. Another variant, designated Hound C, is designed for ECM and has broad lateral antennae and jamming apparatus. The Hound-A has been exported to virtually all the countries of the East European bloc and a number of others worldwide. Large numbers have also been produced in China.

A civil variant of the basic Mi-4 version has been produced for Aeroflot, for general use and freight transport; this was followed by the Mi-4P for passenger transport, which lacks the ventral gondola,

Helicopter: **Mil Mi-8P**
Manufacturer: **State Industry**
Type: **assault transport**
Year: **1962**
Engines: **2 × 1,500 shp Isotov TV2-117**
Rotor diameter: **21.29 m (69 ft 10 in)**
Fuselage length: **18.31 m (60 ft)**
Overall length: **25.24 m (82 ft 10 in)**
Height: **5.65 m (18 ft 6 in)**
Empty weight: **7,417 kg (16,350 lbs)**
Gross weight: **12,000 kg (26,455 lbs)**
Maximum speed: **230 km/h (143 mph)**
Hovering ceiling IGE: **1,320 m (4,330 ft)**
Service ceiling: **4,500 m (14,765 ft)**
Range: **360 km (224 miles)**
Capacity: **28 passengers**

and has a better finish and rectangular side windows in place of the round, military type. The Mi-4P, which went into regular service with Aeroflot in November 1958, can carry up to 11 passengers or eight stretchers and a medical attendant for ambulance duties. The special agricultural version is designated Mi-4S. It can carry a container in the cabin holding 1,000

113

kg (2,205 lbs) of solid insecticide or 1,600 liters (352 gallons) in liquid form, plus dusting or spraying equipment. Although less common than the military one, the civil version has been used in various East European countries.

At the end of the fifties, the Soviet helicopter industry underwent a process of renewal with the introduction of turbine engines. This led to the Mi-8, a successor to the Mi-4 which was developed parallel with the Mi-2 (derived from the Mi-1). The Mi-8 was seen in public for the first time in 1961. It was powered by a 2,700 shp Soloviev turbine, mounted on the cabin roof, and used the rotor, transmission and tail boom of the Mi-4. The fuselage was new, with the pilot seats at the front instead of over the cabin. A second prototype, which flew in September 1962, was powered by two 1,500 shp Isotov TV2s and the Mi-8 entered production in this form. It was later given a five-blade rotor instead of the four-blade system inherited from the Mi-4.

Production of the Mi-8 amounts to several thousand for civil and military use. Together with the Mi-24, the type is now standard equipment for Russia's tactical helicopter regiments and military versions have been exported worldwide.

The commercial variant of the Mi-8, which has large, rectangular windows instead of the round ones of the military version, is used by Aeroflot for various tasks. Three civil variants are known at present: the standard Mi-8P for 28-32 passengers; the general purpose Mi-8T normally used for freight, but with room for 24 passengers on tip-up seats along the cabin walls; and the Mi-8 Salon, a deluxe version for 11 passengers.

The military versions identified by NATO (apart from the prototypes Hip-A and Hip-B) include the Hip-C basic transport and assault version, with double rails at the sides of the cabin for rocket launchers or other weapons; the Hip-D with rectangular containers on external rails and supplementary antennae for electronic warfare; the Hip-E with fairly heavy armament, which is standard equipment for the Russian tactical forces; and the Hip-F, the export version of the Hip-E, armed with six Sagger antitank missiles. Twenty of these transport aircraft can land a battalion of 550 men and, thanks to the large rear loading doors, they can carry small reconnaissance vehicles. Versions of the Mi-8 are in service with many Warsaw Pact countries. In 1981, a new, improved version of the Mi-8 was identified, designated Mi-17. This is powered by two TV3-117MT turbines, each delivering 1,900 shp (2,200 shp on take-off).

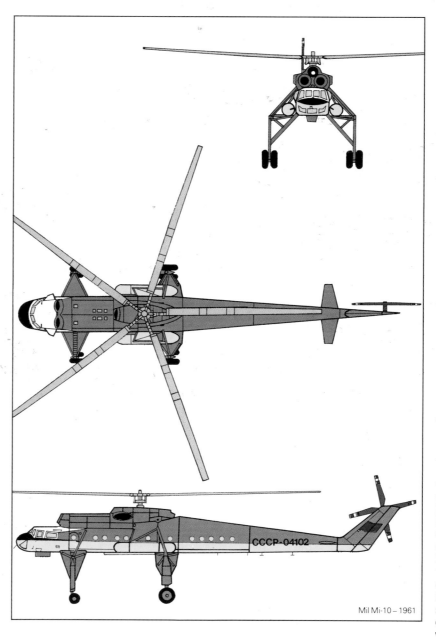

Mil Mi-10 – 1961

Mil Mi-6 (Hook), Mi-10 (Harke) and Mi-10K

The Mi-6, which was the largest helicopter in the world for about 12 years, was also the first turbine-powered Russian helicopter and the first twin-turbine in the world. Work on it began in the mid fifties, and the first of five prototypes flew in autumn 1957.

Production started in 1960 with an initial batch of 30, followed by more than 800 others for both civil and military use. The Mi-6 is used for tactical assault by the Russian armed forces and can carry troops, supplies and entire missile or artillery units. Aeroflot use it both for passenger transport and freight services to remote areas, and as a flying crane for various kinds of work, e.g. laying oil pipelines or pylons, assembling oil rigs, bridge-building. The large cargo hold measuring 12 m long with a maximum width of 2.65 m and a maximum height of 2.5 m (39 ft 4 in × 8ft 8 in × 8 ft 2 in) has a floor capable of supporting a 2,000 kg/m² (409.82 lb/ft²) load, and can carry various types of vehicles or 65-90 passengers, or 41 stretchers and two medical attendants when the helicopter is used as an air ambulance. Bulky loads up to a maximum of eight tonnes can be slung from an external cargo hook. An electric winch can lift up to 500 kg (1,102 lbs) with the aircraft in the hover.

In the fire-fighting version, the Mi-6 can discharge 12 tonnes of water or liquid retardents through the floor in 20 seconds, or more slowly, through two sets of four nozzles. For use as a flying crane or fire-fighter, the two stub wings normally fitted to the aircraft on either side of the fuselage just below and behind the rotor hub are absent. These have a 15 m (49 ft 2 in) span and are detachable. During cruising flight, they can provide 20 per cent of the aircraft's total lift.

The Mi-6, which was the first helicopter to exceed 300 km/h (186 mph), has set no fewer than 14 world records on various occasions in the FAI's E-1 category. These include lifting a 25,105 kg (55,346 lb) load to an altitude of 2,840 m (9,317 ft) and achieving 340.15 km/h (211.36 mph) over a 100 km (62 mile) closed circuit. In addition to allocations to the Soviet armed forces, the Mi-6 has been supplied to the government of Peru and the air forces of Bulgaria, Egypt, Iraq, Indonesia, Syria and Vietnam.

The Mi-10 made its first appearance at the Tushino air display in 1961. Designed as a flying crane, it differs from the Mi-6 in that it has a slimmer fuselage, no auxiliary wings and, notably, a large, tall undercarriage with a track of over 6 m (19 ft 8 in) and ground clearance of 3.75 m (12 ft 4 in), making it possible to load up on the ground using a special wheeled platform if necessary, which can be locked by hydraulic struts. Even outsize loads like prefabricated houses can be carried. The hydraulic struts, without the platform, enable items up to 20 m (65 ft 7 in) long and 10 m (32 ft 10 in) wide to be lifted. The cabin can take an additional load or up to 28 passengers. Closed-circuit television permits visual control of the external load and landing gear, which is particularly important during touch-down. The Mi-10 is in service with Aeroflot and the Russian armed forces; a few have been exported to Iraq. About 55 had been produced by 1978.

The final derivative of the Mi-6 is the Mi-10K, seen in public on 26 March 1966. This differs from the Mi-10 in that it has much shorter landing gear and a thinner tail rotor

Helicopter: **Mil Mi-10**
Manufacturer: **State Industry**
Type: **flying crane**
Year: **1961**
Engines: **2 × 5,500 shp Soloviev D-25V turbines**
Rotor diameter: **35.00 m (114 ft 10 in)**
Fuselage length: **32.86 m (107 ft 10 in)**
Overall length: **41.89 m (137 ft 5 in)**
Height: **9.90 m (32 ft 6 in)**
Empty weight: **27,000 kg (59,525 lbs)**
Gross weight: **43,450 kg (95,790 lbs)**
Maximum speed: **202 km/h (125 mph)**
Service ceiling: **3,000 m (9,840 ft)**
Range: **250 km (155 miles)**
Capacity: **28 passengers; 11,000 kg maximum slung load (24,250 lbs)**

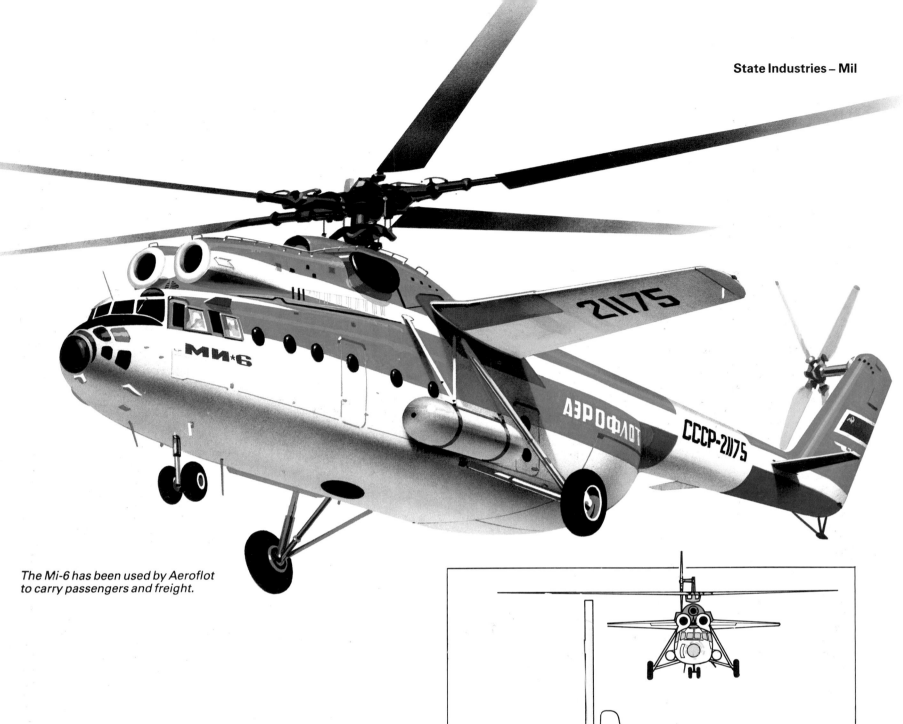

The Mi-6 has been used by Aeroflot to carry passengers and freight.

support structure. A glazed gondola is fixed beneath the nose, with a rearward-facing pilot seat. From this position, the occupant can control the helicopter during hovering and superintend loading and unloading. The maximum payload is 11,000 kg (24,250 lbs), but this can be increased to 14,000 kg (30,864 lbs) by installing Soloviev D-25VF engines, each of which yield 6,500 shp.

Helicopter: Mil Mi-6
Manufacturer: **State Industry**
Type: **heavy assault transport**
Year: **1957**
Engines: **2 × 5,500 shp Soloviev D-25V turbines**
Rotor diameter: **35.00 m (114 ft 10 in)**
Fuselage length: **33.18 m (108 ft 10 in)**
Overall length: **41.74 m (136 ft 11 in)**
Height: **9.86 m (32 ft 4 in)**
Empty weight: **27,240 kg (60,053 lbs)**
Gross weight: **42,500 kg (93,695 lbs)**
Maximum speed: **300 km/h (186 mph)**
Service ceiling: **4,500 m (14,764 ft)**
Range: **620 km (385 miles)**
Capacity: **65-90 passengers or 12,000 kg (26,455 lbs)**

Mil Mi-12 (Homer)

The Mil Mi-12, known as V-12 in the Soviet Union, and by the NATO reporting name Homer, is so far the only helicopter produced by the Mil bureau to depart from the single main rotor plus tail rotor formula. It is to date the world's largest helicopter and flew for the first time in 1968, but did not enter production. The second prototype, which was presented in the West at the 1971 Paris Air Show, set seven load-carrying records in 1969: in February, a 31,030 kg (68,408 lb) load was lifted to 2,951 m (9,681 ft) and the following August, 40,204 kg (88,634 lbs) was taken to 2,255 m (7,398 ft).

The Mi-12 project was started in 1965 with the aim of producing a vertical take-off aircraft capable of carrying missiles or other loads compatible with those of the four-engine AN-22. The bureau chose the side-by-side rotor formula

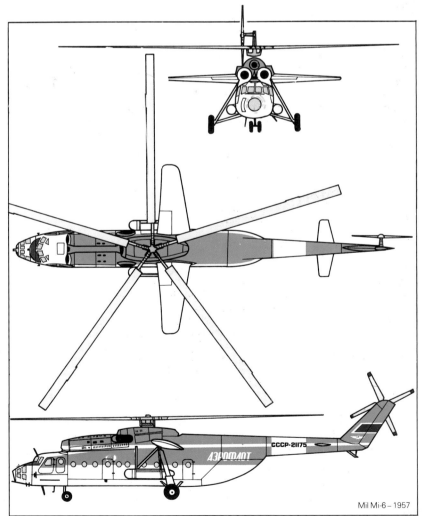

Mil Mi-6 – 1957

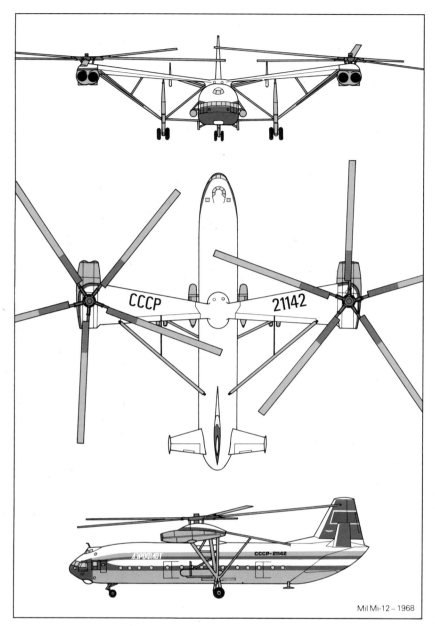

Mil Mi-12 – 1968

wheels on each unit. A large end-plate fin tail unit was mounted at the rear of the fuselage, with moving vertical and horizontal surfaces.

As well as being designed for military use, the Mi-12 was probably intended for service with Aeroflot, especially for deployment in areas of Siberia which are rich in resources but which have very poor communications. Technical problems were almost certainly responsible for development of this aircraft being abandoned in favour of the Mi-26.

Mil Mi-14 (Haze)

Very little is known as yet of the Mil Mi-14, a derivative of the Mi-8, which is now in service with the shore-based units of the Soviet Naval Air Force and in Libya. It appears to have been tested in the Soviet Union at the beginning of 1974, entering service in 1975, and is now in full-scale production. It differs from the Mi-8 in that it has a watertight hull with sponsons and marine-type rudders on either side of the aft portion, into which the rear landing gear units retract. A fairing for the search radar is fitted under the nose, and a dipping sonar or magnetic anomaly detector beneath the root of the tail boom. In all probability, the Mi-14 can be used for over-the-horizon target designation, guidance of surface-to-surface missiles and for search and rescue. It probably has a bomb bay for antisubmarine torpedoes, depth charges and other weapons.

Helicopter: **Mil Mi-14**
Manufacturer: **State Industry**
Type: **amphibious antisubmarine**
Year: **1976**
Engines: **2 × 1,500 shp Isotov TV-2 turbines**
Rotor diameter: **21.29 m (69 ft 10 in)**
Fuselage length: **18.15 m (59 ft 6 in)**
Overall length: **—**
Height: **—**
Empty weight: **—**
Gross weight: **12,000 kg (26,455 lbs)**
Maximum speed: **230 km/h (143 mph)**
Hovering ceiling IGE: **1,600 m (5,250 ft)**
Range: **200 km (124 miles)**
Armament: **torpedoes, depth charges**

Mil Mi-24 (Hind)

The Mi-24 was the first helicopter to enter service with the Russian Air Force in the combined role of assault transport and helicopter gunship. It was first seen in 1973 with the Russian forces stationed in East Germany, and has been widely distributed to Warsaw Pact countries and other allies of the Soviet Union. Many of these helicopters have been used in Afghanistan since December 1979.

There are two main versions of the Mi-24, which has been given the NATO reporting name Hind; one is primarily intended as an assault transport aircraft (yet is capable of carrying a formidable armament), and the other is a helicopter gunship for engaging other helicopters in air-to-air combat, with secondary transport capability.

Thus far, NATO has identified five different versions of the Mi-24. They

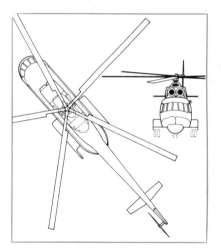

in order to use the engine-transmission-rotor assembly of the helicopters of the Mi-6/Mi-10 series with minimal modifications. Two of these assemblies were in fact mounted at the tips of the two short wings, which had an inverse taper from the root to the wingtips. The engines were 6,500 shp Soloviev D-25VF turbines giving the helicopter a maximum speed of 260 km/h (161 mph), with a 35,400 kg (78,000 lb) load and 500 km (310 mile) range. The large cargo hold measuring 28.15 m long by 4.4 m (92 ft 4 in × 14 ft 5 in) wide could take various kinds of loads, including very bulky ones, as well as troops or handling crews. The fuselage had a conventional, semi-monocoque structure, with large

clamshell loading doors at the rear to facilitate handling of bulky loads. The flight deck was on the upper floor of the cabin and there were six crewmembers. On the ground, the helicopter was supported by large, fixed tricycle landing gear with two

Helicopter: **Mil Mi-12**
Manufacturer: **State Industry**
Type: **heavy general purpose**
Year: **1968**
Engines: **4 × 6,500 shp Soloviev D-25VF turbines**
Rotor diameter: **35.00 m (114 ft 10 in)**
Fuselage length: **37.00 m (121 ft 4 in)**
Overall length:—
Height: **12.50 m (41 ft)**
Empty weight: —
Gross weight: **105,000 kg (231,483 lbs)**
Maximum speed: **260 km/h (162 mph)**
Service ceiling: **3,500 m (11,485 ft)**
Range: **500 km (310 miles)**
Capacity: **35,400 kg (78,043 lbs) or 50 passengers**

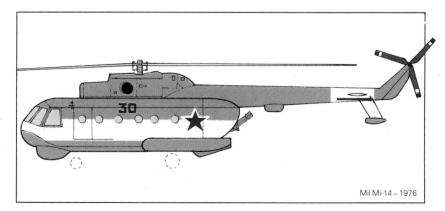

Mil Mi-14 – 1976

The Mi-24 tactical assault transport has been built in many versions with heavy armament.

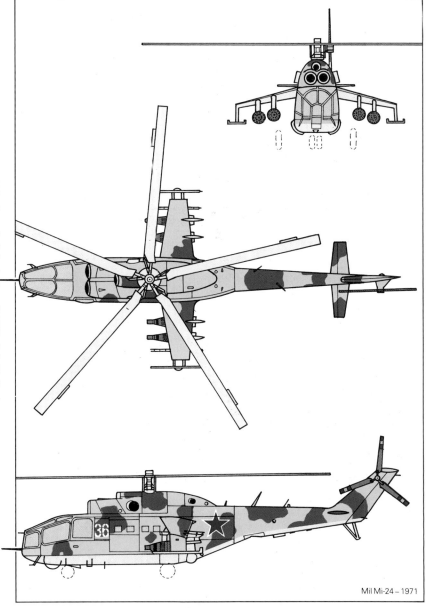

share a common basic structure, powerplant and transmission, but differ in their armament, operational equipment and tail rotor configuration. The armed versions also have a cabin with a double canopy at the front. The known versions are:

Hind-A: Assault helicopter, with an extensively-glazed front section for the four crewmembers (pilot, copilot, gunner/navigator and forward observer). It is presumably designed to land squads of troops, keeping enemies at bay with its weapons. It can also attack armoured vehicles, including tanks. The auxiliary wings, which have a strong angle of incidence and marked anhedral, each carry three weapons stations for missiles or rockets. A machine gun is housed in the nose, with a chin-mounted sighting system. On the first example of the Hind-A, the anti-torque rotor was on the starboard side of the tail pylon, while in more recent examples and on modified aircraft, it has been moved to the port side.

Hind-B: Similar to the Hind-A but with wings without dihedral and with only two weapons stations on each stub wing. The tail rotor is on the starboard side of the tail unit.

This version, which has been built in limited numbers, very probably preceded the Hind-A into production and service.

Hind-C: Basically similar to the Hind-A, but without the machine gun at the front, the fairing under the nose and the missile rails beneath the wingtips. The tail rotor is on the port side.

Hind-D: Basically similar to the late production Hind-A, with the tail rotor on the port side, this variant of the Mi-24 has a completely redesigned nose for use as a helicopter gunship. The two crew (pilot and machine gunner) are seated in tandem under separate canopies.

Helicopter: **Mil Mi-24 (Hind-A)**
Manufacturer: **State Industry**
Type: **assault**
Year: **1971**
Engines: **2 × 2,200 shp Isotov Tv-3-117 turbines**
Rotor diameter: **17.00 m (55 ft 9 in)**
Fuselage length: **—**
Overall length: **17.00 m (55 ft 9 in)**
Height: **4.25 m (13 ft 11 in)**
Empty weight: **4,700 kg (10,362 lbs)**
Gross weight: **10,000 kg (22,046 lbs)**
Maximum speed: **270 km/h (168 mph)**
Armament: **1 machine gun, 4 antitank missiles + rockets; weapon load: 1,275 kg (2,810 lbs)**

Mil Mi-24 – 1971

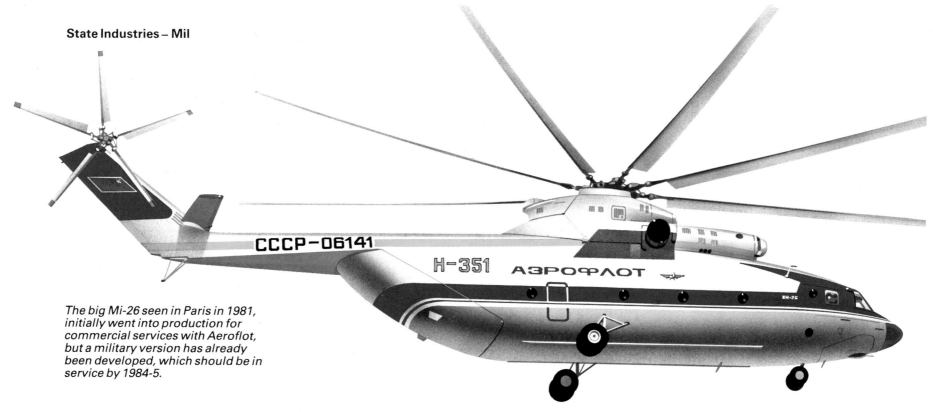

The big Mi-26 seen in Paris in 1981, initially went into production for commercial services with Aeroflot, but a military version has already been developed, which should be in service by 1984-5.

The pilot sits behind and higher up for a better field of view, while the gunner, who is protected by a bullet-proof windscreen in the forward cockpit, operates a large caliber machine gun with four rotating barrels, which is installed in a turret under the nose and allows a wide air-to-air and air-to-surface field of fire. Various types of sensors for use in poor visibility are also located beneath the nose, and probably include radar, high-resolution low light level TV cameras, and possibly infra-red sensors. The Hind-D has the same wing armament as the Hind-A, plus a long probe at the top right-hand side of the forward canopy, which is probably part of a low airspeed precision measuring device to assist the firing of 57 mm rockets. A number of blisters and antennae project from the fuselage and tail boom.

Hind-E: Similar to the Hind-D and intended for the Soviet armed forces, it has been strengthened by replacing a few critical components made of aluminum by others in steel or titanium. The armament includes the very modern Spiral laser-guided antitank missiles, of the "fire and forget" type, instead of the wire-guided Swatters.

Finally, the existence of another armed version developed from the Hind-D now seems certain, which has improved armament and is designated Hind-F. It has also been established that the helicopter referred to by the Russian authorities as the A-10, which has established various absolute speed and rate of climb records in both men's and women's categories since 1975, is a lightweight version of the Mi-24, the front section of which is like that of the Hind-A/C versions.

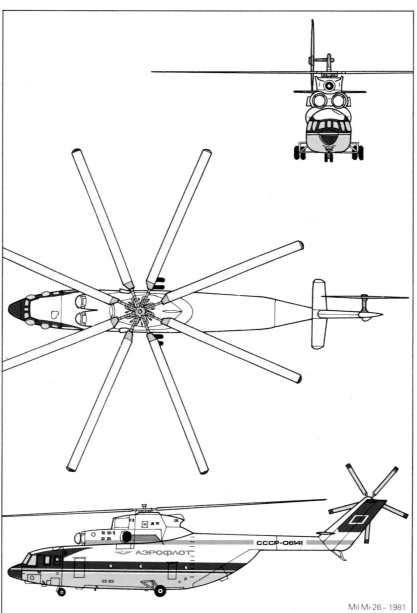

Mil Mi-26 – 1981

Mil Mi-26 (Halo)

The Mi-26, which was seen in public for the first time at the 1981 Paris Air Show, is the result of a specification issued at the beginning of the seventies for a transport helicopter whose empty weight, without fuel, was not to exceed half the maximum take-off weight. It first flew on 14 December 1977 and has two very powerful turbine engines driving a big eight-blade rotor, and a large cargo hold 3.20 m wide, 3.15 m high and 15 m deep (10 ft 6 in × 10 ft 4 in × 49 ft 2 in) with two winches on overhead rails, each capable of lifting 2.5 tonnes. Access to the hold is through a hydraulically-actuated rear loading ramp. The maximum payload is 5,000 kg (11,023 lbs) or 70-100 passengers. The helicopter has a crew of four, with room for an additional handler, and has a full range of navigational electronics and an automatic hover system.

Helicopter: **Mil Mi-26**
Manufacturer: **State Industry**
Type: **heavy transport**
Year: **1977**
Engines: **2 × 11,400 shp Sotarev D-136 turbines**
Rotor diameter: **32.00 m (105 ft)**
Fuselage length: **33.72 m (110 ft 7 in)**
Overall length: **—**
Height: **8.05 m (26 ft 5 in)**
Empty weight: **28,200 kg (62,170 lbs)**
Gross weight: **49,500 kg (109,128 lbs)**
Maximum speed: **295 km/h (183 mph)**
Range: **800 km (500 miles)**
Service ceiling: **1,800 m (5,900 ft) hovering**
Capacity: **70-100 passengers or 5,000 kg (11,023 lbs)**

Smolensk

This little engineless single-seat helicopter was designed in 1946 by M.A. Kapfer. It was towed by a vehicle on the ground up to a speed of about 40 km/h (25 mph) and its rotor started up by a winch anchored to the ground, after which it autorotated. It had a metal tube framework with a canvas skin over the front of the fuselage, a three-blade rotor and a tail unit for directional control. Rotor diameter: 5.74 m (18 ft 10 in). Fuselage length: 4.37 m (14 ft 4 in). Height: 1.76 m (5 ft 9 in). Empty weight: 80 kg (176 lbs). Service ceiling: 180 m (590 ft).

Yakovlev Yak-100

The Yak-100 was developed in competition with the Mi-1, and bore a striking resemblance in size, shape and weight to the American Sikorsky S-51. It did not enter production, however, and in fact Yak-100 was the design bureau's designation, not that of the armed forces. A second prototype of the Yak-100 flew in 1949 and the two helicopters were tested until June 1950, when it was decided to drop the project. Engine: 575 hp AI-26 GRFL. Rotor diameter: 14.5 m (47 ft 6 in). Empty weight: 1,805 kg (3,979 lbs). Gross weight: 2,180 kg (4,806 lbs). Maximum speed: 170 km/h (106 mph). Ceiling: 5,250 m (17,225 ft).

Yakovlev Yak-24 (Horse)

After having designed an experimental helicopter with coaxial rotors and the Yak-100 between 1944 and 1947, the Yakovlev design bureau embarked at the beginning of the fifties on the development of a heavy twin-engine helicopter with tandem rotors. The first prototype flew on 3 July 1952, with the same rotor blades, transmission and rotor hub as the Mil Mi-4. The four-blade rotor of the prototypes was made of light alloy and covered with fabric, but this was replaced by a steel rotor with a metal skin on the production models. The fuselage was of tubular structure, originally fabric-covered, then with a light alloy skin. There were two big end-plate fins on either side of the rear fuselage. The quadricycle landing gear had fully castoring wheels. The cabin of the Yak-24 could accommodate 20 troops or four staff cars or a similar payload.

Final development work on the aircraft was extremely long and complex and full-scale production for the armed forces began in 1955, about 30 months behind schedule.

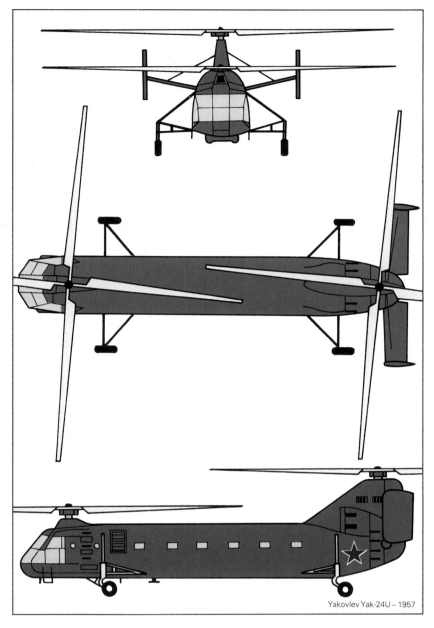

Yakovlev Yak-24U – 1957

In December of that year, a Yak-24 established a world helicopter record by lifting a 2,000 kg (4,409 lb) load to 5,082 m (16,673 ft) and 4,000 kg (8,818 lbs) to 2,902 m (9,520 ft).

In 1957, the Yak 24-U appeared, with modified rotors, a reinforced structure, more cargo room and provision for carrying slung loads. This version was capable of lifting 3.5 tonnes vertically. Aeroflot (the Russian state airline) evaluated the Yak-24A commercial version for 30 passengers, but turned it down. It also rejected the Yak-24K deluxe version for 8-9 passengers, while the Yak-24P for 39 passengers, with two 1,500 shp Isotov turbines mounted above the cabin was never built. About 100 of the Yak-24 (NATO reporting name Horse) were built, although some sources put the total at only 40, and it was used exclusively by the Russian Air Force. Its service life seems to have been beset by numerous accidents.

Helicopter: **Yakovlev Yak-24U**
Manufacturer: **State Industry**
Type: **heavy transport**
Year: **1957**
Engines: **2 × 1,700 hp Ash-82V**
Rotor diameter: **21.00 m (68 ft 11 in)**
Fuselage length: **21.29 m (69 ft 10 in)**
Overall length: **—**
Height: **6.50 m (21 ft 4 in)**
Empty weight: **11,000 kg (24,250 lbs)**
Gross weight: **15,830 kg (34,900 lbs)**
Maximum speed: **174 km/h (108 mph)**
Hovering ceiling IGE: **1,500 m (4,920 ft)**
Service ceiling: **2,700 m (8,860 ft)**
Range: **255 km (158 miles)**
Capacity: **40 equipped troops**

AERO VODOCHODY NARODNY PODNIK
(Czechoslovakia)

This company is part of a Czech motor car manufacturing and aeronautical concern which was formed in the early 1950s. From 1955 to the beginning of 1960 the company produced a series of light aircraft and experimental helicopters, of which only one reached limited series production. Construction of helicopters ceased in the mid 1960s but the company continues to produce trainers.

HC-102 Helibaby

The HC-102 Helibaby, designed by H. Sohleta, was derived from the Model HC-2, the first wholly Czech helicopter to be produced in any numbers. Like its predecessor, the HC-102 was a lightweight aircraft seating two side-by-side in an extensively-glazed cabin. The original powerplant of the HC-2, an 83 hp Praga DH, was replaced on the HC-102 by another Czech-built engine, the 115 hp four-cylinder opposed M-110H. Extensive structural use was made of plastics materials. A few were built for the Czech forces for liaison, observation and ambulance duties.

Helicopter: **HC-102 Helibaby**
Manufacturer: **Aero Vodochody Narodny Podnik**
Type: **trainer/liaison**
Year: **1953**
Engine: **115 hp M-110H radial**
Rotor diameter: **8.78 m (28 ft 9 in)**
Fuselage length: **8.40 m (27 ft 7 in)**
Gross weight: **681 kg (1,500 lbs)**
Maximum speed: **120 km/h (75 mph)**
Range: **175 km (109 miles)**
Capacity: **1 pilot + 1 passenger**

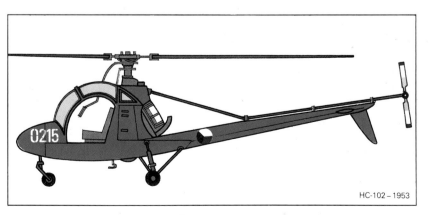

HC-102 – 1953

MORAVAN
(Czechoslovakia)

The Kunovice factory built light aircraft and helicopters during the 1950s.

Helicopter: **Z-35 Heli-Trener**
Manufacturer: **Moravan**
Type: **trainer**
Year: **1960**
Engine: **140 hp M-332**
Rotor diameter: **8.80 m (28 ft 10 in)**
Fuselage length: **8.22 m (27 ft)**
Height: **2.58 m (8 ft 6 in)**
Empty weight: **520 kg (1,146 lbs)**
Gross weight: **725 kg (1,598 lbs)**
Maximum speed: **130 km/h (80 mph)**
Hovering ceiling IGE: **1,800 m (5,905 ft)**
Service ceiling: **3,850 m (12,630 ft)**
Range: **320 km (200 miles)**
Capacity: **2 seats**

Z-35

The Z-35 Heli-Trener, developed by the Czech Moravan works, first flew in 1960. It was a small, two-seat trainer designed for maximum simplicity of structure and maintenance. Apart from the trainer version, the Z-35 was also offered as a single-seater for agricultural use. The prototype underwent intensive trials up to 1964, but demand was insufficient to justify large-scale production and the project was therefore dropped.

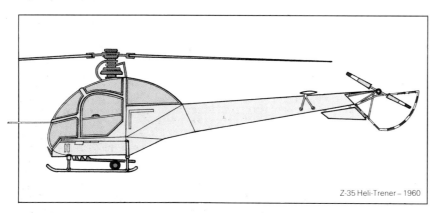

Z-35 Heli-Trener – 1960

WSK
Wytwornia Sprzetu Komunikayinego (Poland)

Founded in 1951-52, WSK-Swidnik began by constructing the Mi-1 under license with the designation of SM-1. In 1957 PZL was absorbed into this concern.

Helicopter: **Kania/Kitty Hawk**
Manufacturer: **WSK-PZL**
Type: **general purpose**
Year: **1979**
Engines: **2 × 420 shp Allison 250-C20B**
Rotor diameter: **14.56 m (47 ft 9 in)**
Fuselage length: **11.95 m (39 ft 2 in)**
Overall length: **17.41 m (57 ft 1 in)**
Height: **3.75 m (12 ft 4 in)**
Empty weight: **2,140 kg (4,718 lbs)**
Gross weight: **3,550 kg (7,826 lbs)**
Maximum cruise speed: **211 km/h (131 mph)**
Range: **500 km (310 miles)**
Capacity: **1 pilot + 8 passengers**

WSK-PZL Kania and Sokol

WSK-PZL has recently developed a derivative of the Russian Mi-2, the Kania/Kitty Hawk with two Allison 250-C20B engines and American instrumentation designed for the Western market. In the United States it was intended to market the aircraft through Spitfire Helicopters under the name Taurus, but the political and financial situation in Poland has delayed both the Kania programme and the latest WSK-PZL project, the 14-seat W-3 Sokol (Falcon), two prototypes of which have been built at Swidnik for trials. Powered by two 960 shp Glusnekov TVD-10 turbines, the W-3 is similar in size and layout to Western designs such as the Aérospatiale Super Puma and Westland 30.

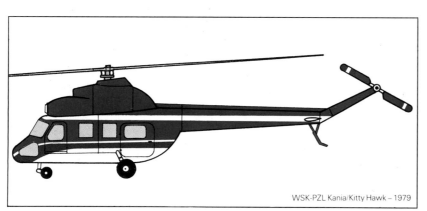

WSK-PZL Kania/Kitty Hawk – 1979

OTHER HELICOPTERS

A B C

1952 American Helicopter XH-26 Jet Jeep. Light single-seater developed at the request of the USAF and US Army. It could be carried in a standard container and assembled in minutes. It was powered by two small pulse jet engines delivering 16 kg (35 lb) thrust each. Rotor diameter: 8.24 m (27 ft). Height: 1.83 m (6 ft). Empty weight: 136 kg (300 lbs). Gross weight: 397 kg (875 lbs). Maximum speed: 144 km/h (90 mph). Range: 168 km (104 miles).

1953 Baumgartl PB 63. A single-seater, the last of a family of experimental helicopters designed in Brazil by the engineer Paul Baumgartl. After the first model with coaxial rotors, it was given a traditional two-blade articulated rotor. Engine: 85 hp Continental C85. Rotor diameter: 6 m (19 ft 8 in). Empty weight: 238 kg (525 lbs). Gross weight: 360 kg (794 lbs). Ceiling: 2,285 m (7,500 ft).

1959 Beja-Flôr. The Beja-Flôr was a light two-seat utility aircraft developed by the Departamento de Aeronaves (PAR). It was specifically designed for Brazilian environmental conditions. The main rotor of mixed wood and metal construction had a flapping movement only and the rotor head incorporated a mechanical-hydraulic stabilization system which reduced flapping to zero on the pitch axis. Two small, intermeshing tail rotors provided control in translational flight and countered torque.

1945 Bendix Model K. Single-seater designed by Martin Jensen, with coaxial, contra-rotating rotors mounted on two concentric shafts about 70 cm (2 ft 3 in) apart. Engine: 100 hp continental C100. Rotor diameter: 7.62 m (25 ft). Length: 3.81 m (12 ft 6 in). Height: 2.97 m (9 ft 9 in). Empty weight: 366 kg (807 lbs). Gross weight: 544 kg (2,000 lbs). Cruise speed: 96 km/h (60 mph). Service ceiling: 3,050 m (10,000 ft). Range: 80 km (50 miles).

1971 Bensen B-8M. The Bensen Aircraft Corporation has been the largest manufacturer of light autogyros since the early fifties, and its aircraft are readily available in kit form. After the first experimental B-7M Gyrocopter, the American company went ahead with mass production of the Type B-8M with a more powerful engine and larger diameter rotor.

Another variant with a rotor brake, swivelling nosewheel and approximately 45 kg (100 lbs) higher gross weight is the B-8M Super Bug, which can start up its rotor on the ground for a vertical take-off. One version of the B-8 is fitted with flotation gear.

1969 Campbell Cricket. The Campbell Aircraft Co. originated as a licensee of the Bensen Aircraft Corporation but developed its own variants of the basic Bensen gyroplane, one of which, the Cricket, went into limited production in the early 1970s powered by a 75 hp Volkswagen engine. Thirty-three aircraft were eventually built, mostly for private owners. Attempts to develop a two-seat gyroplane led to the contruction in 1973 of the Campbell Cougar, a twin-boomed aircraft powered by a 130 hp Rolls-Royce Continental engine. Although test-flown in a single-seat configuration, development was abandoned before the definitive two-seat cabin was fitted.

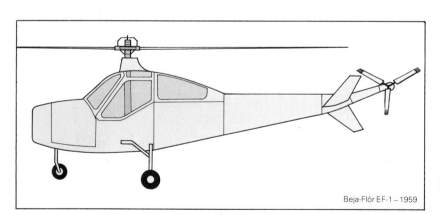

Beja-Flôr EF-1 – 1959

Helicopter: **Beja-Flôr BF-1**
Manufacturer: **Centro Tecnico de Aeronautica**
Type: **utility**
Year: **1959**
Engine: **225 hp Continental E 225**
Rotor diameter: **9.40 m (30 ft 10 in)**
Fuselage length: —
Overall length: **8.75 m (28 ft 8 in)**

Height: **3.15 m (10 ft 4 in)**
Empty weight: **700 kg (1,543 lbs)**
Gross weight: **950 kg (2,095 lbs)**
Maximum speed: **160 km/h (100 mph)**
Hovering ceiling IGE: **2,700 m (8,860 ft)**
Service ceiling: **3,500 m (11,485 ft)**
Range: **270 km (168 miles)**
Capacity: **1 pilot + 1 passenger**

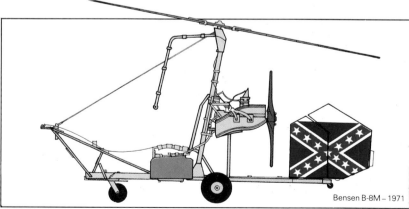

Bensen B-8M – 1971

Aircraft: **Bensen B-8M**
Manufacturer: **Bensen Aircraft Corporation**
Type: **single-seat autogyro**
Year: **1971**
Engine: **72 hp McCulloch**
Rotor diameter: **6.70 m (22 ft)**
Fuselage length: **3.45 m (11 ft 4 in)**
Overall length: —

Height: —
Empty weight: —
Gross weight: **227 kg (500 lbs)**
Maximum speed: **137 km/h (85 mph)**
Hovering ceiling IGE: —
Service ceiling: —
Range: **160 km (100 miles)**

CDEFGH

1976 Cicare CK-1. The CK-1, developed from a family of experimental helicopters, is a two-three seater with a four-blade rigid rotor which makes extensive use of fiberglass. A short production run was initiated in 1978. Engine: 220 shp Lycoming. Rotor diameter: 7.6 m (25 ft). Overall length: 8.53 m (28 ft). Gross weight: 800 kg (1,764 lbs). Maximum speed: 163 km/h (100 mph). Range: 480 km (300 miles).

1969 Cierva CLTH-1. The Cierva CLTH-1 twin-engined coaxial rotor five-seat helicopter was developed in the United Kingdom in the late 1960s by a design team led by Jacob Shapiro, who in the 1940s had been technical director for the earlier Cierva company which had developed the Air Horse and Saro Skeeter. The CLTH-1 was developed from the Rotorcraft Grasshopper of 1962, which was powered by two 65 hp Walter Mikron engines. The CLTH-1 was of more advanced design with fiberglass main rotor blades arranged in a close-linked coaxial system. Yaw control was achieved by differential pitch. Engines: 2 × 145 hp Rolls-Royce Continental 0-300. Rotor diameter: 9.75 m (32 ft). Overall length: 10.51 m (34 ft 6 in). Gross weight: 1,474 kg (3,250 lbs). Maximum speed: 201 km/h (125 mph). Range: 402.30 km (250 miles).

1955 CJC-3. Tandem rotor two-seater, metal fuselage with the engine installed in the center. Fixed quadricycle landing gear. Work on the CJC-3 began in 1952 and the helicopter started test flights in January 1955. The project was subsequently abandoned due to technical problems. Engine: 190 hp Lycoming. Rotor diameter: 6.47 m (21 ft 3 in). Empty weight: 857 kg (1,889 lbs). Gross weight: 1,290 kg (2,843 lbs). Maximum speed: 180 km/h (112 mph).

1958 Doman D-10. Developed from the model LZ-5, this general purpose six-seat helicopter was to have been mass produced with the help of an Italian company — Ing. A. Ambrosini & Co. — but the programme did not go ahead. Engine: 525 hp Lycoming THIO 720. Rotor diameter: 14.64 m (48 ft). Overall length: 17.81 m (58 ft 5 in). Height: 4.93 m (16 ft 2 in). Empty weight: 1,577 kg (3,477 lbs). Gross weight: 2,495 kg (5,500 lbs). Maximum speed: 167 km/h (104 mph). Service ceiling: 6,075 m (20,000 ft). Range: 1,205 km (750 miles).

1952 Doman LZ-5. Eight-seat medium transport aircraft designed to a US Army specification but put to commercial use instead. Only a few examples were built. Engine: 400 hp Lycoming 580D. Rotor diameter: 14.64 m (48 ft). Fuselage length: 11.57 m (38 ft). Height: 3.12 m (10 ft 3 in). Empty weight: 1,297 kg (2,859 lbs). Gross weight: 2,363 kg (5,209 lbs). Maximum speed: 169 km/h (105 mph). Service ceiling: 5,490 m (18,012 ft). Range: 392 km (244 miles).

1952 Dorand DH-011. The engineer René Dorand, of the Société d'Etudes des Giravions Dorand, developed several designs for experimental rotary wing craft using a thermal propulsion system, whereby compressed air was ejected from the blade tips. Engine: Turboméca Aspin I. Empty weight: 540 kg (1,190 lbs). Gross weight: 1,025 kg (2,260 lbs). Theoretical ceiling: 6,000 m (19,685 ft). Range: 200 km (124 miles).

1956 Fiat 7002. General purpose experimental helicopter using the cold-jet propulsion system. The compressed air ejected by the blade-tip nozzles was provided by a 530 hp Fiat 4700 turbogenerator. Rotor diameter: 12.00 m (39 ft 4 in). Fuselage length: 6.12 m (20 ft 1 in). Height: 2.88 m (9 ft 5 in). Empty weight: 650 kg (1,433 lbs). Gross weight: 1,400 kg (3,086 lbs). Maximum speed: 170 km/h (105 mph). Service ceiling: 3,400 m (11,115 ft). Range: 300 km (186 miles).

1952 Firth FH-1. Experimental helicopter built around the fuselage of an unusual fixed-wing aircraft, the 1948 Planet Satellite, with a light alloy semi-monocoque structure. It had a three-blade rigid rotor and tricycle landing gear. It was abandoned before flight testing due to financial and technical difficulties. The engine was a 146 hp Gipsy Major.

1957 Gaucher Remicopter. A light single-seat helicopter with a tubular fuselage, two-blade rotor powered by two ramjets, and a large tail unit with no tail rotor. Powerplant: 2 SNECMA ramjets. Rotor diameter: 5.8 m (19 ft). Fuselage length: 3.20 m (10 ft 6 in). Height: 2.15 m (7 ft). Empty weight: 140 kg (309 lbs). Cruise speed: 130 km/h (81 mph). Maximum speed: 140 km/h (87 mph). Range: 150 km (93 miles).

1954 Goodyear GA.400 Gizmo. An ultra-lightweight single-seat helicopter offered to the American armed forces. Light alloy structure. Two-blade main rotor and tail rotor. Engine: 38 hp Johnson marine outboard. Rotor diameter: 6.10 m (20 ft). Overall length: 6.40 m (21 ft). Height: 2.14 m (7 ft). Gross weight: 236 kg (520 lbs). Maximum speed: 104 km/h (65 mph). Service ceiling: 3,600 m (11,810 ft). Range: 80 km (50 miles).

1981 Helicop-Jet. A light four-seater with Palouste air generator and jet propulsion through the rotor blades. Built by Etablissements Charles Déchaux of Paris. Engine: 500 shp Turboméca Astazou II. Rotor diameter: 9.40 m (30 ft 10 in). Fuselage length: 3.10 m (10 ft 2 in). Empty weight: 450 kg (992 lbs). Gross weight: 1,060 kg (2,336 lbs). Maximum cruise speed: 200 km/h (124 mph). Range 450 km (280 miles).

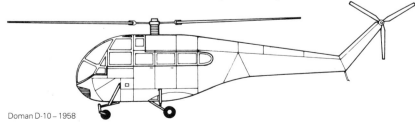
Doman D-10 – 1958

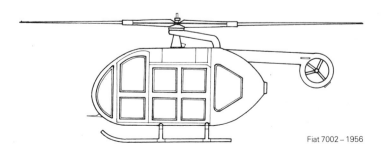
Fiat 7002 – 1956

HLM

1981 Hillman 360. In 1972 Mr. Douglas Hillman of Arizona USA began development of the first helicopter to be powered by a rotating-combustion engine, the Wankel Bee. It flew in July 1975, but was superseded by the Hornet, powered by a conventional 150 hp Avco-Lycoming engine, in 1978. In 1979 Hillman was joined by Rudolph Enstrom, designer of the original Enstrom helicopter, and this led to the development of the Hillman 360, which first flew in 1981. The 360 was a three-seat light helicopter with a two-blade main rotor and a semi-rigid underslung teetering hub; it featured a V-belt rotor drive with a sprag-type overrunning clutch. Development was shelved following Hillman's death in 1983. Engine: 205 hp Avco-Lycoming H10-360-C1A. Rotor diameter: 8.15 m (26 ft 9 in). Overall length: 9.47 m (31 ft 1 in). Gross weight: 998 kg (2,200 lbs). Maximum speed: 185 km/h (115 mph). Range: 2,511 km (1,560 miles).

1949 Hoppicopter Mark II. A single-seater designed by the American Horace Pentecost and driven by a small two-cylinder engine installed under the pilot seat. It had contra-rotating rotors. Engine: 40 hp Triumph. Rotor diameter: 5.18 m (16 ft 3 in). Empty weight: 66 kg (145 lbs). Gross weight: 136 kg (300 lbs). Cruise speed: 97 km/h (60 mph). Range: 113 km (70 miles).

1974 HTM Skyrider. Prototype four-seat helicopter derived from the Sky-Trac, with virtually the same structure and two contra-rotating two-blade rotors, but a new fiberglass fuselage with room for three passengers on a bench seat behind the pilot. Engine: 260 hp Lycoming 10-540. Rotor diameter: 10.40 m (34 ft 1 in). Fuselage length: 7.43 m (24 ft 4 in). Empty weight: 1,015 kg (2,238 lbs). Gross weight: 1,530 kg (3,373 lbs). Maximum speed: 185 km/h (115 mph). Service ceiling: 3,860 m (12,664 ft). Range: 620 km (385 miles).

1952 Hunting P.74. Design for a helicopter with blade-tip jet propulsion. Compressed air was supplied by a gas generator. Three-blade rotor, quadricycle landing gear. One prototype was built in 1956 but failed to fly. Engine: 654 hp Napier Oryx. Rotor diameter: 16.77 m (52 ft 9 in). Gross weight: 3,518 kg (7,756 lbs). Cruise speed: 178 km/h (110 mph). Ceiling: 8,530 m (27,985 ft). Range: 530 km (329 miles). Payload: 10 passengers.

1954 Lualdi ES.53. This single-seater designed by Carlo Lualdi and Sergio Tassotti was the first in a family of light Italian helicopters. It flew at Campoformido in 1954. Only one was built. Engine: 85 hp Continental C.85. Rotor diameter: 7.31 m (24 ft). Length: 6.55 m (21 ft 6 in). Height: 2.60 m (8 ft 6 in). Empty weight: 400 kg (882 lbs). Gross weight: 850 kg (1,873 lbs). Maximum speed: 110 km/h (68 mph). Service ceiling: 2,000 m (7,874 ft). Range: 250 km (155 miles).

1955 Lualdi L-55. Derivative of the foregoing with a bigger fuselage and cockpit seating two side-by-side. Classic configuration with two-blade rotor and stabilizer bar. Engine: 180 hp Lycoming 0360.

1959 Lualdi L-59. Light four-seater derived from the Model L-55, one of which was evaluated by the Italian Army. It used the Hiller-Rotormatic system. Only one was built. Engine: 260 hp Continental 10 470. Rotor diameter: 10.60 m (34 ft 11 in). Fuselage length: 8.98 m (29 ft 5 in). Height: 3 m (9 ft 10 in). Empty weight: 740 kg (1,631 lbs). Gross weight: 1,200 kg (2,646 lbs). Maximum speed: 159 km/h (99 mph). Ceiling: 5,900 m (19,357 ft).

1952 Manzolini Libellula II. Designed by Bordoni, an Italian engineer, and financed by count Manzolini, this little single-seater had two coaxial, contra-rotating rotors. Only one model was built. Engine: 100 hp Walter Minor III. Rotor diameter: 9.00 m (29 ft 6 in). Fuselage length: 4.75 m (15 ft 7 in). Height: 3.30 m (10 ft 10 in). Empty weight: 500 kg (1,102 lbs). Gross weight: 650 kg (1,433 lbs). Maximum speed: 109 km/h (68 mph). Hovering ceiling: 1,250 m (4,100 ft). Range: 200 km (124 miles).

1982 Marquion RM-02. Single-seat helicopter in kit form designed by Roger Marquion of the Gyroclub of Provence. It is based on the experience of an American, Max Williams, and on the Scorpion, but has a taller, longer fuselage. The rotor head is a wholly original design; the tail rotor is taken from the Williams aircraft, but the diameter is increased by about 4 cm (1.5 in). Marquion is seriously considering marketing the helicopter in France. The engine is a 100 hp two liter Porsche.

1952 Matra Cantinieau. Two-seat experimental helicopter designed by Paul Cantinieau. It was unusual in that the powerplant was arranged horizontally above the forward portion of the cabin. The design was reworked in Spain by Aerotecnica (see AC-12/13). Engine: 105 hp Hirth HM-504. Rotor diameter: 8 m (26 ft 3 in). Length: 6.70 m (22 ft). Empty weight: 400 kg (882 lbs). Gross weight: 600 kg (1,323 lbs). Cruise speed: 100 km/h (62 mph). Range: 200 km (124 miles).

1954 McCulloch 4E. Tandem rotor helicopter developed from the Model Jov-3 designed by D.K. Jovanovich. Only one prototype built in 1952. Steel tube structure, fixed tricycle landing gear and vertical tail surface. Engine: 235 hp Franklin 6A-350. Rotor diameter: 7.01 m (23 ft). Fuselage length: 5.48 m (18 ft). Height: 2.82 m (9ft 3 in). Empty weight: 680 kg (1,500 lbs). Gross weight: 1,090 kg (2,403 lbs). Maximum speed: 145 km/h (90 mph). Range: 400 km (250 miles).

1956 Molyneux. First rotary wing craft built in Australia, by Melbourne engineer Molyneux. It had tandem three-blade rotors. Engine: 500 hp. Rotor diameter: 9.14 m (30 ft). Gross weight: 1,814 kg (4,000 lbs). Cruise speed: 145 km/h (90 mph). Range: 560 km (350 miles). Capacity: 5 seats.

1959 Montecopter Triphibian. Light three-seat helicopter powered by jets at the two blade tips. It had an all-fiberglass structure with a small delta wing to improve lift in horizontal flight. Engine: 200 hp Continental 141. Rotor diameter: 10.97 m (36 ft). Fuselage length: 4.65 m (15 ft 3 in). Height: 2.52 m (8 ft 3 in). Empty weight: 545 kg (1,200 lbs). Gross weight: 907 kg (2,000 lbs). Maximum speed: 158 km/h (98 mph). Service ceiling: 4,570 m (15,000 ft). Range: 160 m (100 miles).

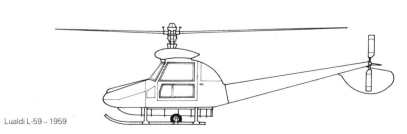
Lualdi L-59 – 1959

NOPR

1947 N.1700 Norelic. The Société Nationale de Constructions Aéronautiques du Nord (Nord-Aviation) built its first helicopter prototype in 1947, in which the head of the two-blade rotor moved both parallel to the aircraft's longitudinal plane of symmetry and perpendicular to it. Engine: 170 hp Mathis. Rotor diameter: 10 m (32 ft 10 in). Length: 7 m (23 ft). Empty weight: 510 kg (1,124 lbs). Gross weight: 800 kg (1,764 lbs). Cruise speed: 130 km/h (81 mph). Service ceiling: 3,000 m (9,842 ft). Range: 350 km (217 miles).

1946 NC-2001. Five-seat helicopter designed by René Dorand with twin, two-blade intermeshing rotors. It made only one flight and was abandoned in favour of other projects. Engine: 450 hp Renault. Rotor diameter: 15 m (49 ft 3 in). Length: 9.7 m (31 ft 10 in). Gross weight: 2,550 kg (5,622 lbs). Cruise speed: 159 km/h (99 mph). Service ceiling: 4,880 m (16,000 ft).

1956 NHI H-3 Kolibrie. Designed and built by Nederlandse Helicopter Industrie N.V., this helicopter was so stable that it could be flown hands-off for at least four minutes. Its endurance varied considerably according to the payload, from about one hour with a single pilot and maximum fuel, to 15 minutes with a 400 kg (882 lb) load. Aviolanda, a Dutch company, was responsible for manufacturing the Kolibrie and built about ten.

Helicopter: **NHI H-3 Kolibrie**
Manufacturer: **Nederlandse Helicopter Industrie N.V.**
Type: **agricultural**
Year: **1956**
Engines: **2 × 25 kg (55 lb) TJ5 ramjets**
Rotor diameter: **10.57 m (34 ft 8 in)**
Fuselage length: **4.00 m (13 ft 1 in)**
Height: **2.57 m (8 ft 5 in)**
Empty weight: **200 kg (440 lbs)**
Gross weight: **650 kg (1,433 lbs)**
Maximum speed: **120 km/h (75 mph)**
Hovering ceiling IGE: **—**
Range: **100 km (62 miles)**
Capacity: **1 pilot + 1 passenger**

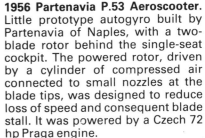

Nord 500 – 1968

1968 Nord 500. After ten years' research, Nord-Aviation developed a small experimental aircraft in 1967, the Nord 500, with tilting ducted propellers. The design was unusual, in that it resembled a helicopter minus its rotors. Behind the body of the aircraft containing the single-seat cabin was a conventional type of cantilever tail. The high wing, with a fixed central portion, had ducted fans on the two outboard sections, which rotated through 90° on the horizontal axis. After the first tethered flights, the second prototype made its first free flight in July 1968, but development was suspended shortly afterwards.

Aircraft: **Nord 500**
Manufacturer: **Nord-Aviation**
Type: **experimental**
Year: **1968**
Engines: **2 × 317 shp Allison 250C-18 turbines**
Propeller diameter: **1.90 m (6 ft 3 in)**
Fuselage length: **6.50 m (21 ft 4 in)**
Overall length: **5.70 m (18 ft 8 in)**
Height: **3.09 m (10 ft 2 in)**
Empty weight: **—**
Gross weight: **1,250 kg (2,755 lbs)**
Maximum speed: **350 km/h (217 mph)**

1955 Omega SB-12. Four-seater with a four-blade articulated rotor and two 200 hp Franklin engines mounted on each side of the fuselage to improve accessibility and cabin capacity. Only two were built. Rotor diameter: 11.89 m (39 ft). Fuselage length: 11.12 m (36 ft 6 in). Height: 3.96 m (13 ft). Empty weight: 1,338 kg (2,950 lbs). Gross weight: 1,905 kg (4,200 lbs). Maximum speed: 138 km/h (86 mph). Service ceiling: 3,450 m (11,320 ft). Range: 250 km (155 miles).

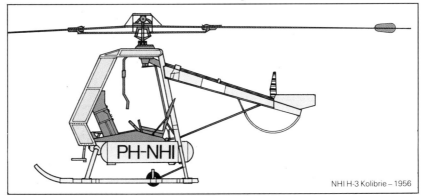

NHI H-3 Kolibrie – 1956

1956 Partenavia P.53 Aeroscooter. Little prototype autogyro built by Partenavia of Naples, with a two-blade rotor behind the single-seat cockpit. The powered rotor, driven by a cylinder of compressed air connected to small nozzles at the blade tips, was designed to reduce loss of speed and consequent blade stall. It was powered by a Czech 72 hp Praga engine.

1971 Phillicopter Mk.1. Light two-seater with aluminum and fiberglass fuselage and steel tube tail boom. Engine: 145 hp Continental 0300. Rotor diameter: 7.92 m (26 ft). Fuselage length: 7.16 m (23 ft 6 in). Gross weight: 748 kg (1,650 lbs). Maximum speed: 145 km/h (90 mph). Range: 370 km (230 miles).

1950 Piaggio PD.3. Experimental helicopter designed by D'Ascanio using parts of an aircraft under construction at the beginning of the war. It had a self-stabilizing three-blade rotor and was tested at Pontedera airfield. Engine: 200 hp Alfa 115. Rotor diameter: 13.02 m (42 ft 8 in). Empty weight: 810 kg (1,786 lbs). Range: 300 km (186 miles).

1975 Robinson R-22. A helicopter with very clean lines and a steel tube and light alloy fuselage, partially covered by a fiberglass skin. The tail boom has a simple, semi-monocoque structure and carries a small tail unit. The powerplant is a Lycoming 0-320-A2B installed at the rear of the fuselage, behind the cabin. Over 300 Robinson R-22s have been delivered to date and production in late 1983 was based on three aircraft a week. The more recent R-22HP version has a 160 shp Lycoming 0-320-B2C engine with a higher compression ratio which reduces consumption and improves performance at high altitude.

R S T W

1962 Rotorcraft Grasshopper. Light two-seater designed to provide a comfortable form of private transport for the price of a luxury car. It was unusual for this category and period, in that it had two engines, initially of 65 hp, then of 100 and finally of 125 hp on the version intended for mass production. It had two contra-rotating, semi-rigid, two-blade rotors, a fully streamlined, covered fuselage and skid landing gear. Engine: 125 hp Continental 0240. Rotor diameter: 8.23 m (27 ft). Fuselage length: 5.60 m (18 ft 4 in). Height: 2.69 m (8 ft 10 in). Empty weight: 645 kg (1,422 lbs). Gross weight: 1,305 kg (2,877 lbs). Maximum speed: 200 km/h (124 mph). Range: 400 km (248 miles).

1966 Rotorway Scorpion. Tiny single-seater driven by a water-cooled outboard marine engine. Two-blade semi-rigid aluminum rotor. Engine: 63 hp Mercury. Rotor diameter: 5.85 m (19 ft 2 in). Overall length: 5.21 m (17 ft 1 in). Height: 1.83 m (6 ft). Empty weight: 172 kg (379 lbs). Gross weight: 272 kg (600 lbs). Maximum speed: 137 km/h (85 mph). Service ceiling: 3,655 m (11,990 ft). Range: 257 km (160 miles).

1966 Scheutzow Model B. Light two-seater, a small batch of which were built with steel tube fuselage and enclosed cabins with side-by-side accommodation. The rotor had the Flexhub system to reduce vibrations. Engine: 165 hp Lycoming IVO 360. Rotor diameter: 8.23 m (27 ft). Overall length: 9.45 m (31 ft). Fuselage length: 7.21 m (23 ft 8 in). Height: 2.49 m (8 ft 2 in). Empty weight: 453 kg (998 lbs). Gross weight: 702 kg (1,548 lbs). Maximum speed: 137 km/h (85 mph). Service ceiling: 4,250 m (13,945 ft). Range: 270 km (168 miles).

1980 Seguin/Adams Wilson. Small single-seat home-built helicopter derived from an American model sold in large numbers in kit form. Two-blade wooden rotor and light alloy fuselage; simple landing gear without shock absorbers. Engine: 52 hp Triumph. Rotor diameter: 6.55 m (21 ft 6 in). Fuselage length: 4.60 m (15 ft 1 in). Height: 1.52 m (5 ft). Empty weight: 155 kg (342 lbs). Gross weight: 257 kg (567 lbs).

1976 Seremet WS-8. Ultra-light single-seat helicopter designed by Vincent Seremet in 1976 and built in Denmark. It had a two-blade main rotor and a pedal operated tail rotor. Engine: 35 hp Kiekhalfer. Rotor diameter: 4.50 m (14 ft 9 in). Overall length: 3.05 m (10 ft). Empty weight: 53 kg (117 lbs). Gross weight: 150 kg (330 lbs).

1964 Simetzki ASRO 4. Lightweight helicopter prototype with two seats side-by-side, of mixed construction with a three-blade articulated rotor. Engine: 100/130 hp BMW 6012. Rotor diameter: 7.22 m (23 ft 8 in). Fuselage length: 5.78 m (19 ft). Empty weight: 210 kg (463 lbs). Gross weight: 465 kg (1,025 lbs). Maximum speed: 160 km/h (99 mph). Endurance: 1 hour, 40 mins.

1968 Tervamaki-Eerola ATE 3. A small single-seat autogyro similar to the models by Wallis, designed and built by the Finns Tervamaki and Eerola. The improved model, the JT-5, differed in that it had a triple tail plane. Several have been sold, including some in kit form. Engine: 75 hp Volkswagen. Rotor diameter: 7 m (22 ft 11 in). Length of fuselage: 3.20 m (10 ft 5 in). Height: 1.90 m (6 ft 3 in). Empty weight: 150 kg (330 lbs). Take-off weight: 260 kg (573 lbs). Maximum speed: 160 km/h (99 mph). Range: 300 km (186 miles).

1967 Thruxton Gadfly. The Thruxton Aviation Co. of Andover, England, began design of their two-seat cabin ES101 Gadfly autogyro in 1964, using a conventional two-blade teeter rotor system with a fixed-pitch pusher propeller driven by a 165 hp Rolls-Royce Continental engine, and a twin boom tail structure. Ground tests of the sole prototype began at Thruxton airfield in 1967 but this autogyro failed to fly and was abandoned. Rotor diameter: 9.14 m (30 ft). Length: 3.35 m (11 ft).

1969 VFW-Fokker H3 Sprinter. Two-three-seat compound helicopter with three-blade rotor with compressed air blade-tip jet propulsion. For horizontal flight, the machine is powered by two ducted fans placed at the sides of the fuselage. Engine: 400 shp Allison 250-C20. Rotor diameter: 8.70 m (28 ft 7 in). Overall length: 9.29 m (30 ft 6 in). Empty weight: 495 kg (1,091 lbs). Gross weight: 968 kg (2,134 lbs). Maximum speed: 300 km/h (186 mph). Service ceiling: 4,000 m (13,123 ft). Endurance: 2 hours.

1965 Wagner Sky-Trac. Family of light general-purpose helicopters with contra-rotating rotors. The three-seat Sky-Trac 3 could lift a load heavier than itself. Engine: 260 hp Franklin 6AS-335. Rotor diameter: 10 m (32 ft 10 in). Overall length: 7.10 m (23 ft 4 in). Empty weight: 760 kg (1,675 lbs). Gross weight: 1,500 kg (3,307 lbs). Maximum speed: 160 km/h (99 mph). Endurance: 4 hours.

Helicopter: **Robinson R-22**
Manufacturer: **Robinson Helicopter Company**
Type: **light transport**
Year: **1975**
Engine: **150 shp Lycoming 0-320-A2B-4**
Rotor diameter: **7.67 m (25 ft 2 in)**
Fuselage length: **6.30 m (20 ft 8 in)**
Overall length: **8.76 m (28 ft 8 in)**
Height: **2.67 m (8 ft 9 in)**
Empty weight: **346 kg (763 lbs)**
Gross weight: **590 kg (1,300 lbs)**
Cruise speed: **174 km/h (108 mph)**
Hovering ceiling IGE: **1,980 m (6,496 ft)**
Service ceiling: **4,265 m (13,990 ft)**
Range: **386 km (240 miles)**
Capacity: **1 pilot + 1 passenger**

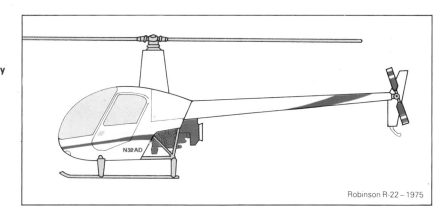

Robinson R-22 – 1975

Photographic appendix

Forlanini's steam-powered helicopter - 1877 (I)

Brennan Helicopter - 1925 (GB)

D'Ascanio's helicopter - 1930 (I)

Cierva C-19 - 1931 (GB)

Cierva C-24 - 1932 (GB)

Weir W.5 - 1938 (GB)

Doblhoff WNF 342-V4 - 1943 (D)

Focke-Achgelis Fa 223 E-1-1941 (D)

Sikorsky R-4 - 1942 (USA)

Hiller J-5 - 1947 (USA)

Agusta A.101G - 1964 (I)

Agusta-Bell AB-47G-2 - 1957 (I)

Agusta-Bell AB-47J Ranger - 1957 (I)

Agusta A.109 - 1977 (I)

Agusta A-129 - 1983 (I)

Bell 533 - 1962 (USA)

Agusta-Bell AB-204B - 1963 (I)

Bell Model 205 - 1963 (USA)

Agusta-Bell AB-206A -1967 (I)

Agusta-Bell AB-212 - 1971 (I)

Bell X-22A - 1966 (USA)

Bell XV-15

Bell 400 Twin Ranger - 1984 (USA)

Bell-Boeing JVX - projected first flight 1987 (USA) ▶

Boeing Vertol CH-47C - 1968 (USA)

Photographic appendix

Bristol 171 Sycamore - 1959 (GB)

Bristol 192 Belvedere - 1960 (GB)

Breguet G.IIE Gyroplane - 1949 (F)

Cierva CLTH-1 - 1969 (GB)

Cessna CH-1B - 1954 (USA)

Fairey Jet-Gyrodyne -1954 (GB)

Fairey Rotodyne - 1957 (GB)

Fairey Ultra Light - 1957 (GB)

Hiller HJ-1 Hornet - 1952 (USA)

Hiller YH-32 Hornet - 1952 (USA)

Hiller H-23A - 1950 (USA)

Hillman 360 - 1981 (USA)

HC-102 Helibaby - 1960 (CS)

Hiller YROE-1 Rotorcycle - 1958 (USA)

Lockheed Cheyenne AH-56A - 1967 (USA)

Kamov Ka-26 - 1970 (USSR)

Mil Mi-2 - 1963 (USSR)

Mil Mi-6 - (USSR)

Mil Mi-10 - 1961 (USSR)

Mil Mi-10 - 1961 (USSR)

Bölkow Bo-105D - 1970 (D)

MBB-Kawasaki BK-117 - 1979 (D)

SARO Skeeter - 1958 - (GB)

Nord 500 - 1968 (F)

Silvercraft SH-4 - 1967 (I)

Sikorsky S-51 - 1953 (USA)

Sikorsky SH-3D - 1967 (USA)

Sikorsky S-61R - 1965 (USA)

Sikorsky S-61 - 1978 (USA)

Sikorsky S-76 - 1970 (USA)

SO.1120 Ariel - 1950 (F)

SO.1221 Djinn - 1954 (F)

SA.315B Lama - 1972 (F)

SA.3160 Alouette III - 1959 (F)

SA.3200 Frelon - 1963 (F)

SA.330 Puma - 1968 (F)

SA.231 Super Frelon - 1965 (F)

SA.341 Gazelle - 1971 (F)

SA.365 Dauphin - 1975 (F)

Photographic appendix

VFW-Fokker H-5 - 1969 (D)

Westland Wessex - 1962 (GB)

Westland Whirlwind - 1959 (GB)

Westland Scout - 1961 (GB)

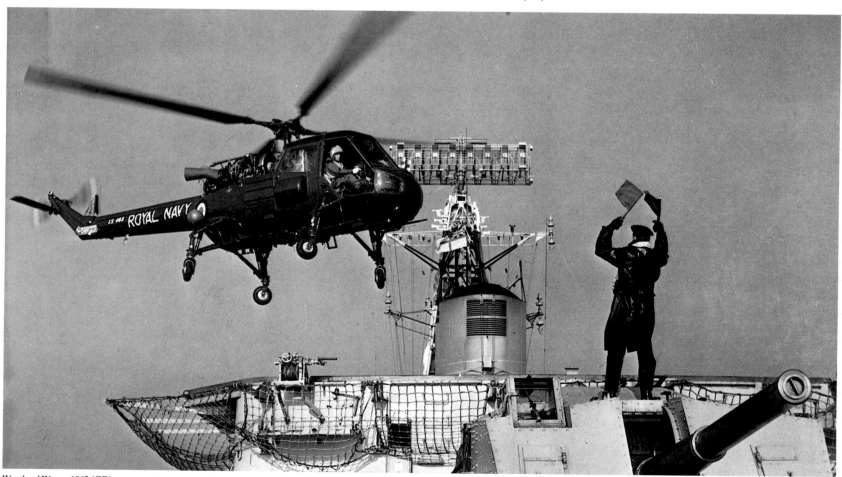

Westland Wasp - 1962 (GB)

Numbers in italics refer to illustrations.

INDEX BY COUNTRY

Listed below are those helicopters which are illustrated in colour.